THE Cost of justice

BY

MIKE GEDGOUDAS

Al –
I hope you Enjoy!

[signature]

12-26-08

Fireside Publishing Company
Lady Lake, Florida

THE COST OF JUSTICE

This is a work of fiction. All of the characters, organizations, and events portrayed in this novel are either products of the author's imagination or are used fictitiously and are not based on any persons, living or dead.

Published by:
Fireside Publications
1004 San Felipe Lane
The Villages, Florida 32159

www.firesidepubs.com

Printed in the United States of America

Cover design by: J. Kyzar-White

First Edition: December 2008

ISBN: 978-0-9814672-8-3

PRAISE FOR:

THE COST OF JUSTICE

As a former insurance defense lawyer and a Supreme Court Justice, I found this story, <u>The Cost of Justice</u>, to be credible and riveting...a thoroughly enjoyable read. Mike Gedgoudas, as an author, is obviously very talented.

Justice Tom Woodall
Associate Justice
Supreme Court of Alabama

While reading <u>The Cost of Justice,</u> I found that I thoroughly enjoyed the read. I felt it was excellent in a number of ways including character and plot development, vivid descriptions, technical expertise, and suspense. Mike Gedgoudas did a great job in wrapping up the story for the reader with the "1-year later" and "2- years later" segments. The action throughout gave the reader enough information to stay closely involved with the plot and characters without signaling the ending too soon. It is a story that will intrigue anyone who enjoys a good mystery and suspenseful drama.

Well written...Well researched...Well polished

Niki Sepsas
Adventure traveler
Freelance writer and novelist

Mike Gedgoudas

ACKNOWLEDGEMENTS

This book would not have been possible but for the help of numerous people, some of whom I will invariably leave out. To those whom I inadvertently missed, please accept my apology. You are all still very important to me. With that said, the following people were instrumental in getting this book into its final form: Carl and Des (I will miss you guys when you go home); Maggie Keller (for opening my eyes to the thousands of grammatical errors that occupied the first draft, and fixing them all); and Lois Bennett, for taking a chance on me.

Also, Niki Sepsas and Justice Tom Woodall for their endorsements and encouragement. A number of friends at RCC and elsewhere who read the manuscript and gave me the willpower to push hard to get this book published: Christine Martin, Bill (Two Feathers) Berkmeier, Larry MacIntosh, Bryan MacMurray, Jennifer Cole, Rich Klimpt, Nikki Christopher, Peg Jones, Ernie Benson, Judge Scott Vowell (a true mentor) and any others who read it that I may have left out.

Eternal thanks to Jan for the cover design and giving me everything I wanted this to be. You are amazing. Everyone at Fireside Publishing, thank you, thank you.

I owe everything I am and was able to become to my incredible family, extended and all: Mom, Len, Grandma and PaPa and Grandmother, Ronnie, Mom and Dad, and everyone else in this huge dysfunctional group that I love so dearly and who make life so enjoyable.

Lastly, thanks to Kim, Bub and Sis, for putting up with me while writing this book. Without their sacrifices of my time, this never would have happened. I hope they will be as generous for the coming books ☺

This novel was inspired by my visit to Biloxi, Mississippi several months after Hurricane Katrina devastated the area. It is dedicated to those who were fortunate enough to be treated properly and have been able to rebuild their lives as well as to those who have not.

Mike Gedgoudas

ONE

Jackson Garrett never expected to end up here, staring into the bottom of his favorite glass, now emptied of the last of the Makers Mark he started only four hours ago.

He had played it so magnificently from the beginning. How so much could disappear so fast was dizzying. Stephanie, the only person in whom he had ever confided during his adult life, was gone. Only the cedar-paneled walls of the study were available this afternoon.

He was alone, very alone.

Winter arrived at different times in Orange Beach, depending on the year. The start of the season became harder to predict when in 2006, it arrived with a whimper in early November then gave way to spring and almost summer with the dogwoods starting to bloom in mid-December. It never lasted that long, especially compared to areas north of the Mason Dixon line, where their idea of winter and South Alabaman's ideas were as opposite as red and blue.

Nature seemed even more confused than Jack this late January afternoon. Only the week before, temperatures had soared to almost eighty degrees, with the local children playing outside in shorts and, in some cases, no shirts. The dogwoods went back into hibernation almost the same day the kids went back into their houses, as the temps barely managed to reach forty. According to Mark Knowles, chief meteorologist at Channel 5, it was here to stay, at least for the next couple of weeks. It was the end of January and winter had sobered the mood of most of the state.

"You stupid son of a bitch," Jack whispered to no one. "You had to do it, didn't you?" he continued, reminding himself of his actions.

Buster was the only one listening now, except the walls of the empty study where Jack sought refuge during his need for reflection. Buster had been there for the last twelve years, never letting Jack down. He was there when Jack officially made the decision that would lead to today, and he agreed then it was the right thing to do. But Buster had lost most of his hearing and all of his sight. Most retrievers didn't live twelve years anyway. Still, it was enough for Jack that he was there.

"You just had to do it," he repeated aloud. "You know, Buster, maybe we deserve this after all," he said self deprecatingly, a bit louder, as Buster lay still at the window. As usual, he was staring through closed eyes at the willow tree that adorned the courtyard just twenty-five feet from the window of the study. "Buster! Do we or don't we?" he asked, still no answer from his friend.

The .38 on the corner of his desk came into focus again.

"You," Jack said to the pistol that had been removed from its hiding place only an hour ago.

"Is this really what it's come to now?"

The gun responded equally as well as Buster. Although the .38 had only been in Jack's life for the last forty-eight hours, it would have astonished voters from coastal Orange Beach to Huntsville, merely ten miles from the Tennessee line, that the sitting Chief Justice of the state Supreme Court didn't own a firearm until two days ago. After all, the NRA was one of his largest campaign contributors. Major newspapers reported all candidates' campaign contributors in the weeks prior to the general election. The NRA was the only one they could decipher, due to political action committees' success in hiding their contributions to candidates by transferring funds through numerous PAC's before reaching their final destinations.

For Christ's sake, Jack thought, the '04 election was virtually sealed with the advertisement of the Chief Justice hunting quail in a south Alabama field, flanked by the governor, who went on to win his second term two months later, and the former Chief Justice, who stepped down after sixteen years on the bench to pursue "personal interests." Justice Powell was passing the torch to the next up-and-coming "conservative judicial mind that would support the values of the people. A justice everyone could be proud of…a justice who would strictly interpret the law, and stand up for the great citizens of this State," according to the voice-over prepared by the same actor the national GOP had used in the state for the last five election cycles.

"I fucking hated that day," he told Buster, again.

But pretending to be what the public wanted was the only way to win in the current political climate. Even, if that meant whoring yourself out to the numbed mindless populace, as Jack had been informed early on.

Seven and a half years ago, Jack's only experience with a PAC was the same as that of lower level politicians. He read about them, and had been asked for donations from various PACs that found his name on their mailing lists. It was a necessity for all players, but the bigger the player, the more dangerous the game, both personally and now professionally. Soon, they'd taken on a much more meaningful role in the life of Chief Justice Garrett.

The meeting was scheduled for four p.m. And, if the news to be delivered by Bob Powell turned out as expected, there would be hell to pay. Unfortunately for the former Chief Justice, he would be first in the firing line.

At three fifteen p.m. Bob called, as promised.

"Jack, we have a decision," was all he said. "I'm on my way, near Foley. Should be there at four- thirty or so."

"I'll have the cognac ready," Jack said finally. "I have the feeling we'll both need it."

"Don't be so pessimistic, my friend," Bob replied. "I'm sure everything will work its way out. I'll see you in a bit."

As he hung up the phone, Eugene Jackson Garrett sat, still staring at the empty glass and the .38. In less than an hour he would know his fate and, quite possibly, that of his friend and mentor

TWO

Les Vance was the senior partner at Gibson Vance, one of the largest defense firms in Alabama. Les had made his way up the legal ladder the way more than half of Gibson Vance's senior personnel had, the old fashioned way – legacy. Through legacy he landed in Sigma Kappa Delta at the University of Virginia, where he graduated with a B.S. in history and later from UVA law school. Fresh out of law school in 1985, he was placed into an associate position at Gibson Vance. When his father, Leslie, died in 1990, he had made partner younger than most in the profession, the usual seven-year program being waived in his case. The legacy had to continue, and to his credit, Les had acquired a reputation as a strong advocate for his clients. His courtroom record was superb, and he was well respected, though not as strongly as his father.

Les presented a formidable persona at six feet two and two hundred ten pounds. Women, attracted by his dark hair and blue eyes, were never a problem for him. While at UVA, he played on the rugby team, and one season of football. He left football after spending most of his game time watching with the other sixty-five thousand people who regularly attended home games. He now reveled in the niceties of affluent life, living in a seven thousand square foot Spanish-style one level home in the Belvedere area.

He met Melanie, an undergrad at UVA from Vicksburg, Tennessee while he was in law school. Melanie had been groomed for her role as Les Vance's wife. Undergraduate school was hunting grounds for her, and she knew it. She proved to be a most proficient hunter in bagging Leslie Vance, Jr. Although he was never called Leslie, at the direction of his father, the family name had to be carried on, and Leslie, Sr. preferred that the "Jr." simply remain on the birth certificate at first. He would have to wait to see if his son could live up to his good name.

Gibson Vance also garnered the majority of the legal work for numerous insurance and corporate interests around the state. Les received a call from Taylor Franklin, in-house lead counsel for Insure Pro, just as he was barking his commands at his staff to set up the conference room's refreshments for the meeting.

The corporate jet had been delayed from Dallas due to the storm front that had gone through earlier that day. Mr. Franklin wouldn't be in until after four-thirty. Les sent the limo to the airport and awaited the arrival of Taylor Franklin. The Gulfstream IV landed ten minutes late and proceeded to AMR Combs private aircraft terminal. Taylor Franklin deplaned into an overcast, damp day. *Typical*, he thought. It seemed every visit in the winter to this redneck city was the same.

Dallas is much more sophisticated, more progressive. Just get me the hell out of here. Why is this damned state so backwards, anyway?

Greeting Taylor was Ben Cunningham, a nineteen year-old college sophomore, who worked as a courier for Gibson Vance. Les asked Ben to drive the limo to greet Mr. Franklin, a task he had performed only once before. Ben knew enough to keep his mouth shut. A brief "Hello, Mr. Franklin," and they were off to the Bank One Building, fifteen minutes from the airport. Ben dropped Franklin off at the main entrance and drove away.

At shortly after five pm, Taylor Franklin arrived at the thirty-fifth floor. The polite young receptionist showed him to the main conference room, though he needed no directions.

Taylor Franklin was a Texas native. After graduating from Texas A&M, he went on to Harvard Law where he graduated magna cum laude. He clerked for the Honorable Leo Gelding at the D.C. Court of Appeals before moving back to Dallas and starting his corporate defense career. For ten years he was Insure Pro's first selection for outside counsel when suit was filed in Texas. Taylor was handsome, well spoken and a gifted advocate. He had seen Insure Pro through some of their most difficult legal crises over the years. By 1995, at forty, he was offered the position of General Counsel at Insure Pro. He had grown tired of

11

representing a number of his highest profile clients, specifically those who ignored his advice. Insure Pro had always relied on Taylor, and it had served them well over the years. The compensation package presented to him was too great to turn down – stock options and base compensation, plus benefits. He was easily lured away from private practice. Taylor realized very quickly that he had made the right decision.

"How was your flight?" Les asked, because he had to, certainly not because he was interested.

"The same as always," he replied. "What is the status on the Garrett matter?" he continued.

"Bob left the JIC and is on his way to see him now," Les said.

"Where is he now?"

"He should be there within an hour or so. Can I get you a drink?" Les asked.

"Coffee, black…and get the rest of them in here now. I want to be out of here by seven," Taylor replied.

"We'll start as soon as we hear from Bob." Les left the room to gather the other partners involved in the Garrett matter. Les was sure there would be no reason to worry about Jack.

THREE

Bob Powell called Jack from The EZ Go Convenience store on Highway 98.

"Just tanking up, Jack. You need anything while I'm here?"

"I'm fine, Bob, see you soon."

"I can't wait to see the place again." Bob tried to make conversation as he waited to fill the tank.

"It hasn't changed much since the last time you were here; see you soon." Jack hung up.

Jack bought the beach property in 1986. It was located across from the front beach properties, and he purchased two and a half acres. After having practiced law for seven years, he had finally made it. It wasn't that he had been the best lawyer of his time. Jack Garrett simply got lucky.

He began practicing law in 1979 at the age of thirty. After graduating from the University of Alabama, he worked several dead end positions in sales, mainly for smaller manufacturing groups. It was enough to pay the bills, but certainly not enough to thrive. He entered law school several years later at his alma mater, and graduated with honors, after having also served on the law review.

He began his law practice with a small firm in Montgomery, the capital city. The majority of the work was general practice. He handled misdemeanor cases, divorce and child custody, and bankruptcy proceedings, along with a handful of probate matters. Several personal injury cases came along, which he enjoyed, too. After two years, he had built a rather impressive client base. Referrals were coming in at a good pace. He finally figured that he was making Stan Yost and Bill Young more money than they needed, and Yost and Young lost their first associate.

Jack decided to give it a go on his own, and he opened his own practice. In 1981, Jackson Garrett & Associates opened for business in the eastern edge of Montgomery. The name was rather misleading, as there were no "associates." But such was the way of marketing a one-man show. Appearance meant everything, and the name mattered not. Jack knew if the client came in the door, he could seal the deal, no matter the type of case.

The office, rented space in an office building off the Eastern Boulevard, was in a modest. two-story building built around 1970. Two offices occupied the second floor – a temp service, and an electronics repair store. Jackson Garrett & Associates had a three-room office on the first floor, facing the parking lot outside. His neighbor in the building was a small mortgage broker who, like Jack, knew the proper marketing strategy, calling the two-person group National Mortgage and Finance.

Jack used the main office and purchased a desk and credenza, along with a couple of high-backed cloth chairs for clients. The walls were adorned with his framed degrees from the University and his certificate from the Supreme Court of Alabama to practice law, signed by each justice on the Supreme Court in 1979.

The foyer was the reception area, with a small black leather sofa and two black leather chairs for clients. The receptionist desk had been purchased at the local Office Depot and assembled personally on a slow afternoon. The phone system was generic, and there were two trays on the receptionist's desk, an "in" tray and an "out" tray. Located behind the receptionist area was a small office that was used as a copy room and file room, home to a small leased copier and postage meter. One five-level filing cabinet was on the wall opposite the copier. Jack kept a mini refrigerator in the copy room stocked with cokes for the clients who requested a drink.

It was here that Jack began the daily grind that supported him and Stephanie. He and Steph married in 1978 during his third year in law school. She had worked as a secretary for a law firm in Tuscaloosa when he clerked there during the summer. She was entering her second marriage, and Jack needed the company.

Being slightly overweight, and having begun to bald in his early twenties, Jack was happy to find an attractive woman who genuinely seemed to love him. Steph supported him in every way during his early years in practice and didn't complain that they lived in an apartment early in their relationship. They eventually bought a small house just outside of town. It wasn't ideal, but it was home ownership.

Jackson Garrett & Associates plugged along, gaining clients along the way. The general practice income well exceeded the pay he had made at Yost & Young. Jack soon began to generate more income annually each year, and fell into a routine, content to stay where he was. He represented plaintiffs and defendants, but he was relatively under the radar in Montgomery. His life changed dramatically in 1985.

* * *

A former client called Jack late on a Friday in June, just as he was about to leave the office. "Mr. Garrett, you probably don't remember me; my name is Eunice Johnson." Jack had grown accustomed to clients beginning conversations this way. But he remembered all his clients specifically. It was a gift he was happy to have.

"Eunice, dear, how are you and Harold doing?" Jack replied.

Eunice Johnson broke down immediately. Sobbing over the phone, she told him, "I lost Harold, Mr. Jack. They took him from me."

Over the next forty-five minutes Jack heard the facts as presented by Eunice Johnson, and he knew he had to sign this case today. "Ms. Eunice, do you still live on 38th Avenue West?" he asked, hoping his Rolodex still held her correct contact information.

"Yes sir, Mr. Jack."

"I'll be there in fifteen minutes, OK ma'am?"

"OK, Mr. Jack."

Jack called Steph to let her know he would be late, and sped over to Eunice and Harold Johnson's house.

It was true.

* * *

Harold Johnson was retired from the Navy. He served in World War II, and had seen action in Europe. He had traveled to Dothan, about an hour and a half drive south of Montgomery, to visit with his daughter and granddaughter for the day. On the way home, Harold was stopped at a traffic light in Troy, thirty minutes from home. He never knew what hit him.

But now, Jack did. The report was right in front of him. An eighteen-wheel truck, carrying flammable liquids, slammed directly into the rear of his Dodge Neon. As Jack would later learn, the car was virtually unidentifiable after the accident. There was speculation that the truck driver had been on medication, or possibly had been driving for far too long. It mattered not to Jack . Ms. Eunice signed a contract with Jackson Garrett & Associates that afternoon.

After completing the appropriate probate forms, and having Ms. Eunice appointed as representative of the estate of her deceased husband, Jack had the lawsuit filed within a day. Discovery followed. Jack learned quickly that the driver of the truck that took Harold Johnson away from his wife of sixty-five years had a seizure disorder. His last run had lasted seventeen hours. He was so exhausted that he couldn't keep his eyes open, so he had taken some pills bought from a truck stop six hours before the accident. The main problem was that they were purchased from someone outside the store. A methamphetamine addiction didn't correspond well with the driver's epilepsy.

The company had full knowledge of their driver's medical history and discovery in the lawsuit revealed that they had reason to believe he had drug problems as well. It was clear that they had tried to cover up their knowledge of the trucker's medical history by doctoring his medical file. There were no other injuries and no other vehicles involved in the accident. After only six months of litigation, First American Casualty and Indemnity issued the settlement check made payable to Jackson Garrett & Associates and Eunice Johnson, as Personal Representative of the Estate of Harold Johnson, deceased, for the sum of fifteen million dollars – a color copy of which would adorn the walls of Jack's office for another five years. Jack wouldn't have to worry about the ensuing litigation between the excess insurers and the company over the concealment of the driver's condition.

* * *

Jack paid cash for the property in Orange Beach and began building his dream home, a Mediterranean bi-level. It included five thousand square feet of living area and sported a red stucco tile roof, certainly larger than most of the residences in the area, but far from being a monstrosity. An iron fence with a double gate surrounding the property guarded its entrance from the front beach road.

The house sat back two hundred fifty feet from the entrance. A circular driveway of various shades of red brick directed traffic around a concrete fountain located in front of the residence. One branch of the drive continued around the right side of the house to the garage, while the other circled back to the main roadway leading to the beach road.

The entrance into the house was just as Jack had wished –two large doors, opening from the middle, and a small front porch with three steps arched in a half circle, proceeding down to the driveway.

The main floor consisted of a large two-story foyer with a spiraling staircase leading to the second floor. The dining room on the left and sitting area on the right both faced the front lawn. The master bedroom to the rear of the house featured vaulted ceilings and opened into the master bath, with a stone lined four-person shower. The walk-in closet, a room in and of itself, could hold Jack and Stephanie's full wardrobes, with plenty of room to spare.

An open floor plan created an aura of relaxation and comfort with the living area tastefully decorated with leather sofas and ottomans, complemented by matching recliners facing the built-in entertainment center. A sixty-inch-plasma television was centered above the gas fireplace providing entertainment for the entire room. Floor to ceiling windows encompassing French doors led to a rear deck of treated pine, stained a deep brown. Thick centipede grass covered the back yard, with several palm trees dotting the landscape.

Jack's study was set off from the garage, on the back right side of the house. The study consisted mainly of reference books, law journals, and an occasional recreational book, though recreational reading was rarely in Jack's schedule. Bay windows overlooked the courtyard adjacent to the driveway, where a two-year-old willow tree replaced the one Jack had planted when the house was first constructed.

* * *

Bob Powell pulled his new white BMW745 into the driveway of Chief Justice Jackson Garrett's house, stopping in front of the double doors. He walked up the three steps to the entrance, took a deep breath, and rang the doorbell.

Jack opened the door and immediately Bob knew this whole thing had taken its toll on him. Jack was wearing blue jeans, a buttoned down white dress shirt and black loafers with no socks. Bob leaned in and offered his hand.

"You holding up, buddy?" Bob asked, genuinely concerned.

"I've told you three times – I'm fine." Jack responded.

Bob could tell that Jack had been drinking. How much he wasn't sure, but he had that look. Bob always thought that Jack had a fondness for the bottle, but he presumed that it never got the better of him. "Let's go to the study, Jack."

"I'd rather we sat in the living room," he replied.

"Very well. You have the cognac?"

"Give me a second." Jack led Bob Powell into the living room and turned to the kitchen to pour the drinks. Bob studied the rear of the house. Dusk was upon them, and landscape lighting in the back yard had just come on.

Jack returned from the kitchen and handed Bob his cognac then sat in the recliner nearest the French doors. Bob took a seat on the sofa.

"Have you talked to Steph?" Bob was clearly procrastinating the conversation. He knew his friend was deeply stressed, but he was also buying some time.

"You didn't come down here to talk about my ex, and we both know it, Bob." Powell clearly knew nothing about his personal life now. Jack assumed the worst and was sure that his old pal was simply dragging the matter out because he was the only person that the JIC could think of to break the news gently to him. "Well, what am I going to be doing tomorrow?" Jack got straight to the point.

"You are going to be the Chief Justice of the Supreme Court of Alabama." That was it. No explanation. Bob sat silently, staring at Jack and trying to discern his thoughts.

"What do you mean?" Jack inquired, looking for some degree of reassurance to make sure he had heard him correctly.

"I mean, the JIC has determined that there will be no action taken; you will resume your duties as Chief Justice." Bob said clearly.

"I was sure that…" Jack was baffled; he couldn't speak. He had been sure his career as Chief Justice was over.

Bob interrupted, "Jack, you know I am not a member of the JIC, so I don't know what the process is…" Bob was lying. Not about being a member of the Judicial Inquiry Commission, for he certainly was not. But the basis for the Commission's determination to exonerate him, he knew full well. "But the decision came down late this morning, and they are taking no action against you, that's all I know."

* * *

Jack leaned back and struggled to make sense of what he had just heard. The constitutionally created Judicial Inquiry Commission investigates complaints of misconduct and professional wrongdoing concerning judges. Consisting of judges, lawyers, and non-lawyers, the JIC had taken action against judges for such things as misleading campaign advertisements and wrongfully incarcerating a witness for his testimony, likely a power trip more than anything else.

Chief Justice Garrett didn't know how the case against him originated. He knew all too well the reason, but how the publicity came about left him completely in the dark.

Two years ago, Jack had attended a judicial conference in Atlanta. These conferences were routine, and judges were treated to them constantly. They were wined and dined, usually by promoters of the conference, who were closely affiliated with lobbyists representing the constituencies that sought to have "their candidate" elected. For appellate judges in Alabama, this meant a free weekend at a luxury hotel or resort, with all the amenities. Although virtually the rest of the country had realized that electing judges on party lines was probably not in the best interests of justice, Alabama held on to the old way of doing things.

Judges over the last several decades campaigned on issues that came before them. Tell the voters outright that they wanted to ban abortion, or expand tort reform, incarcerate drug offenders for life…you name it. If the candidate found a hot issue, he'd tell you how he'd rule on it up front. To hell with the law! If I don't like it, and you agree with me, I'll change it. And it worked.

In spite of the realization that the legislature enacts laws, the judiciary in Alabama continued over the last twenty years, nonetheless, to create laws as they saw fit. Albeit a unique method, it worked. Jack Garrett learned early on how to get around the pesky legislature, and even those juries that people loathe so much.

The "Effective Administration of Justice" seminar was held at the Ritz Carlton Hotel in Buckhead, Georgia, in early 2006. Jack went along with several other appellate judges and, for the most part, kept to himself, as usual. Late Friday evening he went to the lounge located off the main lobby of the five-star hotel. Fridays were big nights at the Ritz. A jazz band played in the lounge, and the upper class Atlantans and business travelers would settle in for a relaxing evening of wine, liquor and music.

Around eleven-thirty p.m., as Jack was listening to the band, a rather nice looking woman approached and asked if the seat next to him was available. Steph had been gone for ten years. He had been too frightened to express interest in the only other woman in his life. Loneliness was something he had come to embrace as preordained. The brunette was friendly and struck up a conversation. It lasted for an hour or more, and the drinks kept flowing. She related her sob story of divorce and failed relationships that mirrored Jack's, so he listened intently.

At one in the morning, she escorted Jack Garrett upstairs to her room, holding his arm to keep him balanced. Jack had virtually no recollections of that evening. He remembered talking to her in the lounge; other than that, most of the night was a blur. The headache he woke with the next morning rivaled anything he had ever known. She was gone, and he was in his own room. Most of Saturday was spent recovering, and Jack missed the seminar, though no one seemed to notice, and clearly no one seemed to care. He returned to Montgomery on Sunday, making the two- hour drive down Interstate 85 back to his house in the city. He felt like he'd been run over by a freight train.

About a month later the story broke, first in the Times, not the largest paper in the state, but it was sure to spread quickly. **CHIEF JUSTICE CAUGHT WITH PANTS DOWN** was the headline in the paper out of Anniston, a medium sized city on the eastern side of the state, about forty-five minutes from Atlanta. An unnamed source had reportedly informed the paper that the current Chief Justice of the Supreme Court had been partying hard in Atlanta and a videotape of his sexual escapades had surfaced. *A videotape! I don't even remember the fucking night, let alone the woman's name, and I certainly didn't video myself.* Jack was completely befuddled. *Who the hell was she? What is she doing? Who is behind this? Surely she couldn't have known who I was.* There were no answers…only more questions.

It wasn't long before the rest of the media outlets had picked up the story. If there was one positive aspect to the matter, it was that the story only ran for a day or so. No pictures were ever printed, only a recitation of the supposed facts - facts which Jack was unsure of, due to his amnesia of that evening. If the video existed, he hadn't seen it, and had no idea where it was, if it existed at all.

It mattered not to the Chief Justice. The complaint of misconduct, or conduct unbecoming a judge was filed. By whom, he was not told. The matter went before the JIC. Jack knew some of the members of the JIC. The appellate judge was Ron Thompson, a Republican from Mobile, who sat on the Court of Civil Appeals. Jack and Ron were acquaintances and shared similar views. He also knew the two circuit court judges, Billy Marshall, from Jackson County, and Sherman Pope, from Madison County. Both supported him in his campaign. The two state bar members, both lawyers from Birmingham, were also supporters, although he knew very little about either. He had no idea who the non-lawyers were.

The charge carried much more political capital than professional consequence, Jack thought. *Hell, half the elected officials had cheated on their spouses, and I'm not even married now.* It was true, although his marriage was dissolved in 1994, the allegations of the unnamed woman, or whoever it was, were sure to have an impact on his public appeal. Voters wanted to elect pure, family men. Granted, by 2010, when the next election was to be held, many would forget about this tryst, except his opponents, who would hammer away at it. *I may not even run again. Private practice can still be entertaining, and I can make a good living.* But Jack had come to relish his position on the high court.

* * *

Having informed Jack of the good news, Bob Powell sat sipping his cognac. It was clear that Jack was relieved at hearing his job was safe. Now was the time for Bob to do what he was paid to do.

"Before I go, there's one thing I need to ask you about, my friend," Bob said as he straightened his posture. He set his cognac on the wrought iron coffee table that separated the two jurists, and commanded the attention of his friend.

"Yes," was all Jack could manage to say. His mind was still spinning, trying to take in the magnitude of what had occurred only a minute ago.

"Jack, as you know, the *Whisenhunt* case is going to be on the docket before long," Bob said matter-of-factly.

"I'm aware it will likely come up, Bob," Jack started, "but we don't expect it for a while." "Hell, Bob, that's the first of the trials and it doesn't even begin for several more weeks."

"I realize that, Jack. But you know as well as I do that, either way, it and the others are going up." Bob was referring to a fact that everyone involved already knew. No matter who prevailed in the cases, the losing party was going to appeal.

No question.

"And you are also aware of the seriousness of those cases?" Bob inquired.

"All cases we review are serious," Jack responded.

"I agree," the former Chief Justice replied. "I've been in your position before, you know. But there are degrees of importance in each case as well."

"What is your point, Bob?"

"Jack, you know the balance is not as it was six years ago." Bob was gaining more attention as Jack began to question internally why this matter had come up at such a time. After all, Bob's interested party might prevail. Barring any errors by the trial judge, Jack knew that he would not reverse such a judgment for the hell of it. Jack sensed that Bob was anticipating a loss, trying to prepare him for the inevitable.

"You have a long career on the bench ahead of you, Jack. But some cases will cry out for attention. There has to be some balance."

"Again, what is your point, Bob?" Jack began to appear agitated.

"I don't want to see any of your contributors backpedaling, Jack. What did you raise for your campaign in '04?"

"You know how much we raised." Jack was puzzled. "Is there something I should know?"

"We're not that different you know, Jack. When I was in your position I derived some of my funding from the same sources that you do now, and I just wanted to make sure you remembered where you came from. I'm looking out for you, and we certainly don't need to find ourselves four to five," Bob said.

"I know where I came from, and I'm well aware of my situation." Jack had been reminded before on numerous occasions. *Toe the party line. Keep your money happy. Blah. Blah. Blah.* Jack was getting pissed at the insinuation that he was being threatened at this juncture, although not officially.

"So, we are on the same page," Bob continued.

"Most definitely," Jack said with conviction.

"Perfect. When will you be returning to the Capital?"

"I'll stay here for another day or so – session doesn't start until a week from now anyway. I need to recoup," Jack said.

"I'll call you next week, my friend. And… congratulations."

"Thanks."

Bob stood up and shook his friend's hand. "I've got to get back home before it gets too late," Bob said as he made his way to the front door.

"Drive safe," Jack said as he watched Bob get in his car.

Bob pulled out of the driveway after spending thirty minutes with the Chief Justice.

Jack returned to the study, with Buster still lying asleep at the window, just as he always was. Jack looked at the .38 still perched at the corner of his desk. *What in the hell were you thinking? Tomorrow I am taking you back.* As Jack picked up the pistol, it felt so foreign to him. *You've never even fired a gun.* He replaced it in its spot in the drawer. *God, that was pathetic.*

***

Bob Powell pulled onto Highway 98. As soon as he passed through the gates of the Garrett property, he called.

"Gibson Vance, may I help you?" The voice was familiar.

"Sheila, Bob Powell. Give me Les, please."

"One minute, sir."

"Bob, how did it go?" Les Vance was sitting with Taylor Franklin in the conference room when the call came through.

"Put Taylor on," Bob commanded.

"Yes sir." Les had known Bob Powell for most of his professional life. He disliked the old man, and was tired of him barking orders. But Les knew better than to make anything of it.

"Well, where are we?" Taylor asked of Bob.

"I'll be there in four hours. Jack's not a problem, any more."

"Are you sure?" Taylor asked.

"Look, Jack was positive that he was done. You should have seen the look on his face when I told him he was still on the Court." Bob was smiling now.

"Did you warn him?" Taylor pressed on.

"Not outright. He knows what's at stake in this situation. I'm telling you, Jack is not our problem."

"What now?" Taylor asked, knowing full well the Chief Justice didn't appreciate the full magnitude of what was at stake.

"Tell Les that you're done. Go check into the Tutwiler. I'll be there in four hours. Call Rick and let him know we'll be ready by eleven tonight." Bob hung up.

Taylor relayed the information to Les. There would be no meeting. He didn't care that Vance was pissed and confused. Taylor also knew that Les couldn't question their decision. He took pride in knowing he held so much control over the man.

After a brief and insincere good-bye, Taylor was back in the limo, headed for the Tutwiler Hotel, three blocks away.

Bob arrived in town and met Taylor as promised at the valet.

At eleven-fifteen p.m., Taylor Franklin and the former Chief Justice of the Alabama Supreme Court took off from Birmingham International Airport. The flight to Dallas Fort Worth International would take less than an hour.

FOUR

The Eunice Johnson case allowed Jack to continue his private practice. Work began on the beach home and Jack was finally out of debt, having made a small fortune with her case. He worked much less than before, feeling he deserved a break. He was happy, at last, but his happiness was short lived.

In May of 1990, Stephanie came home from her afternoon tennis league, her usual routine since quitting any semblance of work five years earlier, and informed him that she was not happy. He had been too pre-occupied with the beach home, work, everything but her. She filed for divorce the next week.

The threat of divorce devastated Jack. Unfounded accusations replaced the truth. Stephanie never mustered the courage to tell him she'd fallen for a younger man, so the act was played out. She had been the driving force behind his success and had made his life easier. Now, she was gone. Stephanie moved from their house in Montgomery the same day she announced it was over, convincing Jack she was serious. Efforts to reconcile, all on his behalf, were met with hostility. After the third pathetic effort, Jack, too, understood the finality of the marriage.

The divorce was brutal for Jack.

Not being a beach person, Steph had no interest in the beach house. She did, however, have an interest in the money. And Jack paid. He thought if he offered enough, maybe she might reconsider. There were more Eunice Johnsons out there. People died in accidents every day. Lightning could strike twice. He could give her even more, but she didn't appear to care.

The proceedings ended with Steph having taken half of Jack's accumulated funds. The court did not order her newfound riches; Jack voluntarily offered them. He still had more than enough money to accommodate his lifestyle anyway. He got the beach house and kept half interest in the property in Montgomery.

Jack was forty-two, divorced, with no kids. He had enough cash to pay the bills and had his beach home. His practice had begun to deteriorate, due largely to his lack of desire to earn new clients. Twelve years of marriage were gone, and he was lonely, again.

Jackson Garrett & Associates continued to operate after the divorce, but lacked zest. Jack gradually recovered from his grief, but the desire to practice law as a sole practitioner had waned.

By 1992 a new opportunity presented itself when Jack was approached by Sims Battle, senior partner at Battle, Palmgren & Hickson. Jack was Sims' adversary in the Eunice Johnson case and the two lawyers had gone into combat on several other matters through the years. Jack's abilities as a lawyer were well known and he was respected, as a person. More than once, Sims had hinted that Jack could be a good defense attorney.

Jack met Sims again in September of 1992 at a docket call. This time they were not opponents. Sims struck up a conversation, asking how Jack had been doing since his divorce. Unbeknownst to Jack, Sims' ex-wife was Stephanie's new tennis partner. Sims got an even worse deal than Jack did out of his divorce. Three children and alimony had left him financially and spiritually broke four years earlier. They exchanged sob stories and a few laughs then Sims convinced Jack that further discussions about a partnership couldn't hurt anyone. They both knew that other trial lawyers had changed sides and prospered.

A number of corporate interests valued having the mind and creative thinking of a former plaintiff's lawyer on their side. Their perspective of the other side was unmatched when compared to the career defense attorney. Compensation was comparable and consistent. Although billing hours would be new, it sure beat the stress of wondering if a payday was nearby.

Sims had built a well-respected firm, with twenty-five lawyers, one of the fastest growing practices in the state, second only to Gibson Vance. His firm actually had a lot in common with Gibson Vance. They shared many of the same clients in the insurance and automotive industries . Gibson Vance handled most of the cases in the northern part of the state, with Sims' group getting the bulk of the southern areas.

Sims had recruited many lawyers from various areas in the southern sector of the state. When it came to courtroom appearances in those areas, it was always a plus to have a lawyer who knew the judge, and every partner and associate who went to court for Sims Battle had that connection. Gibson Vance commanded cases based in federal courts and larger cities, and Sims was fine with that. Practicing law in Alabama was niche marketing. And Sims Battle was well versed in his niche.

Two months of negotiations later, Jackson Garrett became an immediate partner at Battle, Palmgren, Hickson and Garrett. Jack had never been a publicity hound, and had not even paid much attention to the story that ran in the News following the *Johnson* case. But Jack had been used as yet another example of the runaway awards that were falling into the laps of plaintiffs' lawyers in the southern state.

News of the settlement was intentional. Most settlements for large sums were done under a confidentiality agreement. Neither side was allowed to discuss or publish the terms, except as provided by law, such as to accountants or by court order. Jack hadn't thought of doing so, and the omission of the confidentiality provision didn't cause him to raise an eyebrow.

First American Casualty and Indemnity saw an opening and took it. Within a week of the settlement, the terms were leaked to *The Birmingham News*, the largest daily publication in the state. The tort reformers went crazy. "Jackpot Justice Continues," "Trucking Company Pays Fifteen Million for Two Car Collision" and "Montgomery Lawyer wins Lotto in Car Wreck" were the headlines. It was more fodder for the movement that would lead to the Court's eventual turnaround several years later.

In 1992, one of the unknowing poster children of the tort reform movement became a defense attorney, representing the very clients who had been victimized by the system in the heart of Dixie. The truth of the matter was that Jack never fancied himself a trial lawyer. Sure, he had made a rather good living on some personal-injury-type cases, but he had handled other cases as well. The *Johnson* case was an anomaly.

Jack settled into defense work easily. And, he was a popular choice of many Battle Palmgren clients. His reputation, the one he had only recently come to know, had preceded him. Judges, in both federal and state courts, gave great weight to the arguments of the former trial lawyer now advocating on behalf of the defendant. He began to love practicing law again.

Jackson Garrett was winning cases. Most cases.

For the defendants. He was the champion of their cause.

By 1997, Jack had become a well-known litigator on behalf of numerous insurance, automotive and financial groups in the south. When Steve Wilson, the "liberal, trial lawyer backed, casino backed" pawn of the (dying) left wing announced that he was running for a third term, the state Republican Party began its search for an opponent.

Jack's name shot to the top of the list. What better candidate to beat the liberal left-winger than the former poster child himself. He was bulletproof from the left, thanks in large part to poor old Harold Johnson, and endorsed by the right.

He sailed through the primary with ninety percent of the vote. The general election was a bloodbath. Never before in the history of Alabama politics had a sitting Chief Justice been ousted by such a large margin. Eighty-five percent of the voters cast their ballot for Jackson Garrett. He outpaced other Republican candidates by thirty percent, although most won their races as well.

At forty-eight years old, Jack became the youngest Chief Justice of the Alabama Supreme Court. And he took over a Supreme Court that only twelve years before had no sitting Republican justice. In just over a decade, the Democrat-controlled Supreme Court had vanished; it was a nine to nothing GOP stronghold. Like all good things, it, too, would pass.

* * *

The initial impact of the new Court was radical. Jack was not pleased with the disregard for precedent that was exhibited by his colleagues, but he was powerless to stop the flow. Despite his financial backing, Jack still saw himself as a moderate. He was cognizant of the fact that the people of Alabama weren't nearly as partisan as the Court.

29

Jack came to know that, while the people cared about crime and its effects and threats on them personally, the real players were the people who put the judges in office – not the voters, but the donors, for it was they who demanded specific action in specific cases; and it was all about one thing.

Money ruled. Jack realized soon enough that the Supreme Court was about one thing, and one thing only – cash.

His first taste of sour grapes came quickly. *Forrester v. Cypress Insurance* was a simple matter to decide. Wayne Forrester had filed suit against his own insurance company for benefits he claimed were due for a fire that destroyed his home. Cypress denied the claim immediately, claiming that Wayne had set fire to his own home, seeking the proceeds. There was ample evidence of arson, but Wayne and his family were out of town the night of the fire. Cypress argued that Wayne had put his house on the market then suddenly taken it off the MLS listing a mere two months later. This provided evidence, they claimed, that he, somehow, had motive for burning his family's house down, together with every personal possession that they had acquired over fifteen years. Outside of that, no other evidence to support the claim of arson submitted by Cypress existed.

The jury was outraged. Cypress was found liable for bad faith failure to pay the claim and ordered to pay the Forresters the two hundred thousand for their home and an additional hundred grand for contents. Additionally, they were slapped with three million dollars in punitive damages for their conduct.

On appeal, Cypress claimed that there was insufficient evidence to support the claim made by Wayne Forrester. The record on appeal was strongly in favor of the Forresters. The Court had only one issue to decide: "Was discretion abused by the trial judge in allowing the case to go to the jury?" Despite the evidence, the Court in an eight-to-one decision held that there was not enough evidence to warrant imposition of punitive damages.

Jack Garrett was the sole dissenting opinion.

The Court ruled that Cypress had to pay the claim for the residence and the personal contents – nothing more.

Wayne Forrester lost, effectively. After legal fees, he couldn't pay the balance on the house. Foreclosure proceedings ensued.

Cypress celebrated their victory.

After four years of litigation, the Garrett Court had ordered Cypress,, to pay what they should have paid from the beginning. Money bought victory.

Cypress knew it.

Jack knew it.

And it made him sick.

Jack Garrett was the dissenting voice in a number of opinions that followed *Forrester*, most of the time in a predictable eight to one decision.

While his supporters questioned his faithfulness, Jack assured them there was a method to his madness.

Few outside of the legal profession, including a number of those practicing law, had any idea how cases came before the Court. Even fewer understood how opinions came to fruition.

FIVE

After five hours of sleep, Bob Powell woke to the sound of his hotel room's phone.

"Mr. Powell, this is your wake up call." The attendant sounded half asleep herself.

He hung up without saying anything. Bob showered and got dressed. He proceeded down the elevator to the hotel lobby and dined on doughnuts and coffee. Sitting in the lobby, he picked up his cell phone and dialed Taylor.

"Are we on for eight?"

"We're here," was all Taylor said.

"I'll be there in thirty minutes." Bob finished his coffee and left the lobby. He got in his rental car and sped down I-20 for the thirty-minute drive to Insure Pro's home office.

The enormous compound of Insure Pro, located fifteen miles north of downtown Dallas, near Carrollton, employed four thousand people at the home office. More like a small city than an office complex, the massive size of the company required that shifts be worked twenty-four hours a day. There was never a moment that Insure Pro closed down. Staff, in one aspect or another, worked on Christmas Day, New Years Day - every day.

The mega-insurer provided all the extras for its employees, including an on-site child-care center. Several restaurants such as Applebee's, McDonald's and KFC saw locating on the grounds as a profitable venture. Also available were two large exercise facilities, one housing an Olympic sized pool, while ping-pong and billiard tables had been located adjacent to the Fitness Center. Cost had not been an issue in creating the college campus atmosphere.

Insure Pro, the largest property and casualty insurer in North America, conducted business in every state in the union. The company kept a high profile as a major corporate sponsor of many professional sports. The Insure Pro Classic Invitational at Eagle Ridge Golf & Country Club, one of the highest purse pro golf tournaments of the year, drew more spectators over the week than any other event on the tour. Last year's event resulted in more than a million dollars going to local charities.

Bob Powell arrived at the security entrance of Insure pro just before eight a.m. Each employee and visitor had to check in at the main gate before entering. For convenience, personnel had a pass card that could be swiped across the electronic post ten feet before the security guard's shack. As the gate opened, waves were exchanged and the employee sped on through.

Bob didn't have a parking pass; he still lived outside of Birmingham with his wife, Susan. His two children were grown and had moved out of state long ago. He pulled up to the electronic reader, drew his credentials from his wallet and swiped them across the blank metal face of the ID verification system. The gate slid open, and he drove through. The security guard's smile and wave went unnoticed, and unreturned.

He drove to the far end of the compound to the Executive Plaza. The Plaza was reserved for the offices of the highest-level execs at Insure Pro. It was a five story building adorned with gray stone columns and emerald green windows. Private covered parking abutted the Plaza with reserved spots, each delineated with a black marble sign etched with the name of the occupant.

After parking the Lincoln Town Car in his reserved space in the visitor's parking area, located to the right of the Plaza, Bob Powell headed toward the executive offices. Each time he came to Dallas, a different car awaited him. He saw no use in keeping a car in Dallas, even though he was here twice a month. Insure Pro offered to move him and Susan here, but he insisted on staying in Birmingham.

At the Plaza, another card reader was located adjacent to the glass doors at the front of the building. He swiped his credentials and proceeded through the main entrance.

The black marble floors of the three-story foyer were buffed to a high gloss. A twenty-foot steel sculpture resembling razor wire surrounding steel I-beams, offset to the right, had been commissioned by a local artist, as had most pieces surrounding the compound.

The former chief justice got on the elevator and pressed the button for the fifth floor. Only three offices were located on the fifth floor of the Plaza. Taylor Franklin occupied the office at the east end of the floor. Next to his suite was the office of Daniel Spearman, Director of Security. The west end suite belonged to Joseph Kirschberg, the Chief Executive Officer of Insure Pro.

Bob knocked on Taylor's door as he walked in. Taylor and Dan Spearman were lounging on the sofas that surrounded the sitting area outside of Taylor's main office. "Come on in, Bob," Taylor said, as Bob made himself at home, sitting on the third sofa in the circle. "Can we get you anything?"

"I ate already. Where do you want to go to discuss this?" Bob was ready to get to the point. He hoped to be back home by dinner and didn't want to make use of his time by discussing irrelevant issues.

"We're ready to proceed now. Right here is fine with us. Joe's not here today anyway, and just wants the matter handled as we see fit." At Taylor's nod, Dan got up and retrieved the Garrett file from the credenza abutting the windows overlooking the fountain in front of the Plaza.

Dan Spearman was an intimidating force of a man at forty-two and still in excellent shape. He was six feet four and a muscular two hundred thirty pounds. He couldn't let go of the crew cut, although it was likely longer than when he had been in the service He spent his military career in Special Forces, having served time in Bosnia, Granada and other places that he probably wasn't allowed to talk about. Dan looked the part as well, even ten years after he'd left the service.

He was always dressed in a dark navy suit with a red and blue striped tie. He must have owned ten different versions of that same pattern, because, although Bob had known him for some time and certainly had seen him many times before, the tie was always slightly changed from his last encounter.

Dan continued to exercise vigorously. He was in the gym six days a week. Weight routines were alternated every other day, with chest and biceps on Monday and Thursday, back, shoulders and triceps on Tuesday and Friday, legs on Wednesday and Saturday. Cardiovascular training complemented the regimen five days a week. Sundays were taken off. His diet was monitored as closely as his exercise. Bob thought on more than one occasion that one week of Dan's schedule, and he would have a heart attack – no question.

Dan came to Insure Pro in early 2002, stumbled his way in, actually. After his honorable discharge from the U.S. Army, he had tried his hand at private security. While he had the physical attributes, his business savvy was terrible. He had no idea how to market himself, and, more often than not, he would scare away potential clients. If that didn't break a deal, his intimidation would generally step in to ruin it.

He met Taylor Franklin after a workout at Irving Fitness and Training. Taylor admired the conviction that Dan imposed upon his regimen. They struck up a conversation after a joint run on the treadmill, and Taylor asked what line of work he was in.

Dan regaled his military background, with some exaggeration for affect then admitted that his attempts at private contracting had been difficult. Taylor ultimately offered him a position at Insure Pro, in the security department. His early assignments were security detail for Joe and other execs visiting Dallas. He occasionally went on junkets with board members or other officers of the company who preferred to take vacations in countries with less than attractive locals.

Always, he had security detail.

He was well liked by the officers and directors whom he guarded. They always felt safe when Dan was around. Taylor had personally used him on several occasions, and had grown fond of him. Although brutish, he was an intelligent individual who understood his role and, as it evolved, so too did Dan. His lucky break came four years into his tenure with Insure Pro.

Paul Herring, the acting Director of Security and also Dan's immediate superior, was killed in a motorcycle accident. Paul had been an experienced rider, even entering several super bike events in the Dallas area. Speculation abounded when Paul was found lying off the side of Kennington Boulevard, a suburban road that wound its way around the outskirts of the Dallas Fort Worth area. Paul's Harley Davidson, a cruising bike, had left the roadway, his bike and body striking a tree head on. The autopsy revealed no presence of alcohol or drugs, and the area of the accident had never been considered a dangerous stretch.

Paul's death was ruled accidental, and Dan was approached by Taylor to head the Security Department. Joe Kirschberg requested that Taylor head the search for Paul's replacement. Joe trusted Taylor immensely. Though he was General Counsel, Taylor was given wide latitude in making decisions affecting all aspects of Insure Pro.

Dan oversaw a department that employed fifty security personnel. Most of them had been acquired from local security companies or through temp agencies, and then hired full time. The vast majority of their work was menial—patrolling the grounds, policing the Insure Pro property, and the occasional escort of a fired employee from the premises, ensuring that their credentials and access passes were accounted for, in case the recently departed felt a need for revenge. Dan left those tasks to the underlings. Now he had convinced himself, he was essentially an executive.

Dan Spearman handed the file, consisting of two brown shucks filled to complete expansion, to Taylor.

"You are absolutely sure that Jack will not be a problem?" Taylor again questioned Bob for what seemed like the fourth time since his visit to the beach home.

"Jack may be difficult to read, but he is with us, I assure you." Bob didn't come across as confident as he tried to sound.

"We have the old dissents, you know. It would appear that he could flip at any time." Taylor referenced the opinions Bob already knew about, those from his first term.

"Have you read the recent opinions?" the former chief asked.

"I am cognizant of his latest rulings, but he still makes me uneasy. Are you sure we did the right thing with the JIC?" Taylor's job dictated that he be cautiously pessimistic.

"Absolutely. You should focus your efforts elsewhere; somewhere you know a problem awaits us." Bob couldn't have been more satisfied that his work with the JIC had been the right thing to do. His friend had made a mistake and the consequences of his actions did not warrant his removal from office.

"There are four alternatives as I see it," Taylor said. "Coburn, Stanley, Bridges or Callahan. Any ideas, Bob?"

"They're all relatively new, as you know, but I can begin making some calls and see what I can come up with." Bob said, relieved that Jack's name had left center stage.

"We've got several weeks, so call me when you get something." Taylor stood and thanked Bob for his time.

Bob assumed he would be in Dallas for the better part of the day, but was pleased to know he would be home earlier than expected. Taylor shook his hand and wished him a safe flight home. Though puzzled that the meeting had ended so soon, Bob dismissed any concerns quickly, and started out of the Plaza.

Taylor and Dan Spearman watched from the fifth floor window as Bob Powell pulled out of the Plaza and headed for DFW. One of the company's corporate jets would have him home in a couple of hours.

"Poor bastard," Taylor said, as they watched him drive away. "The old man sure thinks he still has power." Dan listened carefully to Taylor–another part of his job. Pulling strings with the JIC meant nothing to Mr. Franklin. It was all a means to an end. With enough scare in Jack of early retirement, he was sure to be a team player. Taylor was preparing to earn his huge salary, again.

* * *

Taylor Franklin graduated from Harvard Law in 1982. He was trial journal editor, a step down from the law review folks, whom he viewed as obnoxious, arrogant assholes anyway. He did a brief clerkship with Judge Ronald Perry in the D.C. Court of Appeals, before returning to Dallas and beginning his legal career at the Dallas based Howard, Adams & Belk. Insurance defense, his specialty, led him specifically to defending fraud and bad faith failure to pay cases. Insure Pro was his first big name client.

He enjoyed his work. Rooting out those greedy individuals who were always attempting to defraud their insurance company by filing false claims, or lying on their applications was fun for him. He became a vigorous litigator and his courtroom record was enviable. Plaintiff's lawyers who saw his name on an Answer knew they were in for a serious fight. Taylor viewed all plaintiffs who sued his client as evil, out to take advantage of anyone who had enough money to pay a verdict.

In depositions, he could be ruthless. More than once he had a claimant in tears, only to press harder, knowing their greed had been exposed – that they were upset because they knew what they were doing was wrong. It was effective and rarely resulted in failure. At worst, a jury would question whether he was correct in his argument. As long as they considered it, it was a good tactic.

In 1986 Taylor Franklin was lead counsel in a series of cases filed against Insure Pro in Houston. At issue was the validity of a provision the company had just added to commercial policies covering several of the area's well-known auto dealerships. The local dealers had suffered when torrential rains caused flooding in the area. The policies at issue covered the actual premises, while other carriers handled the floor plans. Insure Pro had previously covered such damage, and had increased premiums for such coverage at the last anniversary date of each policy.

When the claims were made, Insure Pro pointed to an amendment that had been inserted into the policies at issue, precluding coverage for damage that was "directly caused due to structural failure as a result of inadequate architectural, engineering or construction planning." Insure Pro hired Forensic Engineering, LLC to conduct a structural analysis of the dealership buildings. The results were conclusive.

While the flooding had been substantial, the ultimate cause of the loss was substandard structural planning and construction.

The claims were denied.

Taylor argued, unsuccessfully, that the provisions were valid. Insure Pro was ordered to pay over Twenty Million Dollars by the trial court. He learned early that verdicts meant nothing until appeals were exhausted. The Austin cases were appealed to the Texas Supreme Court.

Taylor Franklin, and therefore Insure Pro, was the benefactor of the Republican revolution in the Texas appellate courts. By 1984, Texas had had enough of outrageous jury verdicts and renegade judges handing out retirement checks to lucky litigants. The majority of the justices on the Supreme Court were heavily backed by, among others, Insure PAC, an active political action committee founded as a means of funneling insurance industry money to political candidates across the country. It just so happened that Insure Pro was InPAC's leading contributor.

The verdicts were "plainly and palpably wrong" and there was no question that the trial judge had abused his discretion under the law. Insure Pro, the initial loser in the Austin litigation, was the victor where it counted – in the end.

Ken Griffin, President and Founder of InPAC approached Franklin, later that year. Joe Kirschberg, the CEO of Insure Pro was looking for a new general counsel at the home office. According to Ken, Taylor was at the top of the list. Joe had been apprised of his brilliant maneuvers in the Austin litigation, and was impressed with his imagination.

Within three months the relationship had been consummated. Taylor Franklin was the new Vice President and General Counsel for Insure Pro.

His salary had been doubled from his private practice.

Stock options were included.

He had use of the corporate jet fleet—and all the amenities.

Taylor had come into his own. He was finally where he belonged.

SIX

The vast majority of laymen had no idea how the Supreme Court worked; even fewer knew how opinions of the Court came to be. The Alabama Supreme Court operated on a random assignment process. When an appeal or other issue that the Court had jurisdiction over came up, the case was randomly assigned to one of the nine justices. An opinion would be drafted and circulated, and, if there was any disagreement with the result reached, the offended justice would write a dissenting opinion. It would then be circulated and the rest of the Court would decide their vote. If the majority agreed with the dissent, it would become the law for that case, and the initial opinion would be the loser. It rarely happened that way, with all nine of the justices being Republicans, but Garrett became known for dissenting from majority opinions, the longer he was on the Court. He advised his backers that he was protecting his future political career from attack, and reminded them that he always ruled in their favor on the important matters.

The workload placed on the justices was immense, certainly more than one person would be capable of handling, and each justice hired three staff attorneys, to whom they entrusted a great deal of the work they were called upon to perform. The little known fact was that many opinions had been authored by staff attorneys and simply signed off on by the elected justice.

Jack's senior staff attorney was Sharon Waters. A divorced mother of one grown son, at forty-four Sharon had been a staff attorney at the Court for sixteen years. Private practice was not in her. After graduating from law school at Tennessee, she accepted a clerkship with then Chief Justice Patton Wilkes She enjoyed the work and was passionate about legal research. and writing. She stayed on with Justice Wilkes until he stepped down. Afterwards, she continued with his incoming replacement.

Numerous justices sought after her over the years, but the Chief Justice had first dibs when it came to selection. Sharon never left the Chief Justice's office, despite having served under two Democrats and two Republicans. She was admired for her intelligence and was unmatched in her legal analysis. For the most part, opinions written by Sharon were given only a cursory review then endorsed. She was bright enough to know if she needed to ask for direction on a given issue, though she rarely needed any.

* * *

Politics in Alabama were not like they used to be as the upcoming election loomed. Voters had become savvy to the bullshit that was constantly thrown at them over the last year, and those who did opt to exercise their right to vote were becoming more informed about the issues and backgrounds of the candidates. Party line voting was a dying method of winning elections, as candidates had to actually have a platform and some semblance of intelligence to convince voters to hire them.

By late 2003, the Revolution that had been completed approximately six years before was in jeopardy. In 2004, seven of the nine seats on the Court were up for consideration. Four of the sitting GOP backed justices were in deep trouble. Two, Graham Dodd and Spencer Cowan, were under investigation by the IRS for tax related matters. That they made more annually than ninety-five percent of the voters didn't help. Justice Cleveland Rogers, a four term Republican, was running for re-election, despite health problems. He had been on the Court for twenty-four years, and was staunchly conservative. The state GOP was concerned about his seat, due to all the ammunition he had provided over the years for his prospective opponent.

Justice Phillip Schoolcraft was a lost cause. The party knew his seat would go to the Dems. Schoolcraft had an affinity for young girls, very young. An FBI investigation led to charges of distributing child pornography, after a search warrant on his home revealed more than ten thousand images of children ages five to nine engaged in sexual poses and acts. Schoolcraft was sixty-four when the story surfaced. He had four grown children

41

and thirteen grandchildren. God only knew what other crimes he may have committed. The Schoolcraft fiasco was devastating to the GOP's judicial candidates. They turned on him instantly, calling for, after a full and fair presentation of the facts, of course, the maximum penalty available.

Protect the children – always a popular mantra.

The six remaining GOP justices had all supported Schoolcraft at some time in their political or professional careers. The thought of how those past endorsements were going to be used by their opposing campaigns made all of them nauseous. Even the weakest political strategist was sure to make each one look as if he supported child molestation. If Cleveland Rogers had provided ammunition for his opponent, Phillip Schoolcraft had provided a nuclear bomb for the Democrats.

Jack distanced himself from Schoolcraft immediately, calling for him to resign. *Fuck the facts. Fuck a trial. Fuck waiting to let the criminal process work. Fuck Phillip.* Jack was publicly and privately outraged at the man. He was not going to let Phillip Schoolcraft cost him his job. Not without a fight. Jack was going to make sure that no matter what ads appeared against him, linking him to the child predator, he would have plenty of tape to rebut the assault.

Bulletproof.

Almost.

The 2004 judicial elections were a victory for the Democrats, but not a bloodbath for the GOP. Of the seven seats up for grabs, Democrat-backed candidates took four. It went pretty much as expected. The national media did pick up on the two percent of Alabama voters who wanted to re-elect a child predator, as the state was always good for a laugh from the rest of the country. Although Alabama had elected GOP-backed candidates in more races than not, there was a vocal minority that confirmed that the State was neither red nor blue.

The new Supreme Court mirrored the population more closely than it had in forty years. Jackson Garrett remained Chief Justice. Ted Foster accompanied him on the GOP side along with Christian Mathis, Andrew Morgan and Jeffrey Stallings.

Democrats taking office included Alan Coburn, James Stanley, Mac Bridges and Elizabeth Callahan. only the second woman elected to the High Court, and the first Democratic woman to hold such a position in the history of the state.

The new Supreme Court began to issue significantly more moderate opinions than it had in the past. Lively debates occurred, as the justices settled into their roles. Jack enjoyed the new spirit of moderate judicial thought that he'd always wanted.

Surprisingly, Jack had yet to cast a deciding vote. Few unanimous opinions emerged as, one or more of the opposing viewpoints invariably crossed over and supported the opposition. Apparently, the '04 elections had inspired a sense of reconciliation among the members of the Court. The people had spoken. They did not want extremes; they wanted justice.

The Supreme Court listened.

Helping the newfound atmosphere of bipartisanship on the Court was the fact that there had not been any massive verdicts to come up for review or any polarizing issues. Jack was pleased, and it seemed that all the justices were content to work together toward a truly just cause. There was a sense of calm. Peace.

**

September 17, 2005, would witness the second most deadly and by far most costly natural disaster in the history of the state. Hurricane Peter would spin into a ferocious, tightly packed monster. When the eye would come ashore with a direct hit on Gulf Shores, Alabama, at three twenty-five a.m., virtually the entire lower third of the state would be evacuated. Only emergency personnel would remain to search for those dumb enough to stay, mainly several major network TV crews, a handful of stubborn residents who had nowhere else to go, or wouldn't leave their homes if God himself demanded it, and, of course, The Weather Channel folks.

Hurricane force winds would extend some forty to fifty miles outward from the center of the storm – tropical storm force winds another hundred miles out. About two hours before landfall, forecasters said Pensacola, Florida would receive the direct hit. A late turn to the northwest would send it straight for the densely developed tourist area of Gulf Shores.

43

SEVEN

Jack weathered the storm at his home in Montgomery. He would normally have been at the beach home, as court was not in session. But he obeyed the mandatory evacuation order and returned to the capital. He contacted his staff attorneys to make sure they were doing the same. Mark Boudreaux, the youngest of his crew, had returned to his parents' home in Jackson, Mississippi. He was thirty-four and unmarried. Mark did a brief stint in defense work before applying for the staff attorney position. Jack surmised he had aspirations to become a judge himself. Whether or not he had the stomach for the politics remained to be seen, but he had a keen legal mind.

Clayton Brackin took his wife and daughter and headed north to his in-laws in Nashville. Thirty-eight year old Clayton and his wife Jan, two years younger, graduated from law school together in 1998. Both took positions as associates at Smith, Pike & Fipps in Montgomery. Clayton decided it would be best if they spent some time apart, so their relationship could grow and survive. He professed to love Jan dearly, but needed some time to himself.

Several attempts at litigation proved too much for Clay. Waves of anxiety overtook him even before the most basic of court appearances. He worked himself into a frenzy before a motion docket and made himself vomit. Figuring he had a minor illness, he wrote it off. The second time a motion to continue triggered the nausea. This could have been handled by phone.

Another trip to the men's room.

When the third effort proved no different, he accepted the fact that he needed to stay out of the courtroom. Jan suggested he apply for the staff position. Clay took her advice and proved to be an excellent lawyer behind the scenes.

Sharon, an attractive woman with shoulder length brown hair and green eyes, had lived in Montgomery since finishing law school and beginning the clerkship that would lead to her career as a staff attorney. A tall woman with long firm legs, one might have assumed she had been a volleyball player in college. They would have been wrong, of course. But she did exercise daily and was very fit. She especially enjoyed jogging and swimming.

She was always dressed professionally, usually opting for navy blue skirt and jacket with a white Laura Ashley blouse. If she felt wild she'd don a crème pantsuit and black scarf. She was respectful of the 1998 establishment where she worked, and dressed appropriately at all times.

Sharon lived alone in a two-bedroom house located off the Eastern Bypass. It was a pleasant, safe neighborhood filled with garden homes constructed during a residential boom in the late 90s. Each house had a two-car garage located in the front, directly next to the entrance. The brick front house with siding covering the remainder of it had a small back yard, separated from its neighbors by six foot dog-eared fencing. Sharon enjoyed spending time in her herb garden located just off the concrete patio that sat outside the living room. Bright colors covered the walls, and the furniture had come from Ikea. It was ultra contemporary, with modern sculptural lighting that provided ambient shades across the room.

A 42-inch flat screen television perched atop a painted black buffet. The entertainment area contrasted nicely with the vibrant colors that surrounded it. She complemented the TV with a Bose Surround System, and kept her CDs alphabetically arranged in a cabinet in the buffet.

Most men would have been surprised that a single woman had gone to the expense Sharon did for audio-visual equipment, but it proved to be her companion when not at work. Besides, she was a huge Andrea Bocelli fan. And nothing sounded like Andrea through a Bose system.

She kept the modest home, immaculately clean. With no one else there, it took a minimal amount of maintenance.

Jack called her the afternoon before Peter was set to make landfall. "Sharon, have you been keeping track of the forecast?" His voice was polite and sincere.

45

"Yes, Your Honor. They are predicting it may turn towards Mobile, pretty much anywhere from Mobile to Destin." She had followed the Weather Channel like the rest of the state.

"The last time one this strong came through, power was out for quite a while, and I wanted to make sure you were OK." Jack was genuinely concerned. And maybe a little lonesome himself.

"I'll be fine, Your Honor." She said, appreciating his concern.

"Sharon, we've been working together for a long time. Please call me 'Jack.' Save the 'Your Honor' crap for the office."

"Yes, sir, Jack." She smiled and half giggled, hearing herself call him by his first name.

"And watch the 'sir' part too, Sharon; I'm not that much older than you, you know." Jack chuckled a bit himself. "Look, do you have a generator?"

"No."

"Fireplace?"

"It's eighty degrees, Jack."

"I meant for cooking, dear. They made those homes all electric, right?"

"Yes. We are all electric. Why do you ask?"

"My place is five miles down I-85 from you. I've got gas heat, and a generator. There's plenty of food, and some wine that I just can't bring myself to drink alone. There are four bedrooms and more than enough room if you want to be alone. But I thought you might like some company, especially if we get closed in for a while." Jack's offer had no ulterior expectations.

"I don't know if that would be such a good idea," Sharon said, contemplating his offer. Company did sound nice, and she knew that she and Jack shared similar legal philosophies. Beyond that, she knew very little about him other than that he was a pleasure to work for.

"If you want, I'll even let you sleep with Buster." Jack laughed out loud.

Sharon giggled again, "Well, with an offer like that, how can I refuse?" She came to the conclusion that any adult conversation beat listening to the neighborhood kids going crazy in the streets if the power was knocked out and there was no Nintendo. "I'll throw a few things together and leave in an hour or so."

"Excellent. I'll start working on some dinner." Jack gave her directions to his house.

He smiled.

The Chief Justice looked forward to having dinner with someone other than a lobbyist or politician. It seemed like forever since he had dined with someone who wasn't looking for something in return.

* * *

In Carrollton, Texas, the Emergency Response Unit at Insure Pro moved at full throttle. The director of the unit, Max Donnelly, seldom strayed from studying the printouts coming in every thirty minutes from the National Hurricane Center in Miami. Max had spent several months there learning about forecasting these storms and cultivating a relationship with the director. The Hurricane Center provided their expertise to all major media markets, as well as the larger insurers in the gulf region and Atlantic seaboard.

According to Walter Cole, Chief Meteorologist at the Center, landfall would likely be somewhere between Panama City, Florida, and worst-case scenario, New Orleans. He assured Max there was less than a five percent likelihood of New Orleans being hit. Peter would have to make a substantial move that all but one computer model had excluded to hit the crescent city. Walter sighed with relief that New Orleans would be spared.

As the hours passed, the projected path continued to narrow. It became clear that landfall would occur somewhere in southern Alabama or northwest Florida. Max requested his staff to identify all available adjusters and claims personnel available for storm duty. Within twenty-four hours, he needed people on the ground, ready to provide emergency assistance checks for housing. Some would be donated to the Red Cross and National Guard for aid in delivering food and water.

A sizable group of local claims personnel from Alabama, Mississippi, Louisiana, Tennessee and Georgia would be first responders for Insure Pro. Damage assessments for the company would be handled by senior claims representatives later. By the end of the night, three and a half hours before Peter delivered his wrath,

47

Max had an army of two hundred fifty claims specialists on standby. They were just waiting for his order.The next several weeks were going to be busy.

And, expensive.

* * *

Sharon arrived at the Chief Justice's house at six p.m. The sun had just started to fall toward the horizon. Deep blue skies had greeted the sun that morning. Later in the day narrow bands of wispy high clouds had begun to gradually appear, floating across the southern sky from east to west. By late afternoon, the cloud bands had become more frequent, which, when set against the darkening sky of dark orange with red hues, set the stage for a brilliant sunset.

It was hard to believe that a disaster was hours away.

Sharon rang the doorbell. Buster announced a visitor was at the door, and she heard Jack shout out he was coming.

Jack opened the door dressed in blue jeans and a white button down dress shirt. Black loafers. It would have been his standard casual attire, but for the chef's apron. No funny quotes. It was a plain blue apron, neatly tied around his neck and waist.

"Thanks for coming," he said, as he welcomed her in and took her suitcase. "I hope you like salmon." He placed her bag next to the stairwell leading upstairs.

"I'm allergic to fish," Sharon said with a straight face.

"I'm sorry. I didn't ask..." Jack's expression of utter shock was interrupted by her laugh.

"That was mean. I'm sorry." She caught a glimpse of a smile returning to his face. "Absolutely. I love salmon." She sat at the counter abutting the kitchen.

"Wine?" Jack offered.

"Yes, thank you."

Jack's house was located in Mt. Meigs, about fifteen miles from the downtown area of the capital. He had purchased the two-level home, built in 1980, from the original owner after selling the house he and Stephanie had lived in with its haunting memories of her. He appreciated the peace and quiet of the rural area. The main level consisted of the master bedroom set off from the living room in the rear of the house, with the kitchen and small dining room located on the left, down the hallway from the entrance. For added convenience, a half bath and closet were located just inside the front door.

The kitchen, a gourmet cook's delight, contained new appliances, including a Viking stovetop and oven set into the island across from the refrigerator and cabinets. The island had a breakfast bar made of granite, which backed up to the living room. Jack loved to cook and spent most of his time there. Otherwise he settled in the sitting area of his bedroom, reading. The main level with its hardwood floors and sparse furnishings made it clear that this was a place to stay and not much more.

Sharon knew that the beach home was his retreat. He had spoken of it often, and she imagined it was paradise.

The bedroom door was shut. Sharon assumed that, like most single men's bedrooms, it was probably a wreck, but she was wrong. Jack had cleaned the room thoroughly, but he had put Buster in there when she arrived.

Jack poured a glass of Chardonnay and handed it to her.

As she took her seat, he returned to the dinner preparation. After Sharon accepted his invitation, Jack hurriedly began planning a meal, finally decided on salmon, with a lemon dill sauce, accompanied by roasted asparagus and red potatoes. By the time she arrived, he had carefully laid the food out for cooking.

She was thoroughly impressed. *Is this a date?* To a degree it felt like it. But this was her boss, after all. She was coming to escape the inconveniences of Peter.

Nothing more.

Enjoy the dinner. Have fun.

Jack completed his kitchen duties and showed her to the small dining room table that had been set just across from the breakfast bar. Sharon had finished her first glass of wine and sat down opposite Jack.

He served her first, then himself. He returned to the kitchen and pulled another bottle of wine from the rack.

"I'm a lightweight, Your Honor." Sharon questioned whether Jack was trying to get her drunk.

"Just one glass with dinner, and I told you to call me Jack. I've been saving this bottle for two years," Jack was insistent. "It

49

was a gift to me from an old friend. It's a 2003 Silver Oak Cabernet, and you can't find this anywhere. I was instructed that it was only to be opened for special occasions." Sharon could tell Jack was serious.

"What's the occasion then?" Sharon inquired.

"By all likely appearances, a new beach home." Jack laughed nervously. It was his first realization that his baby would probably be gone by this time tomorrow.

"OK, a glass with dinner," Sharon agreed.

Dinner was excellent. She enjoyed every ounce, cleaning her plate. The wine was magnificent. The dinner conversation revolved around work. They discussed cases, past and present. Other justices' philosophies were debated. It was like being at the Court, only in a different location. After dinner, Jack requested that she keep her seat. "I've got a little dessert for us as well," he said, returning to the kitchen. Sharon kept her seat quietly.

He cleared the table, then went to the refrigerator and removed two four-inch ramekins. He returned to the dining area and placed one in front of Sharon, setting the other where he had been sitting.

"What's this?" Sharon asked.

"Homemade crème brulee," Jack said proudly.

"Are you serious?" She was impressed that he could have guessed her favorite dessert.

"Mostly," Jack admitted. "It's actually store bought, but you have to complete the mix, sprinkle the sugar, and crystallize it. But other than that...homemade." Jack removed the culinary torch from his back pocket and leaned over. A push of the button and he was browning the sugar on Sharon's dessert.

It reminded her of Highlands Bar & Grill. She had been there several times with friends in Birmingham. Highlands was local legend with national accolades. The chef was from Cullman, a small town in north Alabama. He had created a masterpiece with his dream. Highlands featured southern foods, prepared and presented in a fashion that only Frank Stitt could perfect. Rabbit, quail, duck, venison, grits, peas and beans were staples on the menu that changed daily. The restaurant had been ranked in the top ten nationally by several gourmet magazines.

And the crème brulee. Some folks came just for dessert.

Jack had gotten close. But close was good enough tonight.

He cleared the table and began to clean up. Sharon got up and was beginning to help with the dishes when he stopped her. "Please, relax. I'm used to it. Give me a minute and I'll be done." He was persistent and she retreated to the living room.. After he finished putting the dishes away, he joined her.

They sat on the sofa, talking.

Slowly Jack led the conversation away from work and soon began to feel more comfortable. Sharon provided an attentive ear, something Jack really needed. He told her about Stephanie and his early years practicing at Garrett & Associates. He left out the night in Atlanta and the JIC inquiry that followed. But other than that, he essentially opened the book on his life. It felt good.

She appreciated his gesture, and regaled him with her stories as well. She talked about her son and how proud she had been of him. She'd had Keith at an early age, eighteen, and he was grown and living in Nashville, where he operated his own martial arts studio, teaching children and adults jujitsu. Sharon and Keith kept in touch on a regular basis, and managed to see each other once every month or so. She mentioned her ex, and the divorce, but was not bitter in her recitation. She'd decided to keep her married name, as she had become known by it to practically everyone. Sharon had grown to accept her history without being ashamed of it. By 11:30 they both were exhausted.

"Might as well see where it is," Sharon said, referring to the looming disaster they had avoided for the last several hours.

"I suppose so." Jack said with less enthusiasm.

They turned on The Weather Channel for a last look.

Gulf Shores.

Shit. You've got to be kidding me. Jack couldn't hide his concern. He knew that the area would likely be affected, but a direct hit was supposed to be in Florida. Being on the western side of the eye would have been preferable.

"I'm sure everything will be all right," Sharon tried to reassure him, knowing that the news was disheartening.

"I guess we should turn in," Jack said, getting off the sofa.

She rose and started for the stairwell, up to the guest room.

Jack stopped her as she started up. "Thank you," he said, grasping her right hand, holding it on top of his. He cupped his left hand on top. "I'm glad you came."

The look of gratitude on his face told her that he meant what he said.

Sharon leaned forward and kissed him on the forehead. "Good night, Jack." She turned and headed up the stairs to her room.

Jack went to the master bedroom. Buster was asleep at the window, as usual. He patted him on the head, and crawled into bed.

Even though his paradise was in danger of being destroyed, it had been the best night he'd had in years. He fell asleep quickly.

* * *

Peter made landfall as a Category 4 hurricane.

Not since 1979 had a storm this strong struck the state. Hurricane Gregory had devastated Gulf Shores more than two decades ago. Most of what now existed in the area had been constructed after 1985, when the memories of Gregory had waned and people began having confidence in investing there again.

Beachside condominiums, some constructed prior to revamped building codes enacted in the mid 90s, were completely destroyed. The storm surge was estimated to be at twenty feet, bringing water up to a half mile inland, farther in lower lying areas. Older constructions were taken out from the bottom with the initial surge. Winds that reached one hundred thirty-five miles per hour finished the vacation retreats. In a stretch along highway 98, every existing structure disappeared, washed back into the gulf when the waters receded.

Initially water damage took the blame for devastation only to the beachside properties. A small number of those, mainly condominium high rises built up to code, remained. They did so with substantial damage. Some had to be completely razed. Inland damage wasn't as easy to discern. Salt water was detected up to three quarters of a mile inland. Water or wind, or both, had destroyed much of the gulf coast region in south Alabama.

Upon making landfall, Peter proceeded to turn to the east, traveling at twelve miles per hour and heading due north. It was downgraded to a Category 3 within thirty minutes of the eye wall completing its transition over land. Thirty minutes later, Peter was changed to Category 2. By this time, the majority of the storm was over land. The eye wall was still easily identifiable. He was almost thirty miles inland, picking up speed, and tornadoes became the new threat.

Peter picked up speed early in the morning and, by the time he was approaching Montgomery, the capital city, he was still classified as a hurricane. Montgomery and Birmingham, ninety miles to the north, experienced tropical storm force winds. As quickly as he arrived, within twenty-four hours, Peter was gone, soaking north Georgia and the Carolinas with massive amounts of rainfall.

His destruction traversed the entire state. Some communities escaped unscathed. Others, especially in the southern part of the state, lost everything. It defied logic to the emergency first responders. In the gulf region, some communities had areas of complete destruction, with neighboring homes fully intact. Peter chose his victims carefully, it appeared, unleashing his fury on them. Virtually the bottom half of the state was left without power. Random outages were reported as far north as the Tennessee state line.

As was always the case, those who lost nothing thanked God for sparing them. Those who lost everything thanked God for sparing their lives. Those who lost loved ones praised God, knowing He had a plan and that, although they grieved, God would give them comfort and strength.

In all it was estimated that thirty-five thousand families had lost their homes, all of which were in the gulf coast area. More than one hundred thousand homes sustained damage.

One hundred fifty souls were dead statewide.

The financial impact was estimated at fourteen billion dollars.

Insured damage estimates were three to seven billion dollars.

The reconstruction effort, which would have to wait for the initial clean up, would take years. Those less fortunate would live .in. trailers .provided .by .the. government. for .an .indefinite period of time. Some would leave, never to return.The affluent would start rebuilding immediately.

* * *

By six in the morning, Insure Pro had a hundred claims representatives on the ground in south Alabama. Peter was churning through the central part of the state, still causing damage. Initial assessments were grim. Although local authorities and National Guard troops were trying to maintain control, curious sightseers, adjusters and looters roamed the streets – unnoticed for the most part.

Insure Pro representatives followed orders to the letter. The first task was to document as many insured properties as possible, as soon as possible—photographs, videotape, camera phones and anything else that worked. By whatever means available, they were to provide evidence to the company—evidence to support a decision.

Insure Pro garnered more than half of the market in the region for property and casualty insurance. Rough estimates reflected that, of the more than thirty-five thousand properties that were destroyed, the company insured twenty thousand of them. The figures were staggering from a loss standpoint for one company.

By the time the homeowners returned, their company's investigation would have been largely completed.

The claims process would begin.

For some, their experience would land them in commercials supporting their insurance company, to be aired on national television. One would even debut during the Super Bowl.

For too many others, it would be a nightmare.

* * *

The Chief Justice woke at seven a.m. Late for his routine, but he was coming off one of the best nights in recent memory. He opened his bedroom door to find Sharon standing in the kitchen, dressed in jeans and a rugby shirt. She was at the cook top and steam was rising to the ceiling.

"Good morning," she said, turning her eyes to him briefly, then redirecting her attention to breakfast.

"You must be kidding me," Jack said, with a smile on his face. "Excluding Waffle House and McDonald's, no one has made breakfast for me in years." Apparently the morning had picked up where last night had left off.

"It's the least I could do." Sharon was pleased that her boss appreciated her gesture.

She made bacon and eggs, and opened some canned biscuits, finishing up as Jack came out of the bedroom. "Have you seen the news?" she asked.

"It can't be good. I heard the generator come on about an hour ago." Jack figured that if the power had gone out in Montgomery, all hell must have broken loose further south.

"You may want to check it out." Sharon knew Jack was not going to like what he was about to see.

Jack turned on the television, able to do so thanks to the generator and his satellite. He went straight to The Weather Channel. After all, he knew they had the idiots who were willing to risk their lives for any storm, anywhere. Face time was invaluable for them, and with Peter they got plenty.

Peter was making his way north through the state, after the eye wall had gone right through Jack's wonderland. The video was awful. From what he could tell, the water had penetrated deep into the coastland. Though no pictures of his area were shown, he recognized several landmarks. Water had made its way to King's Tavern, which was almost a half-mile inland from the house. *The whole thing could be under water. Years of memories. Gone.* Jack began to realize the magnitude of what happened while he slept. He went to bed happier than he had in years, and, within hours, he was right back where he started.

Sharon turned the TV off. "Let's eat," she said, trying her best to redirect him.

Jack sat down, but she knew he was lost in his thoughts. She didn't bother to say anything. It wouldn't matter anyway.

Jack ate his breakfast quietly, thanked her for the gesture, and excused himself to his bedroom. Sharon returned upstairs, where she would spend the rest of the morning. She wanted to pack her bag and return home, but the power was out and the solitude of Jack's upstairs beat sitting in the dark. At least she could keep up to date on the situation further south to pass the time.

By mid afternoon, Jack had come to the realization that there was nothing he could do about the beach home, and he didn't want Sharon to feel uncomfortable. He went upstairs and knocked on the guest bedroom door. "You feel like playing a game?" he asked through the door.

Sharon opened the door, looking relieved to see that he was more himself. "Sure, why not. What do you have?"

"Some old ones, scrabble, monopoly, those types," Jack said, looking for anything to take his mind off things. They settled on Scrabble. They played the rest of the afternoon, and conversation gradually returned to matters other than Peter.

Sharon spent one more evening at Jack's house before power was restored at her place. She returned home the next morning. It had been the first time in years he had companionship, and for that he was grateful. Within hours of her departure, he was lonelier than before.

EIGHT

Max Donnelly's crew performed at their usual level of professionalism in south Alabama. Within days of the storm, more than two hundred Insure Pro employees were hustling around the disaster area. As promised, a number of them were on loan to relief agencies. Their work was all for PR purposes. The real task was determining what properties insured by Insure Pro were damaged or destroyed, and how. Within two weeks Max had his list ready for the claims department.

Insure Pro's claims analysts were aware that the inland properties would be paid in full. There would be no question that wind damage alone had been the culprit. They had to identify the structures closer to the water. By the end of the tally, it appeared that, of their twenty thousand insured properties destroyed in the area, approximately three thousand were in the zone. That's where the attention would be focused. Max assigned two hundred storm duty claims representatives, all pulled from California and Arizona, to the task. They were given geographical areas to investigate, based on the company's database of insured residences in Alabama's gulf coast. They wanted to get in and out as quickly as possible and get the evidence back to the company. With ten properties assigned to each specialist, it would be a fast operation.

Three weeks after Peter had come and gone, Insure Pro had the photos and video of the three thousand parcels in the zone. Some claims would be filed later, but the company had a good idea of who would be asking for benefits. The company issued a form letter to every policyholder who they had determined had been affected according to their records.

Dear _____ :

    Your family at Insure Pro wishes to take this opportunity to send our sympathies to you and your family during this trying time. We hope that this letter finds you safe. According to our records, your insured property with Insure Pro may have sustained damage as a result of Hurricane Peter.

    We want you to know we are working diligently to determine the amount of damage you have sustained. We have experts reviewing all available documentation to the company so that we can pay valid claims as soon as possible. It is our goal to complete this process as soon as possible so that our policyholders can receive the benefits to which they are entitled.

    If you have any questions, or wish to submit any documentation which you feel would assist us in our investigation, please call the Hurricane Peter Hot Line at (888) 63PETER. (888) 637-3837. Upon completion of our investigation we will be in contact with you. Thank you for your patience and understanding during the claims process.

Sincerely,
Insure Pro

The letter was not signed by anyone, and was mailed to the resident's address at the insured property, as well as to any other residence on file at Insure Pro for the named property owner. If their estimates were correct, around eighty to eighty-five percent of the three thousand properties in the zone were vacation homes. The majority of these homeowners would receive the letter at the alternate address.

***

Les Vance paid a courier at the firm to go to Gulf Shores to check on his beach home one week after Peter struck. His instructions were to photograph the entire premises, as well as videotape the area. He left on a Monday morning and was back at Gibson Vance by noon Tuesday.

Les couldn't believe what he saw. Nothing was left of his vacation spot other than a concrete slab. The entire structure, a two-story stucco home located across the street from the front beach properties, had disappeared. Decorated like many of the units in the area with bright colors and ocean themes, it was a place where he took his family at least four times each summer. They spent spring break week there as well, and an occasional long weekend at other times.

Les' house was less than a quarter mile east of Jack's property. Although they weren't friends, Les had seen the Chief Justice on occasion during visits. When his courier returned to Birmingham, he told Les that there was another gentleman taking photos of his property as well. When asked who he was, he simply said he was an investigator. Les assumed that he was working for his insurance company, and assured the boy that there was no problem. Les called several friends who had places at the Gulf to see if they knew the status of their investments. A few had been down themselves, but most were going to wait until things cleared out.

He knew it would be a waiting process for his insurance proceeds to be approved, and he was heading to the mountains for spring break anyway.

* * *

Jack received his letter from Insure Pro within three days of the postmark. He expected to receive something soon and was somewhat pissed off that it was handled in such an impersonal manner. He wrote it off, knowing Insure Pro had insured thousands of properties in the area; he realized that it was a logistical nightmare, and it was only the first step in the claims process.

Jack took a couple of days away from the Court, the week after Peter hit, and went to check on his Orange Beach home. Like most people who had owned places at the Gulf, he was shocked at the devastation. The lot next to his was empty. Two

59

weeks before, there was a beautiful three-story home with a deck on the third floor that had views of the water. Jack had known the new owners, Harvey and Helen Averitt, for a couple of years. They bought the home from the original owners, but still lived in Baton Rouge. However, they did visit often. They were nice people and now their beach home was completely destroyed.

On the other side it was no different. Nothing but a slab remained of the one-level block foundation house belonging to Bruce Gathings. Jack didn't know him well, but everyone who had a place here was friendly, largely because they always saw each other while getting away from the daily grind.

Jack had been lucky, if you could call it that. His two-story home had been reduced to a one level. The second floor was gone, ripped away by Peter's violent winds. Portions were scattered around the back yard. The second floor had consisted of three bedrooms, designed as guest or children's rooms. They had been simply furnished with queen sized beds and a chest of drawers in each room. Jack found a piece of the bed frame in the larger room lodged into the base of one of the few palm trees that had survived. Little of the actual structure itself was present. The main level was intact. Upon inspection, it appeared as though the entire second floor was simply removed from the flooring joists up. He imagined a massive chain saw essentially cutting the house in two.

What remained of the first floor was a mess. Mold and mildew was already beginning to grow. From what he could see, the water had intruded four feet into his house. Not much more than a week ago, what was left of Jack's dream home was sitting in the Gulf of Mexico.

The better part of Orange Beach also was – to some degree.

* * *

Six weeks after Peter left his mark, the clean up was moving along at a better than expected pace. Sand that had found its way across Highway 98, the front beach road, had been removed and deposited back on sections of the beach. A substantial part of the debris had been taken away, though plenty of work remained to be done. If any positive aspect could be found in the situation, it had to be that the Gulf Shores area wasn't stretched out along a wide swath. Had this been farther east – Pensacola, or Destin for that matter – damage would have been strewn about over a much larger area.

In Texas, Taylor Franklin called a meeting of the Vice President of Claims, Southern Division, and his Regional and Division Claims Managers. They needed to get to work on Peter. After some thought, Taylor moved the meeting, originally scheduled to take place at the Plaza, to Hugh Capelli's office.

Hugh was the VP of Claims, Southern Division. His region included everything from New Orleans to Jacksonville, Florida, including every mile of coastal Florida. Hurricane season was his biggest headache. He came to Insure Pro from Western Indemnity and Casualty, where he had led their National Claims Training Center. At fifty-four, he had spent the last thirty-two years of his life in the insurance business. He started out in claims, working as a property damage adjuster, quickly making his way up the ranks. By thirty, he had decided to try sales, and opened an agency in Denver. Five years later he was bored.

He returned to Western Indemnity's corporate office in Phoenix as the new Vice-President of Claims, Western Division. His territory encompassed everything west of the Mississippi River. Born and raised in Brooklyn, Hugh was tough nosed. He accepted nothing less than a hundred percent from his employees making him difficult to work for. His reputation for using foul language was well known in the company, but he got results. Further, he was careful not to cross the line with his obscenities. Racial slurs or sexually explicit comments were never used, at least not in the presence of co-workers. His last five years were spent at the Training Center, where he instructed everyone, from regional and divisional claims managers to new hires on claims policies and procedures.

Taylor Franklin lured Hugh away in 2000. Taylor had met Hugh at InPAC's annual Donors Gala, held in Las Vegas. The gala was nothing more than yet another opportunity to request contributions, but it was looked forward to every year because of the party that accompanied it. Taylor thought that Hugh was just what Insure Pro needed in claims. After returning to Texas, he asked Dan Spearman to run a full background on Mr. Capelli. Other than an arrest for assault at age nineteen stemming from a bar fight, which had been expunged from his record for youthful offender status, he was clean. *What teenage Brooklyn kid hadn't broken someone's nose?*

Taylor contacted Hugh a month later and inquired about his interest in making a career move. Shortly, negotiations began and within two weeks, Hugh came to work for Insure Pro in his present position, with substantial increases in salary and benefits.

The Kirschberg Claims Building was located two buildings down from the Plaza, toward the entrance to the compound. Taylor arrived to find Hugh in his second floor office with his four underlings sitting at a table in the conference room.

"Have we got the numbers on Peter?" Taylor asked Hugh as he took his seat next to him.

"We have estimates that should be pretty close," he replied, pointing to his Southern Division Claims Manager.

"Let's hear it," Taylor said to Keith Gunn, who was ready with the information.

"Worst case scenario, we have nineteen thousand that need disbursement within the next sixty days, one thousand in the zone. Best case would be seventeen thousand for disbursement, three or so in the zone." Keith knew the numbers were subject to change, but they weren't far off.

"The seventeen, are those total loss estimates?"

"Yes sir. Repair cases will exceed that substantially, but we assumed we'd let our local adjusters handle those."

"We will. How far inland do we expect the zone to extend?" Taylor asked Hugh.

"No more than three quarters of a mile, maybe less," he replied.

"So, at most we have three thousand in the zone, correct?"

"At most," Hugh said.

"How fast can we get the checks issued for the seventeen thousand that we know of?" Taylor had a plan in place before Peter ever existed, and he was cognizant of the fact that a number of claims needed immediate attention as well.

"As soon as we receive the proof of claims, get the cursory review and policy confirmation, they can be out within a week," Hugh responded.

"Pay them as soon as you can, Hugh. Those people need their money and I don't want anything holding it up any longer," Taylor said.

"Keith, get your local guys together, along with any storm duty folks we have assigned to those areas. Call every agent who wrote business in those classifications and get them to start getting loss forms and supporting documentation. I also want a letter out to everyone outside the zone that we have completed our investigation and are waiting on the proper documentation to be submitted so that payment can be issued." Hugh directed his claims manager.

"I'll get started on it immediately," Keith said.

"Thank you gentlemen; I need a minute with Hugh, please," Taylor told the group. Hugh Capelli's four assistants gathered their files and left his office. When the door closed behind them, Taylor got up, went over and locked it.

"I want a list of every policyholder in the zone. Nothing is done on any of those claims until I say so, understood?" Taylor was firm in his tone.

"Understood."

"We need to get Roger on the phone," Taylor said. Franklin picked up the phone and dialed the number for Roger Stoltz.

"Forensic Engineering, this is Wanda. How may I direct your call?"

"Wanda, this is Mr. Franklin. Give me Roger."

"Right away, sir."

Taylor was staring out the window when Roger answered.

"Wondered what took you so long," Roger said

"We're ready to go. I need you here first thing next Monday." Taylor stood, still staring into the parking lot below.

"Fair enough. See you then." Roger Stoltz hung up.

NINE

Life began to return to some semblance of normalcy for Jack. A new session of Court began, and he easily got back in the swing of things. The cases being reviewed were less than interesting, mainly death sentences that he didn't feel like deflecting down, more so that he could have something to do than because they deserved his time. It had been three months since Hurricane Peter, and he still hadn't heard from his insurance company, but it was a lengthy process, and it would all be over soon. Sharon had returned to her usual self. She never mentioned their time spent together at his house since she left, and Jack assumed that it must not have meant as much to her as it did to him. She surely couldn't have been that lonely.

As the weeks dragged along, Jack began slipping into a deep depression. Gradually, he began to deflect more and more cases back to the appeals court. Sharon noticed the reduced workload and finally decided that she needed to approach him. He was sitting at his desk, reviewing a brief, when she walked in.

"Your Honor, is everything all right?" she asked, knowing damn well it was not.

"I'm fine, Sharon. What's on your mind?"

"I don't mean to pry, but you haven't seemed yourself lately. I just wondered if there might be anything I could do." She was genuinely concerned about him.

Don't act like you care so much.

He stopped himself, realizing that Sharon had done nothing to deserve a chastising. Besides that, she was right.

He wasn't himself.

He needed to get away. She needed to go with him, but he could never ask her.

And Jack couldn't handle the embarrassment of a rejection.

"I've had a lot on my mind recently, that's all," he finally admitted.

"Why don't you take some time off? Get away and relax."

Come with me.

Say it.

Say it…

God, you're pathetic.

"Maybe you're right." Jack silently chastised himself for sounding like a schoolboy, letting his true desire be overruled by fear. "A little time off couldn't hurt."

"Go then," she said. "You need to recharge. Have some fun for a change; you haven't done anything in a long time, Your Honor."

Jack spent the rest of the afternoon angry with himself for not having the balls to ask her. He had to leave the capital. It would drive him crazy if he didn't.

By the time he had made his way home, he knew exactly what he needed to do. He picked up the phone and called Walter Broussard. Walt had been his best friend in law school, and they still kept in touch, though much less frequently in recent years. Walt had called him after the election to congratulate him on his victory. It had been more than a year since they had gotten together, but every time they spoke, the conversation picked up where it had left off, as if they lived across the street from each other. Walt was just what Jack needed right now.

Walt answered the phone on the second ring.

"How you doin' ya coon ass?" Jack's effort at a Cajun accent was pitiful, but heartfelt.

"You gotta be kiddin' me. Dar ain't no way dat dis a Soopreme Coat Judge," Walt didn't have to try, though he overdid his own accent for affect. He was a born and bred Cajun, and very happy to hear the voice of his old buddy.

"How've you been, my friend?" Jack said, giving up on the drawl.

"Been great. How's things in the big city, Chief?" Walt replied.

"I'm all right, I guess."

"All right…don't sound so good to me."

"Just thinkin' that I might be in your neighborhood in the next week or so, if you're going to be around," Jack offered, inviting himself as subtly as he could.

"Ain't nobody finds himself in my neck of the woods, unless they lost," Walt said with a laugh. "You know you're welcome any time, just say da word." Walt never changed. No matter if he was busy as hell, when a friend needed to get some R&R,

Walt always made himself available. He never met a stranger, and could always find something to talk about.

"How about next weekend," Jack said eagerly. "I could come for a long weekend, say Thursday or so."

"You welcome to come when you like, and stay as long as you want." Walt couldn't have been more serious. "You tell me what you wanna do. Fishin', huntin', you name it. But drinkin' we shall do."

"Thank you, Walt. Let's make it Thursday then. I'll try to leave around noon and should be there around six."

"Can't wait, buddy."

Jack hung up and realized that he had almost forgotten about Sharon. Getting away was definitely what he needed, and if anyone could help get his mind straightened out, Walt was the guy.

* * *

Within days Taylor received the list of all properties in the zone from Hugh Capelli. The "zone" consisted of a parcel of land in Gulf Shores wherein the company figured the surge had been most prominent. Each insured property in the zone was a potential denial due to the exclusion in the company's policy for flooding. They would also look at alternative reasons for denying them, just as a backup. There were three thousand potential problems, and he had to go through each and every one. He'd made a list of his own, hoping that he had remembered all the important names, but the only way to be sure was to compare it against the official printout, downloaded from the Insure Pro database. The time consuming effort, would be well worth it.

This was a task that couldn't be delegated. He planned to spend as much time as necessary to determine what roadblocks might exist. There would be no rest until he had them all identified. Once again, Taylor Franklin was earning his keep.

The process took longer than expected. Ten hours a day, checking and crosschecking names, addresses and alternate addresses. The IT department had no program that could simplify the matter, and they couldn't be involved at any rate. Taylor spent the next nine straight days going through the data. By the end of day nine, he was confident that he had identified every one. He would have been done in half the time, but for the perfectionist in him. There was no room for error.

When he finally completed his mission, he called Hugh. "Tomorrow, ten a.m. I've got them all."

He went home and, for the first night in almost two weeks, he slept.

* * *

Jack arrived at Walter Broussard's place shortly after six on Thursday evening. Walt, born and raised in Kaplan, Louisiana, graduated from LSU and attended law school at Alabama. He'd always known he would return home, but the Capstone was the only law program that offered him a scholarship. He and Jack met during orientation, hitting it off immediately. Jack was amused with his accent and sense of humor. As their friendship grew, he respected Walt's intelligence as much as his wit.

After graduation, Walt did return home, opening his own practice in Lafayette, sixty miles west of Baton Rouge. He took what he could get, as did every new lawyer going it alone. Over time, he built a successful practice negotiating oil and gas leases for landowners in his hometown and neighboring areas, and occasionally representing injured offshore workers.

Twenty years later, he'd had enough of Lafayette so he moved back to Kaplan to tend to his terminally ill mother. After a year at home in Kaplan, his mother died, and Walt came to the conclusion that it was where he belonged. He formally closed his Lafayette office and re-opened in Kaplan.

Kaplan was a throwback to times when life moved at a slower pace. With a population of only four thousand, it was a place where no one locked their doors at night. The local newspaper listed every criminal charge of the week in the Saturday Times, right down to Mary Comeaux, who was clearly guilty of running one of the two red lights in town. A traffic jam in Kaplan meant that it took six minutes to go from one side of town to the other, as opposed to five.

Along the Gulf of Mexico, twenty miles south of town, no beach communities or developments existed, just raw landscape filled with marshland and nary a hill in sight. At nighttime the Milky Way was prominent in the sky, and by daybreak the intermittent sound of shotguns rang out from the duck hunters sitting in blinds throughout the marsh. From any point in town, one could see for miles across open rice fields. For Walter Broussard, Kaplan was heaven on earth. For anyone else seeking solace from the frantic pace of city life, it was even better.

* * *

"Walter! What we be eatin' tonite?" Jack didn't bother knocking. He'd been to Walt's place before and learned that no one did. He announced his presence as he walked in.

"Give it up bro," he heard from the back of the house, as Walt came around the corner. "It's almost sad to hear you try, you know." Walt was pointing at Jack with a grin on his face.

"My apologies," Jack said, reverting to his traditional southern dialect.

Walt retrieved two beers from the refrigerator and maneuvered his two hundred sixty pounds into a too-small chair at the oak dining table in the kitchen. He rubbed a grubby hand across the beads of sweat on his forehead and smoothed the hair framing his receding hairline. His usual attire consisted of sweat pants and a t-shirt, unless he was at the office. It was easy to imagine why he could pass, as he did every year, as Santa Claus at the local school for disabled children.

"How long do you plan on staying, my friend?" Walt asked, hoping Jack was able to stick around for a while.

"I don't know," his guest answered. "How about we just take things as they come? I'm not on a schedule."

"I hear you, Jackson; how about we go out to the porch?" Walt got up and grabbed his beer, heading toward the door.

Jack followed him outside where they took a seat at a wrought iron table with matching chairs.

During the next two hours, the old friends caught up on important happenings in each other's lives. Jack updated Walt on the political climate in Alabama, the never-ending search for campaign financing, and some of the more unusual cases that he had opined on for the Court. He wanted to mention Sharon, but couldn't bring himself to do so. Walt listened for the most part, but did share some memories of his mother. Mostly though, he listened. He sensed Jack desperately needed that. His friend was his guest, and like every other hospitable coon ass, Walt would ensure that his friend got what he needed out of his stay.

By midnight, Jack was already letting the stress go. Both men were tired, and Walt suggested they turn in.

* * *

Hugh Capelli arrived at the Plaza exactly as directed and proceeded to the fifth floor to Taylor's office. His boss leaned back casually in his executive brown leather chair, feet propped up on the credenza that rose from behind the desk. The matching hutch had three twenty-four inch high display shelves, arched at the top and separated by wood paneling. Recessed lighting filtered down from the interior roof of the piece.

The far right display had a picture of Morgan, his seventeen-year old daughter, a knockout who could have had any boy she chose from Cathedral Christian Academy, the private school she attended. Her long blond hair and sea blue eyes came alive in the senior class picture, emphasizing attributes that made her the object of affection for many of the boys at the school. But, as far as Taylor knew, she was more interested in her grades and cheerleading. She had been accepted to Yale and Princeton for next year, but a final decision had not been made.

The left side contained a photo of Trent. The typical twelve-year-old posed, in uniform with his baseball bat, ready to swing, and had a huge smile on his face. Taylor knew that his son's dream of playing major league baseball would eventually have to give way to reality, but he was proud of his son nonetheless. Trent participated in everything twelve-year-olds were into—sports, sports and more sports, and he was a good kid.

The center display held a beautifully framed portrait of Dee. It was a mirror image of Morgan, twenty-five years older. Deanna and Taylor married right out of school and their marriage had been the envy of all her friends. Taylor was the perfect husband, and Dee the perfect wife. If they ever fought, no one saw it, and few believed it ever happened. Dee had been a homemaker for the majority of their marriage. She worked for a couple of years initially, but they decided she should stay home when Morgan arrived. Being a mom trumped working any day.

Dee made Taylor's life easier. She enabled him to do what he loved to do, and he was eternally grateful to her for it.

"So you have completed your review, sir?" Hugh asked, taking a seat in one of the chairs placed in front of Taylor's desk. "It feels like I have cross checked the goddamn thing five times."

"And what do you want me to do?" Hugh was there for instructions only. As usual, there would be no input from him, no questioning of Taylor's judgment.

"Out of the three thousand homes in the zone, I've identified a total of three hundred eighty two that will be fast tracked." Taylor continued flipping through his notes on the zone claims.

"How quickly do you want them completed?"

"Work up the same letter that went out to the seventeen thousand others a couple of weeks ago. Send it no later than the first of next week. As soon as you confirm addresses and alternate addresses, identify every contact location you can find. If you don't find an address other than the one at the property itself, get Investigations involved and tell them to find one. Call phone numbers to confirm good addresses. I don't give a shit how you do it; just get it done." Taylor was not being rude to Hugh. He knew Hugh's affinity for language, and they spoke in the same manner most of the time. "Then sit on them until I tell you otherwise. I'll let you know when they are to go out. I want them in final form."

"And another thing, Hugh," Taylor continued. "Sign the damn things this time. I don't want any more shit to deal with."

"Yes sir."

Unlike Hugh, Taylor had soon realized his own task would be too time consuming for him to do alone and enlisted the assistance of ten employees from data entry. He informed their supervisor that he needed ten bodies for an urgent task. and, as always, his request was honored with no questions asked.

The recruits were corralled into a windowless room in the claims building. Each was provided a portion of the list of zone properties, three hundred per head. Parameters were set forth by Taylor in a makeshift orientation. They were instructed to cross reference each name on their list against preset criteria to see if a match occurred. Insure Pro employees, including officers, directors, agents or counsel, were first, followed by contributors donating a minimum of ten grand. Also included were U.S. Senators, House members, any member of the federal judiciary, along with state legislators and judges. Last were the major contractors, and subcontractors employed by the company in the region, including owners, officers and directors of those entities.

Once each employee had gone through the comparisons, they were ordered to provide Mr. Franklin with all hits. If there was any question as to whether a property qualified for consideration, it was to be included, and Taylor would make the final decision.

They did their job well, and found a total of four hundred sixteen matches. Upon further review, Taylor eliminated thirty-four of them as unnecessary. The remainder was the chosen ones. There would be no record of the ceremony. None of the employees participating were given enough information to understand the nature of their assignment. To them, it was nothing more than comparing data fields on a computer screen. As a precautionary measure, each employee was required to sign a confidentiality agreement, providing for immediate termination and specified damages for disclosure. Speaking out would cost them their jobs and more. Considering their present compensation, there were no options other than compliance.

Taylor was fairly confident that he had managed to preclude any problems outside of the predicted number of lawsuits that the bean counters had already assessed. Only one name caused him any concern.

TEN

Jack woke to a delicious smell permeating Walt's house. He threw on some clothes and made his way to the kitchen, where the aroma was even better. Walt had heated up some boudin, a mixture of rice and sausage dressing encased in pig intestines. While it sounded like something out of a reality game show, it was actually very tasty. The intestines were not eaten; they were simply a thin cover to hold the goodness together. Once you got over the thought of the outer shell, it was easy to eat your weight's worth. Waffles with maple syrup accompanied the appetizer.

They ate breakfast at the kitchen table, watching the local morning news program. The bright morning temperature felt easily twenty degrees higher than back at home. After breakfast, Walt asked whether Jack would be interested in going for a ride.

"Where to?" Jack asked.

"Nowhere in particular; I just thought we could cruise around and maybe you could educate me a bit."

"That's a fine idea," Jack said, "just to get out for a while." They grabbed their jackets and hopped in Walt's truck for a drive to no place in particular.

As they started off, Walt asked. "You enjoy being on the Court, Jack?"

"Sure."

"That wasn't a yes or no question, buddy," Walt replied, "I want to know about it all, what you like, what you don't. Educate me. We don't do things the way you folks do up there, you know."

"I thoroughly enjoy being Chief Justice" Jack said as he began the lesson. "As far as reviewing appeals, researching the law, interpreting it and rendering decisions, I couldn't dream of a better job. My decisions can mean life or death, winning or losing, several dollars to millions of dollars. It's a tremendous responsibility I take very seriously. I give my full attention to everything I do on the Court. I have wonderfully talented people working for me, and I trust them implicitly. If judging was all there was to it, it would be the best job in the world."

"If? What's the drawback?" Walt asked.

"If it wasn't for all the goddamn politics," Jack replied. "Are you really interested about all this bullshit, or are you just trying to humor me?"

"I'm serious, Jack. Tell me what it's like. We've got nothing but time here, unless you just want to drive around staring out at the marsh for the next while."

"If you insist." Jack was well schooled in the politics of the judiciary and was always happy to share his views, as long as it was with someone who wasn't looking for favors, worse yet, ammunition.

Walter clearly fell into the former category.

Jack proceeded to give him something of a crash course in Alabama politics from his personal perspective.

Alabama was one of only seven states in the country that still elects its Supreme Court justices by way of partisan elections. Thirteen or so states still had elections, but no candidate was branded with a party label from the inception. Most states had recognized the inherent problems with partisan judicial elections years ago. Lagging behind the rest of the country in most other categories, it wasn't difficult to imagine why Alabama brought up the rear in jurisprudence matters.

The first problem, as Jack explained, was that money remained the primary concern. Everyone knows already that money rules in politics. The difference was that most states had done their best to remove politics from the judiciary. While that concept, in and of itself, is impossible to achieve, it can certainly be minimized. The concept is that if a judge is not answering to a particular party or block of voters, presumably he or she would be more inclined to follow the law, rather than interpret it in a light most favorable to a given group. The constituency of every judge should be the people as a whole, not a segment thereof.

Political parties put enormous pressure on their candidate to perform in a manner that is in line with their viewpoint. A justice should not be pressured into such a position. But that's the way it worked back home. And if a prospective jurist wanted a chance to sit on the bench, he had to ride the political wave that was peaking at the moment. In the 1980s that usually meant being a Democrat. The tide turned such that GOP candidates were the new fad years later. Both parties took advantage of their monopoly on the Court, and the results were inequitable for one group or another.

Justice was not served.

When the Democrats were in control, traditional GOP interests suffered. When the reversal took place, it was essentially payback time. Democrat based interests had their turn being the stepchild. The process repeated itself over and over. Jack rode in on the Republican wave that had recently begun to recede, but he had played it close to the vest, and had done, in his humble opinion, a remarkable job at keeping a moderate legal ideology, while not offending either his financial base or that of the opposing party.

There were many aspects to the GOP that troubled him. He was well aware of the hypocrisy involved in taking campaign contributions from the very interest groups that he found so vile, but it was a necessity for survival. Of particular disgust to him was the Christians for Conservative Justice Council. The name was misleading, as was virtually every name of a political action committee.

The CCJC was nothing more than a front for an extreme right wing group whose two primary goals were abolition of abortion and the revival of mandated prayer in public schools. The CCJC also had sold its platform to thousands of churches in the state, thus acquiring a massive base for fundraising. The reality was that few church members who had made donations to their cause had any real knowledge of their agenda. Not necessarily because they were unintelligent, more so because they were misinformed. CCJC had attempted to have the legislature pass a law that forbade any medical provider or facility performing abortions from operating within 2500 feet of a church or school. Unless you were in a national forest, there was no place in Alabama that wasn't within the prescribed radius of a church or school.

Fortunately for Jack and the other justices, the U.S. Supreme Court had already ruled on both matters, and they were bound by that decision. That didn't stop CCJC from trying to get the Court involved anyway. They failed in the legislature, thus keeping the matter out of the courts, much to the surprise of CCJC and the relief of the Garrett Court.

Complicating the matter for prospective judges, most of the so-called "Christian" PAC organizations had banded together, sharing mailing lists, donor information, and other pertinent information. Telling the good from the bad was impossible.

Alabama had a massive churchgoing population, and, as Jack explained, still did. At the Sunday services prior to every major election, churches would pass out voter guides to their respective congregation. They usually were in the form of a sample ballot remarkably similar to the official ballot that would be distributed the following week. Many of the recipients simply took the sample ballot given to them into the polling place and marked the official one accordingly. Churches certainly weren't the only organizations influencing the vote. Unions got in on the game for the other side. People weren't voting their conscience; they were doing what they were told.

One woman in north Alabama had worn a pin to work indicating her support for a certain candidate that her boss disliked. He had issued his own voter guide to his employees, specifically stating that a vote for her candidate's opponent was in the best interest of the company's financial health. She was fired. Politics was that volatile here.

The money was the biggest problem of all. A recent article in the Wall Street Journal illustrated the point. Though Alabama tended to bring up the rear when it came to many national comparisons such as education, percentage of high school graduates, percentage of population earning more than the poverty line, and percentage of other social issues, the state was the undisputed champion when it came to the costs of the state Supreme Court races. The total costs of the last court elections in '04 reached a staggering twelve million dollars. It started back in 1994 with the revolution on which Jack piggybacked into office.

National tort reform movements, spearheaded by the U.S. Chamber of Commerce, began pouring millions of dollars into states whose Supreme Courts had struck down tort reform legislation. The money was provided by insurance companies, manufacturers and banks, for the most part. The previously Democrat controlled Alabama Court had done just that to a package of laws capping damage claims, and restricting access to the courts for certain claimants. The prior Court had determined that such caps, were unconstitutional. With only a handful of states electing judges on party lines, Alabama became an important testing ground.

The '94 elections were the most costly in history, and the most vicious. One ad that likened a candidate to a skunk brought a misconduct charge against the sitting Justice, a Democrat, who was ultimately defeated. That trend continued through the most recent elections where Democrats had gained four seats back. The Schoolcraft incident led to a barrage of successful ads telling the voters of those candidates who supported a pedophile. Jack's last campaign had raised and spent a total of more than one and a half million dollars.

"One and a half million bucks! You can't be serious?" Walt was amazed at what he was hearing.

Jack continued his lesson.

Jack knew when he took office in '94 that there was a problem in the judiciary in Alabama. It wasn't that prior Courts had struck down tort reform laws. It was that a handful of verdicts were unreasonable. It just so happened that those verdicts grabbed the national spotlight. Had the prior Courts simply issued reductions in the awards, the pressure likely wouldn't have been so great. But they didn't. Cries of businesses fleeing the state, and a pending economic exodus were made by the reformers. The reality was that the state's economy was thriving, and several major automotive manufacturers had built new production facilities in the state.

The campaign worked. The revolution of 1994 was a complete success with the total dismantlement of the Democrat led Court. The Alabama model was exported to other states with partisan elections that had a history similar to Alabama's, with identical success.

"If you don't mind me asking, Jack, how much are you making a year?" Walt jumped in.

"My annual salary is ninety-seven a year."

"So you raised over one and a half mil, for a position that pays you less than a hundred grand?'

"My supporters did."

"And who are they?"

"For the most part, insurance companies and the like, just as I mentioned earlier."

"But I thought you fancied yourself a moderate."

"I've been on both sides of the fence, as you know. But you can't straddle the fence for a judicial election at home."

"I assume that the people who got you in office expect something in return for their 1.5 mil?"

"Of course they do. Anyone who thinks otherwise is either naïve, or just plain stupid."

"So you give them what they want? That doesn't sound like you, Jack."

"I rule in accordance with the law as I understand it to be. I have dissented from a number of majority opinions. It just didn't matter; we had a nine-zero majority until the last election."

"Didn't that upset your contributors?"

"It's come up, but they have been appeased."

"I don't get it."

"That's a complicated matter, Walt. One I'd rather not get into."

"So, now that you have four new voices on the Court, what's going to happen when something gets sticky?" Walt asked.

"So far, nothing has. But my principles are what they are. Besides that, the overall political climate in Alabama is always evolving, just as it is now. For example, Jeff Stallings is a good judge. He's bright, educated and, from what I can tell, a principled man. But he won his last race by a mere thirty-five hundred votes over a Democrat they put up with no experience in the practice of law, for Christ's sake. He was a career law professor with no credentials outside a classroom, and he almost won. That tells you a lot about the mindset of our electorate."

"But if you were to cross over on a ruling, what then?"

"I'd probably lose my funding, or at worst, a new candidate would challenge me in a primary, with plenty of money from my old base."

"And you'd be a goner, huh?"

"Walt, I truly love the job I have. I feel like I can make a difference in my career. Money isn't the issue for me; I have plenty to live on if I need to." Jack started, then paused for a moment, looking out the window at the rice fields, and finally said, "I just don't know if I have the stomach for the politics any longer. It's a brutal, cutthroat environment, and I know, deep down, that's not what I'm made of."

"You're a good, honest man, Jack. I've always known that. I have no doubt that you will always do what is just and right. Things have a way of taking care of themselves, you know."

"I want to believe that, Walt, I truly do."

The friends drove through the marshland in southwest Louisiana, not saying a word for another ten minutes. Walt perceived that the Chief wanted to convince himself that Walt was right, and he hoped to find the optimism within himself.

Finally, Walt said, "I hope you don't mind, but I've taken the liberty of scheduling something I think you might need."

"What, an intervention?"

"Of sorts, you could say. We are having a good old-fashioned crawfish boil tonight at the house, and you, my old friend, shall be the guest of honor." Walt was smiling.

"I had a feeling that I couldn't come down here without you pulling some kind of shit on me." Jack's face eased into a grin. "How many folks do you have coming?" Jack had attended one of these parties, and usually it seemed as though half the town had stopped by at some point during the evening.

"Just a small one this time, no more than thirty or forty." Walt started laughing. "You may remember one or two, but they're all good people here. There's not a one wouldn't give you the shirt off his own back if you needed it."

"I don't doubt that for a minute."

They started heading back to Walt's to relax for a while before the festivities that were scheduled for later that afternoon. It was going to be the first time in a while that Jack had been around that many people who didn't know him, and certainly weren't asking for something from him. He found a great deal of relief in that knowledge. Walt Broussard was providing him exactly what he needed.

ELEVEN

Roger Stoltz arrived at the Plaza just as instructed by Mr. Franklin. Taylor knew he was a bit early when the guard at the main gate called to ask if he was approved to enter. Roger made his way to the rear of the property and parked in visitor parking. He knew his way to Taylor's office.

He exited the elevator and went directly to Taylor's suite. He knocked on the closed door, and waited for a response.

"Come on in, it's open."

Roger entered to find Taylor at the conference table in the middle of the office, pouring over paperwork. "I thought there would be others here," he said, glancing around the room.

Roger, lead engineer at Forensic Engineering, LLC, also served as the company's named incorporator in the Secretary of State's office. Both a native Texan and a Houston native, he attended the University of Texas for undergraduate work, and remained there to obtain his masters in structural engineering. Roger spent his first twenty years as an engineer for an Austin firm. It was a safe place for him, so he resigned himself to his place in life, content to collect a paycheck every two weeks.

After eighteen years of it, a change of heart began to occur. Roger realized that he had become too complacent. He wanted to advance his career, and earning potential. He began a personal consulting business, without the knowledge of his superiors. It was easy at first, just taking an hour or two after work. The money was great, and he was beginning to have fun again.

That all ended when he was subpoenaed to testify in a civil case that he had provided consultation on back in Houston. Roger had taken some time on weekends to go down for site visits, and had put in the rest of his research time at home, after hours, of course. But now he was required to be out of town for a week. His testimony was key for the defense; if he was suddenly unavailable, his consulting career was over. He never forgot his conversation with defense counsel that followed.

"I may have a problem with the trial schedule, sir."

"What kind of problem?"

"You know my work schedule, sir, and I can't be gone for the whole week. Paul doesn't know anything about this." Paul, CEO of Allied Engineering, was Roger's direct superior.

"Damn it Roger, you have to be there. Without you, we have no case,"

"I'm stuck here, sir. I don't know how I can possibly get off."

"Let me put it this way, Roger. You come down to Houston and do what we're paying you to do. You get us through this case, and I assure you that you'll have more than enough business. Allied will seem like a job waiting tables at fucking Outback. I promise you, your new career will be unbelievable. You don't follow through with your obligations to us, and you will never have a consulting job again in Texas, and I assure you, I know every carrier around. Word gets out fast, you know."

It was a threat, but Roger knew that what he had heard was true. If he truly wanted to have a consulting career, he had to go the distance. It was blind faith he would be giving here.

Roger concocted a story for Paul that his mother was having surgery and needed him in Houston for her recovery. He figured he could at least try to play both sides for as long as possible. He knew he was in trouble when his fifth day on the witness stand was over and the end wasn't in sight. He called Paul with a lame excuse. Paul demanded he come back to Austin for a new project that was assigned to him. His day of reckoning had arrived.

His job at Allied Engineering was over; that much was clear. It was impossible for him to abandon his testimony now. His future as a consultant hinged on this case, according to his client.

Roger left the witness stand after seven days of testimony and drove himself straight to the hospital where he was admitted. He had none of the risk factors, and recently had been given a clean bill of health, but he was sure that he was in the middle of a heart attack. The doctor informed him that he had, in fact, suffered an attack. But, it was an anxiety attack.

Roger's testimony was superb, and the jury ruled in favor of his client, he was later informed. Upon returning to Austin, his belongings were already packed for him. Paul had apprised him of his termination by phone. His last visit to Allied lasted five minutes. Roger Stoltz picked up his personal effects and returned home.

True to his word, Taylor Franklin began hiring Roger on a routine basis for expert testimony. He also encouraged other insurers, both in and out of the state, to hire Roger for consulting gigs. Roger's business took off, and he knew he had made the right decision. His only problem was a lack of staff and a proper office to handle the volume that was coming his way. By his assessment, eighty percent of his income was coming from Insure Pro. Within six months, he had an office, six associates and a support staff of fourteen.

"There's no need for anyone else, Roger," Taylor began. "I've got a final list of properties in the Peter matter for you."

"How many are we talking about?"

"Just over twenty-six hundred."

"That's less than I would have expected."

"I need to send letters on them within the next several weeks. Can you get them all done?"

"Three weeks? That's not a lot of time for that many, even if we distribute it to every associate and focus solely on those. Plus we have to do site inspections."

"I want every body you have on it. And there are a large number of them that are mere slabs now. They can be grouped together for the site inspections." Taylor knew that Roger understood the importance of this project. Roger was only called to his office for special occasions.

"Where are the files?" Roger asked.

"Hugh has a copy made for you. Get your courier over to claims and they'll be ready this afternoon."

"I'll get everyone ready and get started."

"Good. I'll call you in a week or so for an update." Taylor turned back to his files, not bothering to see Roger out.

He left the Plaza and called Wanda. "Tell everyone we have a firm meeting at three-thirty this afternoon. Whatever they're doing, they are to put it aside."

"Yes sir."

Roger pulled out of the Plaza and started the drive back to Irving, and the home office of Forensic Engineering, LLC.

* * *

Arriving back at his office, Stoltz proceeded straight to the conference room. The files from Insure Pro were on their way He wanted to make sure everything was cleared out for the new project. He called his team in for a dry run before the documents were delivered. Roger had hired his six associates on his own. They were all reliable men and dedicated to their profession.

The office of Forensic Engineering was substantially less impressive than those of Insure Pro. Roger had a fairly small, one-level building in an industrial part of Irving. It resembled a strip mall more than a professional office building. But outward appearance was unimportant. Clients didn't come to him; he went to them. He didn't entertain or have open houses. Each occupant designed and paid for the individual office's décor. As such, furnishings in most cases were practical and inexpensive.

The team assembled within half an hour, giving the employees time to finish their working projects. The meeting began at three p.m. Roger started by informing his men seated around the conference table that Insure Pro had a major assignment for them. Within the next forty-eight hours, he informed them, they would all be in south Alabama. Most of them had already assumed that Hurricane Peter would eventually have them scrambling. Like Roger, they were simply waiting on the call.

The Ryder truck pulled into the parking lot at three-thirty pm, and fifty boxes of paperwork were transferred into the main conference room. Hugh Capelli had already had the documents arranged in a manner that enabled Roger to separate the boxes into geographical plots. Stoltz commanded each man's attention.

"We leave for the gulf coast in the morning. You have photos of the properties, addresses and instructions. This is not a new situation, gentlemen; you know the drill. I have assigned each of you a total of approximately four hundred cases." He heard a collective sigh, assuming that his team had predicted a lengthy stay in the damaged area.

"Each of you has an area that is conducive to a quick entry and exit. Most of these properties have been declared a total wash." The team understood what he meant. They had seen the news reports like the rest of the country. There would be large areas of total devastation, requiring little time for a site investigation. "Don't get me wrong, this will take some time, but I assure you it's not as bad as you think." Roger was hoping his aides would accept him at face value.

The boxes of documents were allocated and distributed to each member of the team. "I'm taking the largest number of cases, so I don't want to hear any bitching from anyone," Stoltz said, standing up from the table. "We'll be staying at the LaQuinta in Foley. I have our rooms reserved. We leave first thing in the morning. Are there any questions?"

After no response, Roger finally said, "Good. I'll see you tomorrow evening. Call me en route if you need me." He called Wanda and instructed her to get his cases loaded into his trunk. The site inspections were necessary for the investigation, but Roger dreaded having to spend so much time looking at empty lots. It all seemed so useless to him. He knew his opinions already, but he couldn't testify persuasively without having been there. He hoped for a good night's sleep. After tonight, there likely wouldn't be one until he came home.

* * *

Jack spent the rest of his vacation relaxing and enjoying the escape that only a place like Walter Broussard's could provide. The crawfish boil was a huge success, and Jack was sure that he met half the town. There were no strangers; everyone acted as though Jack was born and raised with them.

Walt prodded him over and over about life outside of the office. He finally gave in the day before he was set to return home. Walt always had a way to get people to open up, and Jack's defenses were down. Deep inside, he wanted to talk about her; it just took the persistence that only a friend like Walt could provide to pry it out of him.

"There's something you're not telling me, buddy," Walt said on his last night in Louisiana. "And you're not leaving until we get to the bottom of this."

"What makes you say that?"

"I know you. I know something's up – I just can't put my finger on it."

After going back and forth several times, Jack gave in. He told Walt all about Sharon. He spoke of her brilliant mind, her beauty, sense of humor and the way she had made him feel more alive than he had in years. When Walt finally asked if he had told her of any of those things, Jack replied, "What am I supposed to say, Walt? She works for me, and she certainly hasn't shown any signs of interest in me."

"But you haven't tried."

"Why should I?"

"What are you afraid of, rejection?"

"Give me a break, Walt. I'm not a fifteen year old kid."

"No you're not, Jack. But you've raised almost three million dollars and conducted two winning campaigns for one of the highest offices in your state. You've given numerous speeches, stumped on the campaign trail and endured God knows what being thrown at you from your opponents along the way. I find it hard to believe that you're frightened of being turned down by a woman at this point in your life."

"Cut out the bullshit. What's your point?"

"I don't know much, Jack. I'm a simple soul," Walt began, "but I've learned a thing or two about life along the way. If you'll hear me out for a minute, I promise I'll let it go, no questions asked."

"Fine."

As Walt sat down on the sofa, his demeanor changed. Jack saw the transformation in process, and fell into the recliner.

"I've lived a good life, Jack. I've always tried my best to do good toward others, and take care of my own. I've seen my share of loss. Mama and Pop will always be with me, I don't only know it – I feel it," Walt continued.

"Losing your parents is something you expect will happen as you get older, but when Katherine died, a big part of me died too, and I thought I'd never see a good day again." Walt's wife died in a car accident, ten years before, and Jack had traveled to be with him after the funeral.

Jack remembered seeing his friend in more pain than he could have ever imagined, and he hurt for him.

"If there's one thing I've learned through all the misery that accompanies life, it's that you have to take advantage of every opportunity that God presents. Sometimes, it just doesn't happen, and if that's the result, maybe He didn't have that in His plan. But I firmly believe that He wants us to try to make the best out of the circumstances that we find ourselves in. Maybe it's a test, maybe it's not, and hopefully we'll get the answer to that some day. As far as I can tell, buddy, we have one go around on this big spinning ball that we live on, and I intend to make the best of my time in the game."

Jack was quiet, listening intently to his friend. He never took Walt for a philosopher, but his message was taking hold, Walt continued, "I try to look at every situation I find myself in as an opportunity, even the less pleasant ones. I don't want to wake up one day and find myself eighty years old saying that if only I'd have done this or that – I'm going to do it all, everything that I can."

Walt paused for a moment, took a deep breath and exhaled. He looked Jack square in his eyes and said, "I may be wrong, Jackson, but I think, at your very core, you're the same as me.

You just haven't realized it yet. Think about it on that drive home of yours, and I bet you'll agree."

Jack stared back at Walt. "I don't know," was all he said.

"I'm not asking you to admit to anything, just planting a seed for thought." Walt stood up and headed towards the kitchen. "I'm beat, and you need to get some sleep."

* * *

Jack returned to Montgomery the following day. He thought about Walt's words the entire trip home.

You are just like him. Just talk to her.

What have you got to lose? Nothing.

Well, maybe.

Life at the capital went on much the same as it had before. Jack returned to working and saw Sharon on a daily basis. He said nothing. The time wasn't right anyway, he had convinced himself, over and over again. The days stretched into weeks with Jack reverting to his same old self, complacent in his solitude.

Sharon continued to do her job, perfectly as always. She had thought, on many occasions, about the time she'd spent at Jack's during the storm. He was a good, honest man, and attractive for his age. She, too, had become accustomed to living on her own, but in the back of her mind had not given up on the prospect for a future relationship. Her career left precious little time for dating, and it wasn't as if Montgomery had a large supply of single men. Although Jack Garrett would have been an ideal man for her, he was, after all, her boss. She certainly couldn't insinuate interest to him, lest she find herself looking for a new source of income if the feeling wasn't mutual. And she had no indication that it would be.

TWELVE

Roger Stoltz and his crew returned to Texas after spending a month at the gulf coast of Alabama. His staff had suspected that his estimate of how long the process would take was low, and more than one expressed their frustrations at having been gone from home so long. Roger didn't enjoy the boring trip any more than they did. With numerous properties having been completely wiped off their foundations, there was little to actually investigate. Those that remained intact, or partially so, left little evidence of what Peter had actually done to them.

After the best night's sleep he'd had in a month, Roger called Taylor Franklin notifying him of his return. Taylor instructed him to be at the Plaza the following morning for a review.

He arrived as instructed and proceeded to Franklin's office.

"You have the documentation you need, Roger?" Taylor asked as he walked in.

"There wasn't much to see in many cases."

"Do you have enough to form a rational basis for an opinion?"

"That depends on what exactly it is you want me to be able to say."

"Any denial has to be based on the surge or design, Roger. You should know that."

"It's a tough sell, sir. Based upon what I found, the surge was twenty feet or so. The weather folks can give more exact numbers on that. But this storm had substantial wind velocity in this area. It appears that most of the damage was wind related."

"Not good enough!" Taylor screamed at Stoltz. "You will have an opinion that supports us, damn it, and you will testify to it if need be. Do you understand me?"

"I can say anything you want me to, sir, but that doesn't mean a jury will buy it."

"That's not your problem, now is it?" Taylor had already had enough of Roger Stoltz. "You just get to work on preparing for discovery; I'm sure we'll have several suits within the next month or so. Leave it to me to sell it."

"With all due respect, sir, it's a weak…"

"I said, get yourself ready." Taylor interrupted. "Everything you have is because of me, Roger. Surely you don't want us to find someone else to do your job, do you?"

"No sir." Roger knew he was right. If it weren't for Taylor Franklin, he would have nothing, and there was no doubt in his mind that if Taylor wanted to ensure he had no more work in the future, he could make it happen.

Roger left the Plaza feeling more nauseated than he had in years. *I don't like the way this is going.*

He returned to Irving to notify his team that they were to work on nothing but the Peter cases until further notice. He had not been intimidated about testifying again since the Houston case with Insure Pro years ago. He was already starting to get that feeling again.

* * *

Taylor made the short walk over to the Kirschberg Claims Building and went straight to Hugh's office. Hugh had his back to the door, working on his desktop, when his boss walked in.

"We're ready for the letters to go, Hugh."

"Which ones do you want us to send, sir?"

"All of them. First priority will be the approvals I provided, but I want the denials sent out immediately thereafter, a day at most, not weeks." Taylor had already proofed the notification letters while waiting on Roger to get back from the coast. That was a pre-requisite to getting the letters out.

The plan was rather simple, in theory. Taylor knew reasonably early that the claims of those in the zone would be denied, except of course, for those claimants pre-approved by him for various reasons. Of the approximately two thousand seven hundred remaining claims, the risk assessment had been as expected. There would be lawsuits, a number of them. The estimate was that somewhere around ten to twenty percent of the remainder would just accept their losses and write it off as another good screwing that life sometimes doles out. Many others would be settled for far less than policy limits – litigation costs and stress tiring them into submission.

The holdout cases would be tried. That's where Roger came in. With Roger's testimony, Insure Pro had a legitimate, arguable basis to deny those claims. While the company might end up paying some of those claims due to a verdict, there would be no cause of action for bad faith failure to pay, which potentially could result in millions in punitive damages. Some of those cases, Insure Pro was sure to win; the losses would result in nothing more than payment of policy proceeds.

By his calculations, Taylor Franklin was going to save Insure Pro in excess of four hundred million dollars by himself. The rewards would be substantial.

* * *

The Chief Justice assumed that the letter from Insure Pro was simply to request additional information with respect to his claim. It had only been a few months since Peter, and he knew it was a statistical nightmare for an insurer that had so much business in the region. He was fine with waiting it out while things worked themselves out. He brought the letter, along with the power bill and junk that made its way into the mail on a daily basis, into the kitchen. He opened the letter from Insure Pro first.

Dear Mr. Garrett:

We have completed our investigation into the loss at your property located at 2450 Sunset Drive, which occurred on or about September 17, 2005, and have reviewed the proof of loss submitted by you in support of this claim. Based upon our investigation, we are pleased to inform you that your claim for benefits under policy no. 37859327 has been approved for payment. You will be receiving a check for the structure damage claim within the next fourteen (14) days.

A local claims adjuster will be contacting you within the next seven (7) days to confirm the amounts due under the contents provisions of your policy. We hope that this is not too much of an inconvenience, but ask your patience in this process. There are many thousands of claims, which we are reviewing, but we hope to have your claim concluded within the next thirty (30) days.

Thank you again for placing your trust in Insure Pro. It has been a pleasure assisting you during this difficult time. Should you have any questions in the meantime, please call your agent, or local claims department with any questions you may have.

Sincerely,

Hugh Capelli
Vice President, Claims
Southern Division

Jack was amazed that an approval had come so fast, but he had always received prompt attention in dealing with their claims department. If his being the Chief Justice was to blame, he could live with that perk. He had originally assumed it would be many months before he could even think about rebuilding his dream home. Now he could start sooner.

He began to get excited thinking about the prospect of being back in his paradise before the end of the year.

* * *

Les Vance got a call from Melanie while he was at the office. Her screaming and babbling made her almost incoherent. He managed to calm her down long enough to get the gist of what had happened. The Vances received a letter from their insurance company regarding the beach property.

The claim had been denied.

Les was in shock. He told Mel to fax the letter to his personal fax machine in his office immediately. It arrived within five minutes with no cover page – it was brief and to the point.

Dear Mrs. Vance:

We have completed our investigation into the loss sustained at your property located at 5470 Sunset Drive arising out of damage that occurred on or about September 17, 2005, under policy no. 86455137. Our investigation has determined that the loss sustained by you was not a covered loss within the meaning of your policy with Insure Pro.

Based upon our investigation, it has been determined that the damage to your residence was caused by flood, or in the alternative, was a direct result of inadequate engineering, architectural and/or construction design or completion, which are excluded from coverage under your policy.

We regret that this decision was not more favorable, but we are only obligated to pay claims that meet the definition of a "covered loss" as described in your policy. Should you have any questions regarding this matter, please feel free to contact your local claims office. We thank you again for your business, and wish you the best of luck in the future.

Sincerely,

Hugh Capelli
Vice President, Claims
Southern Division

Les was furious. *Those bastards. They don't know who they're dealing with.* He rose from his desk, went over and slammed his door shut. He returned to his desk, unable to sit, hit the speakerphone and dialed the direct number.

"Mr. Franklin's office, how may I help you?"

"Put Taylor on, tell him it's Les Vance, and if he's not there, find him now." Les didn't shout at Taylor's assistant, but it took everything he had not to.

"One moment, Mr. Vance."

"Les, how are you, my friend?" Taylor was more friendly than usual towards Les, but he had finally put his plan into motion and was proud of himself. Besides that, he knew Les was going to be assisting him down the road, and Kathy had indicated that Mr. Vance sounded perturbed when she answered.

"What the fuck is going on, Taylor?"

"What do you mean?"

"I mean, we just received a denial on our beach house claim. That's what I fucking mean."

Taylor was stunned. "You got a WHAT?"

"A denial, and let me tell you…"

"Calm down a minute, Les," Taylor interrupted. "There has been some kind of mistake, and I will get to the bottom of it immediately." Now Taylor was raising his voice. Not at Les, but at the prospect that someone had completely missed something.

"I'd better hear something from you by lunch, Taylor, or we're going to have…

"You absolutely will," Taylor interrupted again, not wanting to get into a pissing match. "I'll call you back within the hour."

Les slammed the phone down, still reeling with anger.

* * *

Taylor called Hugh as soon as he hung up with Les. "Hugh, what the hell is going on over there? I just got a call from Les Vance in Birmingham, and he received a denial letter." Taylor was firm, not yelling, yet. "Pull up his address."

"I don't have an address for him."

"What do you mean, he got our letter. You have to have something."

"Not in our system."

"Cross check it against any Vance you have for the Peter claims."

After several minutes of silence, Hugh said, "There are two Vances, a Calvin and a Melanie."

Shit.

"Get me the file on Melanie. I want it in my office now."

"Yes sir."

The courier arrived with the file minutes later, out of breath from running over from claims. Taylor looked through the file and knew immediately why the error had happened. Les and Melanie had put the beach property in Melanie's name several years ago for tax purposes. Les' name wasn't listed in their system any longer. When Taylor was reviewing files for approval, cross-referencing against his list of policyholders, he just missed it, and Les Vance slipped through the cracks. Taylor had met Melanie on several occasions, but it didn't register when her name appeared. He had reviewed so many files that it was possible it wasn't even his mistake; one of the data entry folks could have overlooked it just as easily. It mattered not as it was still on his dime.

He closed the file and called Les. "Les, Taylor here. We owe you an apology. There was a mistake in coding over in the claims department. That may sound odd, but we have thousands of claims being processed at this time, and I'm sure yours won't be the only one that comes up as incorrect."

"So, it will be corrected then?"

"I'm taking care of it personally."

"Look, I know I was rude when I called, but the denial came out of nowhere and…"

"You have no need to apologize to me, Les, you had every right to be pissed, I'm just sorry it happened. I will get it fixed and get you a letter by the end of the day."

"Thank you."

"No thanks are necessary, and, again, I apologize for the error."

Taylor knew that thanks were in order, for it was his call that approved a claim that otherwise would have been denied. He called Hugh and instructed him to get the revised letter approving the claim of Melanie Vance on his desk immediately. He would send it to Les personally with yet another apology.

By the end of the week, nearly three thousand people would have already received or would soon get the same letter Melanie Vance opened earlier this morning. The first lawsuits were likely less than a month or so away.

* * *

Jack contacted the claims office and finalized his proof of loss, setting forth the contents in his house that were lost or destroyed. Within a month his check was delivered via certified mail. While he was waiting on the funds to arrive, he contacted the contractor who had built the original beach home. The architectural and design plans were still there, and he wanted to rebuild the house just as it had been. The contractor was eager to begin working on reconstruction, and informed Jack that he'd get started on clearing the lot within two weeks. Construction would begin in a month, at most. Jack was going to be back at the coast before he knew it, and he couldn't wait.

* * *

Stephen Whisenhunt received his denial letter around the same time as the other several thousand homeowners did. Like most of them, he was outraged. He had been paying premiums to Insure Pro for years, and had never even made the first claim for benefits. It came as a surprise when he opened the letter, and his wife, Sue, broke down in tears knowing that their vacation home would not be covered. Breaking the news to the kids would prove no easier for them.

Unlike many of the others though, Stephen had some connections. After a few calls, he was told that he might want to talk to William Bucknell Padgett. Buck was a fairly well known trial attorney with his main office in Mobile, Alabama. He was born and raised in Bay Minette, about 50 miles from the coast.

Buck had been practicing law for thirty years, mostly in south Alabama. He was on a first name basis with most of the trial court judges in the area, and, in the smaller counties, was sure to know some percentage of potential citizens who were called to jury duty on any given matter. Buck Padgett was known for his courtroom attire, which always included his cowboy boots, brown slacks and tweed jacket.

Padgett had the southern drawl down to an art form. It was no act, as anyone who knew him would attest. He was the consummate southern man – strong, witty and, in his profession, what most would call a bulldog. He was relentless with adverse witnesses and prepared for a case like no other. Buck would go to any expense necessary to represent his clients, and no document was left unread. Many a small mistake by a defendant was pounced on by the bulldog. When he lost, it was always the fault of the client, that much he was sure of.

Buck received Whisenhunt's call late on a Wednesday afternoon.

"Mr. Padgett, my name is Stephen Whisenhunt. I was referred to you by Bradley Willis in Birmingham."

"Please call me Buck, Mr. Whisenhunt. Bradley told me to expect your call, what can I do you for?"

"It's regarding our beach home and Hurricane Peter." Buck was generally apprised of Stephen's predicament during his conversation with the referring lawyer. "Our insurance company has denied the claim under our homeowner's policy, and we're not satisfied with them at all."

"I'd be happy to look into it, sir, where do you live?"

"We're in Tuscaloosa."

"Any chance we could meet first of next week?"

"I'd be happy to come to your office, sir. I want to get this handled as soon as possible."

"How about Monday after lunch, let's say one-thirty?"

"I very much appreciate it. Thank you for your time, and I look forward to meeting you next week."

As Buck placed the phone down, he smiled. He knew that there would be many cases, against many companies, arising out of Peter. It was his hope that he'd get the first shot at those greedy sons of bitches.

* * *

Stephen Whisenhunt made the trip to Mobile as scheduled and arrived at Buck Padgett's office a half hour early. Buck returned from lunch to find him in the lobby. Padgett & Keeler had a two-story office in downtown Mobile, decorated in a western theme complete with the stuffed bison and elk that Buck had bagged in Colorado, which were mounted on the walls of the two-story foyer. Padgett & Keeler employed ten lawyers, four of whom were partners. Support staff numbered thirty, including their full time investigators. Buck greeted Mr. Whisenhunt and led him upstairs to his office on the southeast corner of the floor.

Buck's office was large, but rather plainly decorated. His desk was covered in paperwork, as was the conference table in his study area to the rear. His prized fourteen-point buck hung on the wall opposite his desk, framed by several certificates that Stephen didn't bother to read. "Have a seat, please," Buck offered. "Tell me what we've got here."

Pursuant to his request during their initial phone conversation, Stephen had brought with him a copy of his policy, pictures of the beach home both before and after the storm, the denial letter from Insure Pro, as well as the original building plans. They had built the home in 1990 after years of savings. It had, like so many of the homes Peter destroyed, been their dream vacation home.

Buck met with Mr. Whisenhunt for the better part of two hours, poring over the documents. Stephen had discussed the matter with a friend of his who was an engineer, and he had left him with the feeling that something wasn't quite right. By the end of the meeting, Buck expressed his interest in pursuing the case for them.

"You know they're not just going to roll over on this," Buck told him.

"I don't know what they're going to do," Stephen replied.

"They'll fight like hell. And it won't be fun for you or your family. But I assure you one thing; we're going to give them all they can take, and more."

"I've heard that about you; that's why I'm here."

"I don't want to play around with this, Steve. It's my intention to have a lawsuit filed in the next two weeks, with your permission."

"I'm leaving it in your hands, Buck. You have my permission to do what you think is necessary."

Buck Padgett filed the first case against Insure Pro from Hurricane Peter. The case was filed in early December of 2005.

* * *

Taylor Franklin received a copy of the lawsuit within two weeks of filing. Insure Pro was monitoring every new case filed in Baldwin County via their electronic notification system. Any member of the system simply logged on to the state's judicial system mainframe and searched all new filings by county. It was no surprise that they had been sued, and Taylor was looking forward to defending the cases.

He vaguely recognized Buck Padgett's name. Taylor had not gone into battle against him, but he was sure that the name was somehow familiar. After some simple research, Taylor knew how the name had struck a chord. Buck had obtained three of the five largest jury verdicts in Baldwin County's history. Buck had been fodder for tort reformers for years.

A worthy opponent.

THIRTEEN

It was during the early stages of the Whisenhunt litigation when Jack made his unfortunate excursion to Atlanta that would result in the Judicial Inquiry Commission proceedings. For well over a year the details of that night remained a mystery to him.

Insure Pro, and Taylor Franklin specifically, fully appreciated the power that the Alabama Supreme Court wielded over them. When it came to civil lawsuits, they were the final word for all intents and purposes. Rarely would the U.S. Supreme Court accept an appeal in such matters, as those were historically left for the states to decide.

Mindful of this situation, Taylor had instituted a program after the 2004 elections specifically directed at the Alabama Supreme Court. With four Democrats having been elected, and the balance of power possibly heading toward a swing in the wrong direction, Franklin decided that they needed to keep running tabs on the lady and gentlemen who would be ruling their fate.

Insure Pro would investigate the backgrounds of each and every sitting justice, determining their hobbies, interests, family life, affairs, drug or alcohol problems, arrests, speeding tickets...everything that they did or had done in the past. Any potential issues that could provide leverage would be maintained and, if needed, exploited. Dan Spearman was placed in charge of the program that was never given a formal name, and whose existence was known only to Dan and Taylor. Information gathered was only to be used if necessary, and only in the direst of situations.

Spearman would update Taylor occasionally if new information surfaced or if a source had any leads. Taylor wanted to remain as far out of the loop as possible to insulate the company, as well as himself. He trusted Dan immensely, and Spearman owed his entire professional career to Taylor. Dan took his newfound responsibility seriously, and worked diligently to impress his boss. Spearman figured he knew more about the justices in Alabama than their spouses did, and knowledge was power.

In mid-January, Dan received a call from his source at the Court, notifying him that Garrett and Jeff Stallings would be attending a conference in Atlanta. Spearman notified Taylor that he needed some time off, which he routinely granted his security director due to his schedule. Dan had an opportunity and it was worth taking. He had done his homework and, if his intuition was right, he might be able to get some dirt. He went to DFW International later that day to purchase a round trip ticket to Hartsfield International Airport.

As he approached the ticket counter, he informed the agent that he needed to get a flight to Atlanta.

"We have a flight leaving at 4:10 p.m., arriving in Atlanta at 7:05 p.m."

"That's fine, I'll take it."

"And your return date, sir?"

"Friday, please."

"I have one available flight returning Friday, January 14th, leaving Atlanta at 9:00 a.m., returning to Dallas at 11:50 a.m."

"That will work as well."

"The round trip fare will be seven hundred eighty-five dollars, how will you be paying, sir, and may I see your identification, please?"

"Cash." He gave her eight hundred dollar bills and his identification.

"One moment, sir, while I process the tickets."

"Thank you, Mr. Sullivan. Have a nice trip to Atlanta."

He had three days to accomplish his mission.

At 4:10 p.m., American Airlines flight 1416 left the gate in Dallas heading to Atlanta, with Ronald Sullivan on board.

* * *

Construction had begun in Gulf Shores and it was all Jack could do to keep from driving down every weekend to check on the status. He'd made several trips already and was pleased at the progress. Based upon the estimate, completion was scheduled for mid-June, earlier than he had expected. By the middle of January, they had already managed to get the frame up enough that it began to resemble a house again. Jack thought that in the next couple of weeks he would begin shopping for new furniture, fixtures and appliances.

When he returned home from his weekend visit to the coast he was more excited than he had been in some time. The thought of planning for the new home meant he would have something other than Sharon to occupy his mind for quite a while, which was a welcome change, considering he had yet to implement the Broussard method of life.

He returned to the Court on Monday and was approached by Jeffrey Stallings, the youngest GOP member of the Court, about a judicial conference at the Ritz in Buckhead, ten miles north of downtown Atlanta. Jeff was taking the opportunity to get out of town since his wife had taken their young twins to Virginia to visit her parents for a week.

"Why don't you make the trip, Jack? It could do you some good." Jeff was sincere in his request, and it would be nice knowing someone from home during the conference anyway.

"I've got a lot to do with the beach house."

"You've got plenty of time for that. Besides, nothing beats staying at the Ritz." Jeff had a point. When it came to luxury hotels, nothing even approached the elegance of the Ritz Carlton. "It's a short conference anyway."

Jack pondered it for a while and finally gave in. "I suppose it might do me some good to get away for a bit."

"Great! Do you want me to drive or do you want to?"

Jack was hoping he wasn't simply looking for a ride. "I'll just drive on up myself and meet you there. I don't know when I'll leave, and I might take off early," Jack said, assuming that it was a deal breaker.

"Fair enough, I'll see you Friday afternoon."

With his only out gone, Jack called the Ritz and booked his room for the conference the following weekend.

* * *

Ron Sullivan arrived in Atlanta in the early evening on Tuesday. He took a cab from the airport and went to the Hyatt Regency in Buckhead. By the time he got to the hotel it was almost 9:30 p.m., and he was quite tired after the day of traveling. There was no time to rest; he had to get to work.

First he called his contact in Atlanta, Kip Anderson. Kip and Ron met two years ago when Ron had gone to Georgia for a gun show. Ever since his time in the military, he had been an aficionado of firearms, and enjoyed traveling the country to see what the latest and greatest thing on the market was. Kip owned The Platinum Oasis, a strip club in Roswell, also north of Atlanta. Kip had taken Ron to his club one evening and they hit it off, drinking until three in the morning, and then having some fun with several of the girls who stayed after work.

Although Ron didn't partake, drugs were available. Most of the dancers were strung out on one thing or another, and Kip was a recreational user, usually only with the girls when he was horny. Ron was shocked at the amount of drugs available, but assumed that Kip had some kind of deal with the local authorities that kept them off his back.

When Ron got ready to leave that night, Kip gave him his card, writing down his cell and home numbers, and told him if he ever needed anything from him to call. Ron called intermittently to keep up to date and cultivate the contact for future assistance, but hadn't talked to him in six or seven months.

As Ron sat in his hotel room, he pulled Kip's card out, hoping that he was still in business, and even more so, still alive. Kip answered on the first ring, "Hello."

"Kip, Ron Sullivan from Seattle. How are you , my friend?"

"Well, well," Kip said. "It's been a while. What are you doing these days?"

"Same old, same old – you know the drill. Listen, I'm in town for a day or so, and was wondering if you could hook me up?"

"Why don't we get together, Ron? I can have a party ready any time"

"I'd love to, but I don't have much time and I'm on a busy schedule. Can you help me out?"

"What are you in the mood for?"

"I was thinking one of your older ones, one you can dress up and who can hold a conversation."

"Sophisticated, huh? You know most of these girls have their issues, but I think I can get what you need."

"How soon? I need someone by tomorrow."

Kip went silent, thinking for a moment. "I've got the perfect girl. I can send Cara whenever you want. Where are you staying?"

"I'm at the Hyatt Regency in Buckhead, room 2018. Have her here at 8:00 p.m."

"How many hours do you want?"

"Let's make it three."

"Normally, she'd run fifteen hundred for three hours, but for a friend, we'll make it an even grand."

"Thank you, my friend." Ron knew there was nothing else he could do until tomorrow, so he ordered room service and watched television for a while. After he finished eating, he was asleep within ten minutes.

* * *

The following day, after eating a small breakfast, he headed downstairs to the Hyatt's exercise room. Following his usual hour and a half routine, he showered and returned to his room.

He waited.

Cara arrived on time and knocked on the door. When Ron opened it he was surprised at what Kip had sent. She was a beautiful woman, dressed in a long black, tight-fitting dress. It certainly didn't suggest her occupation. She was a brunette, in her early forties, but could have passed for thirty-five. Cara had long legs and, from what he could tell, a rather nice breast enhancement. He welcomed her into the room.

"Kip said you were a friend of his?"

"I am."

"I don't mean to be rude, but can we get the details out of the way?"

Ron knew what she was talking about. He pulled the cash out of his pocket and placed it on the table next to her. She didn't bother to count it; this was a friend of Kip's and surely he wouldn't short change her. She sat on the edge of the chair, and started to unzip her dress.

"Hold on," Ron said, trying not to be alarming.

"What's the matter, baby, are you nervous?"

"That's not what I'm interested in, sweetheart."

"Oh, and just what do you want, baby?" Cara assumed that Ron had some type of fetish he wanted indulged.

"I have a business opportunity for you."

Cara zipped up her dress, realizing that apparently Ron really wasn't interested in sex after all. "I'm listening."

Over the course of the next three hours, Ron Sullivan explained to Cara the details of the job he wanted to hire her to perform. He identified the target, explaining that he was a lonely person, likely to be an introverted type when surrounded by people he was unfamiliar with. Cara listened intently to the proposal, nodding her understanding occasionally, but keeping quiet for the most part.

Over the course of the interview, Ron questioned her about her background.

Did she have any children?

Family members in the area?

Did she have a career or other job outside of the business?

Criminal record?

Boyfriend or lover?

He went through a laundry list of potential problems that she might present. Other than periodic drug use, which he expected, and to a degree welcomed, Cara passed with flying colors. By the end of his time with her, he was satisfied that if anyone could get what he wanted, she was his girl. And if she failed, he would prove impossible to track down, an apparition in the mind of a call girl.

When the interview had come to a close, Cara asked what the salary was for her position. "Ten Thousand upon delivery," he said. The look on her face told him that the pay was acceptable.

"We have a deal," Cara said as she walked over to the table and retrieved the fee Ron had surrendered when she arrived. Before she left, Ron obtained all her phone numbers and her address. He told her to keep everything to herself. If she failed to comply with his instructions, there would be no payday. He would call her in two weeks. Cara wasn't provided with a way to reach him.

Ron had achieved all that he could in Atlanta, and he had a day to spare. He stuck to his routine and got some extra sleep before catching the flight back to Dallas.

* * *

Whisenhunt v. Insure Pro was in its infancy, but things were already beginning to heat up. Initial discovery had been sent by both sides, and in usual fashion, both had objected to every request made by their opponent. This was a feeling out period, and neither side was getting much of a feel for the other.

Buck Padgett informed his clients that this was a standard procedure in these cases, and assured them that the action would pick up, eventually. Multiple trips to the courthouse to argue petty motions were the norm. Insure Pro had more than enough cash to fund the litigation, and they were going to put as much pressure on Buck as possible to make him spend equally. Repeated hearings also padded the billings for Gibson Vance.

Taylor Franklin was listed as co-counsel in the Whisenhunt case. Les Vance and Luther Abercrombie were named as counsel of record. Luther had been a partner at Gibson Vance for twenty years, and was a seasoned veteran. Taylor was admitted via Gibson Vance *pro hac vice*, a process that allows lawyers not licensed in the state to participate in a case under the license of the registered attorney. It was a practice that Taylor had engaged in numerous times. Although listed as co-counsel, Taylor would take the lead role when they got further into the proceedings. He didn't bother to travel to the state for routine matters.

By Buck's estimate, the discovery process would last nine to ten months, maybe more. There were experts to locate and hire. They would have to be given ample time to complete their investigation and formulate opinions. Depositions of numerous individuals would be scheduled – the parties, experts and god knew who else. Hell, even the local weatherman could find himself receiving a subpoena in a case like this. They hadn't even gotten their initial responses from the other side yet. Buck had played this game many times and, more often than not, he came out the victor. He was perfectly fine to wait it out.

* * *

105

Cara Patterson felt like two weeks had already gone by, when in reality only four days had passed. She was ready to get paid, but the rules had been explained explicitly. She still didn't know the identity of the man she met at the Ritz, but she had her ideas. The most logical was that he was rich, and his wife was getting the goods on him to use in the soon-to-be-filed divorce proceedings. Any other possibility was too far fetched.

The knowledge that someone was willing to pay her ten grand for her talents only confirmed her belief that the night had gone even better than planned. She reviewed the tape on a daily basis, making sure she'd gotten everything that was asked of her. She was sure she'd hit the jackpot.

Ignoring her instructions, Cara contacted one of her clients, a younger man with a less than appealing appearance whom she had seen for about a year. He owned his own business, was single and had enough money to spend a grand a month for her company. At 5'10" and 330 pounds, he didn't turn many heads. Other than that, she only knew that he was good with computers, because he offered to repair hers when it went down. She'd brought it with her to one of their appointments and watched him work his magic. It was the only magic he could work, but he was a steady customer, and the regular income had been useful.

She asked Tim if he could work on a tape she had made. He didn't like seeing her with another man, but he wasn't ignorant of her job duties either. In addition, he was accustomed to her preferences when it came to her career. Tim didn't want to lose the closest thing to a relationship he'd ever had, so he reluctantly agreed. Tim did as she asked and, for his assistance, she rewarded him with a free session. Cara would usually spend two hours in the shower after an appointment with Tim. That night, since he'd given her a golden ticket, she only spent one.

* * *

Ron Sullivan called Cara just as he said he would, two weeks to the day after their meeting. "Do you have what we discussed?"

"I do."

"I'd like to pick it up tomorrow."

"You just tell me where and when, baby."

"Hyatt Regency again. I'll call you tomorrow afternoon with the room number."

"I assume you'll have something for me?" she asked.

"As soon as I get what I want."

"You will."

Dan left immediately for DFW to get a flight to Atlanta. The first available flight was the next morning. Ron Sullivan was back in Atlanta at noon the next day, headed for the Hyatt. He called Cara as soon as he got to his room, and instructed her to come immediately.

She got herself ready, and an hour later knocked on the door of room 1348.

Ron opened the door, "Come in dear. Do you have it?"

"I thought you'd have something for me, Ron?" Dan wasn't into playing some movie scene out, so he pulled out the cash from his briefcase and laid it on the bed. He kept the knife in his belt behind his back in case she had decided to pull a stupid trick. He would have preferred his weapon of choice, but airline regulations and his short notice trip prevented it.

This time she counted the money. When she was satisfied, she removed the disc from her handbag and handed it to him. She gathered the funds and turned towards the door and Ron stopped her.

"Wait a minute. I need to verify this," he said.

She stopped and sat on the edge of the bed, smiling confidently. "Go right ahead."

Ron placed the disc in his laptop and pulled up the start menu. After directing his computer to open the file, he sat back and waited. Within moments, he found what he was looking for. After a short viewing, he closed the top shut.

"It's been a pleasure doing business with you," he said.

"Anytime. Am I free to go?"

"Have a safe trip home, Cara." She showed herself out.

Ron waited for an hour before checking out and returning to the airport. He had been in Atlanta for less than five hours and was ready to leave. He caught an early flight back to Dallas and was in his bed by ten that night.

He could cross Jackson Garrett off his list. The Chief Justice was sure to be an ally of his employer for years to come.

* * *

The following morning, Dan watched the tape in its entirety. While the Chief Justice had broken no laws as far as he could tell, his conduct was less than appropriate for a man in his position. Under no circumstances would he want such information in the public domain, not because of the behavior per se, but the fact that public perception means everything in judicial races. Dan knew from Taylor that judges in Alabama ran on the family values ticket; they were wholesome, decent people. If the voters suspected otherwise there was no way to win.

Dan had originally planned on taking his newfound material to Taylor first thing, but, after further reflection, he decided he would sit on it for a while. There was no need to use it now anyway, and Taylor had plenty on his plate with the ongoing litigation in Baldwin County. He went to the office and filed the disc away with the dossiers he had created on the other judges.

Dan had managed to dig up materials on seven of the nine sitting Supreme Court justices already. Granted, some of the info was minor – like the dropped domestic abuse charges that were filed against Mac Bridges, stemming from an altercation with his intoxicated mother-in-law – but there was always the possibility that it carried some weight. In fact, most of the information he had obtained had never made it into the public arena. The judges had connections too, and they were protected to the fullest extent possible.

FOURTEEN

Construction in Gulf Shores was way ahead of schedule by March, and Jack thought they might be able to move the completion date up to the end of May. He had laid out the floor plan and was satisfied that he had purchased the perfect furnishings for the new house. Fixtures had also been determined, and he was just waiting on the contractor now. His excitement continued to grow, and he had even decided on a time to implement Walt's suggestion. His life was beginning to take shape again and he began to look forward to each new day with vigor.

* * *

Buck Padgett was in the middle of discovery, and still had not received any real information from Insure Pro. He predicted that it would be early summer before the order to produce documents would cause them to comply.

In the meantime, Buck had begun to assemble his trial team. His structural engineer was out of Jackson, Mississippi, as was the construction expert. Both had already made their initial site visit to the Whisenhunt property and had provided him with their preliminary findings. The initial results were positive. He had delegated some research matters to underlings in the office, and expected more answers in the near future. At the last hearing, the trial court judge had issued a scheduling order, setting forth time frames for the litigation. He hadn't planned on a quick trial in the case anyway, but he wanted to be able to put some pressure on Insure Pro. The scheduling order didn't help him. The parties were given until the end of the year to finalize all discovery matters, including depositions. The trial date was set – February 18, 2007, almost a year away.

* *

The news hit Jack Garrett like a hammer between the eyes. When the first paper printed the story about his tryst in Atlanta, he thought it was some kind of practical joke being played on him by a mischievous friend, except for the fact that it had already made its way onto local news broadcasts. The unnamed source had supposedly provided the video, to whom he didn't know, but someone claimed they had it. Apparently, the actual footage was too graphic to be shown on television, and for that he wasn't sure whether to be thankful or more frightened. Although it was more than three years to the next election, this was sure to be the beginning of the end of his political career.

Reporters called his office and were instructed that the Chief Justice had no comment and that investigation was continuing. He mulled over the thought of a lawsuit against the media outlets reporting the case, but he had not seen what evidence they had to support the story. He had no choice but to find out what they had, but some things had started to become clearer.

* * *

The news hit Taylor Franklin and Dan Spearman equally as hard.

"How in the hell could we not know about this?" Taylor called Dan at home, wondering why they weren't in charge of such information from the outset.

"I have no idea, boss." Though Dan certainly knew more than he was willing to share, he was truthful about how the story had broken without his knowledge. More than that, he was incensed that Cara, presumably, had broken the deal.

"I want you to get to the bottom of this now." Taylor now realized that a huge piece of collateral could have been theirs, and it was out for everyone to use.

"Yes sir."

Dan put the phone down and dug into his files, searching for the contact information for Cara Patterson. She owed him some money now.

* * *

It took Cara little more than two months to blow the salary she had earned from Ron Sullivan. A couple of shopping trips and catching up on her late rent took most of it. Party favors ate up the rest. She had been anticipating Ron's call for days. When the phone rang, she assumed it was him; it was the only number that had ever registered as a block on her caller ID.

"Ron?" she answered.

"Do you realize what you've done?" he replied. There were no 'hello's from either party.

"I realize full well what I've done, but I think you might want to hear what I have to say before you run off at the mouth."

"You don't take a tone with me, miss. You had best come up with some cash; otherwise there had better be a good goddamned explanation."

"I'm not giving you any 'tone' and, if I were you, I'd shut up for a minute and listen."

Ron was audibly pissed, but had no choice but to hear her out for now. "Well, what is it?"

Cara explained the course of events that had led to the publication of the Garrett tapes, and ultimately to Ron's call. She reminded him that he hadn't provided her with any way to get in touch with him after he had left, back in January. She had called directory assistance in Atlanta, but there were no listings for him, and he never bothered to tell her where he lived. She also told him that she had additional information that he might be interested in purchasing from her.

"What have you got?" he interrupted.

"More footage," she said.

"Of what?"

"I'll get to that." She proceeded with her story – Ron also hadn't told her anything about the man she was to meet that night. He provided a photo, and some background information about personality, but that was it. The photo was the only thing that helped her identify the man. Her job had been carried out as instructed until they got to the room. That's when things strayed. He was completely shit-faced, and Cara finally asked him what he did for a living – out of curiosity. All he managed to tell her was that he was a judge, what kind she didn't know and didn't care. They partied hard for a couple of hours, and she did what she was asked to do. When he passed out, she checked his wallet and got his name from his Alabama license.

Cara managed to arouse him enough to help him get to his room. Then she left, mission accomplished. When she reviewed the video that had been acquired, she realized that more than just the sex had been recorded.

"What else do you have?" Ron asked.

Cara told Dan about the additional activities that she said had taken place that evening. "I didn't think the camera was on, but apparently they were recorded as well.

It took a minute for what she'd said to settle in with Dan. *There's no way in hell she's got that on tape.* "You didn't show me anything about that when I picked up the tape," he finally said.

Cara could tell from the change in his tone that he was interested now. "You hired me to try and get him on tape having sex," she replied. "That's what you paid me for, and that's what I delivered. You got exactly what you wanted, and I held up to my end of the deal, just as you did."

"What did you do with the other part of the video?"

"I edited it and gave you what you asked for."

"You did?" He questioned her ability to perform such a task.

"I realize that you have some kind of stereotype about women in my business, but I assure you I have more talents than just that." She was lying, but Ron would never know she had been incapable of the edit. After Ron had left, she began researching the name that was in the wallet and discovered that he was a Supreme Court judge.

Still of the opinion that this matter revolved around a divorce proceeding, Cara figured the additional footage was certainly worth more to Ron than what she had previously received. "I assumed you'd be interested in acquiring the other footage, but had no way to get in touch with you. So I farmed it out to the media over in Alabama."

"And you got paid again?"

"Why not, I have bills to pay too you know. Besides, if you're not interested in the other footage, I'm sure someone would be. And if you want your money back, just tell me when and where." She was bluffing but, if push came to shove, maybe Kip could help her out. "I assumed, and correctly so, that once it came out on the news, you'd get the word and call me."

"What are you asking for?"

"Fifty."

"Fifty grand?" There was a hint of surprise in his voice now.

"I'm a business person too, you know."

"Give me two hours, and I'll call you back."

"Fair enough."

As soon as the call ended, Dan picked up the phone and called Taylor. Dan had a contact in Atlanta who had inside information on the Garrett tapes. According to Dan, the owner of the tapes had leaked a segment to the media in Alabama, essentially seeking to test the waters on the value. The owner was interested in a private party transaction, but was considering taking it to the national media – CNN, NBC, ABC, CBS, FOX – whoever the highest bidder happened to be. According to his source, fifty grand would buy the video from the owner, but they needed an answer soon.

Dan knew that if Taylor had been aware of his involvement from the beginning, his job was most likely over. Though he trusted Dan, carelessness like this couldn't be tolerated. Dan's hole was getting deeper by the moment, and Taylor could bail him out with an agreement to purchase the video. Dan had paid Cara out of his own pocket, knowing that when the original video would be used, his boss would reimburse him for his efforts. Now it was getting out of control, and Dan didn't have that kind of extra cash; otherwise, he would have gone to Atlanta and cleaned the matter up.

Taylor evaluated the decision in his head. If the national media or even regional media picked the story up, Garrett was done. He would be out of office immediately, probably resigning on his own. Governor Mike Holliday would then appoint a new chief justice to serve out Garrett's term. Though Holliday was a conservative governor, there were certainly no guarantees that the new appointee would be solidly on their side, especially in light of the gains made by the Democrats in the last election. A moderate appointee on behalf of the governor was more likely to appease the voters . After running through the possibilities,

Taylor came to the conclusion that Garrett would be a better asset on the Court than an unknown appointee, and a shoo-in for their cause with the damning evidence they would hold.

"Go ahead and get it," Taylor informed him. "It'll take a couple of days to get the money."

"Yes sir." Dan felt the burden lifting off his shoulders as Taylor approved the transaction.

Ron immediately called Cara back and informed her that he would be in Atlanta three days later to complete the deal. He also issued her a stern warning that if she were holding anything else back on him, there would be dire consequences. She assured him that she was not.

Three days later Dan was back in Dallas. He destroyed the disc that had cost him ten thousand dollars and replaced it with the only copy of the video portraying Chief Justice Jack Garrett in an Atlanta hotel room, engaging in conduct that would cost him his job if it ever surfaced.

* * *

As quickly as Jack's life had begun to thrive, the tides turned in the other direction. The sex tapes were taking their toll on him. His colleagues tried to encourage him at work, while secretly condemning him behind closed doors. More than once, he had almost convinced himself that a resignation would be best. Had it not been for Walt, he would have been off the Court weeks ago.

When the story broke, Jack called his friend to fill him in on what had happened. When Walt heard Jack's version, the only one he needed to hear, he urged him to stay strong, and persevere. It was a difficult effort, and was getting harder by the day. The news stories faded quickly, as they always do, but the JIC had been apprised of a complaint. Jack was never told who had filed it – those issues were kept confidential – and it didn't matter to him anyway; the damage was already done. His initial reaction to file suit was discarded when his personal attorney was shown a copy of the video. Jack didn't want to see it, and accepted his lawyer's advice to let the matter go.

When the JIC sent their formal letter notifying him of the complaint, and asking for his explanation, all he could do was reiterate that he had no recollection of the events of that evening. They would do as they wished with him, and he had resigned himself to whatever fate they imposed.

The worst part of the whole ordeal was telling Sharon. She, like the rest of them, had read the papers and seen the story when it ran. Within days of it breaking, Jack called her into his office. "I know you're aware of the reports."

"I am, Your Honor."

"Sharon, right now I don't know what to do. I want you to know that what they are reporting, that's not me. I'm not saying the reports are untrue, I'm just saying that that's not me." He told her about his lack of memory and his embarrassment at the situation. She listened to him intently, showing concern. But he couldn't tell whether she was genuine or not. His blinders were still on. "I need very much for someone to believe in me now, and I don't know if you can or not," he said, staring at the floor of his office.

"Jack, I know that's not who you are, and, whether you want to believe me or not, I do believe you. This Court needs you," she replied.

He wanted desperately to hear her say that she needed him, not the Court. Nevertheless, she had managed to lift his spirits to some degree, and he came to the conclusion that he would press on for now.

As the weeks passed, the story of Jack's Atlanta escapades faded into a memory for everyone but him, and his boring life resumed itself.

* * *

By the end of May, Buck Padgett was required by the Court's order to provide Insure Pro with the names of the experts he intended to use in the Whisenhunt case. In addition to their names, he had to set forth the opinions they had on the cause of the damage to the property, and the basis for those opinions. He was spending money hand over fist now. The experts charged by the hour, and his engineer alone was racking up one hundred fifty per. Unlike Buck, they didn't get paid only if they won, and he had already sent over ten grand to the guy. Buck had grown increasingly fond of the Whisenhunt case as discovery progressed. Their vacation home had washed away like many of the others but, according to the experts, it wasn't because of flood or design problems. Buck had been apprised that, as a matter of fact, the Whisenhunts' house had been not only up to code, but built too strong. It was the first time in his career that he had even heard of such a theory.

Armed with his experts' opinions, Buck sent Les Vance and Taylor Franklin a summary of their expected testimony. The defendants had thirty days to provide their expert information to Buck. From then on, they'd get into the meat of the case.

* * *

Billy Grantham at Grantham Construction called Jack on June 1st to inform him that they had completed the job. Although Jack had stayed in periodic contact, he hadn't talked to him in a month. Billy told him that the landscaping contractor would be on site for a week or so, but he was welcome to start moving in the furniture and anything else he wanted.

The news brought Jack's mood around again. He went to the coast the following weekend with a rented truck full of furnishings. When he arrived, the house was just as he expected with the exception of some minor changes in color, mainly slightly darker shades of paint. It was his dream home again. He hired some local day laborers to help move the furniture and, within a day, the house was filled. He had pre-arranged for the local Lowes to deliver the appliances, and they had arrived the following morning. There were still small items in Montgomery, mainly towels, linens and a few pieces of artwork, to bring down. But overall, it was ready to inhabit again. A trip to the grocery store was in order, but he had brought enough with him to get him through a day, and it could wait.

He returned to the capital for the following week and called Walt to tell him the good news. Walt was excited for him and, as usual, pressed him on the situation with Sharon.

"Have you said anything yet?"

"Give it a rest, will you," Jack replied.

"You know as well as I do that every house could use a woman's touch, Jack. The way I see it, this is as good a time as any. With God as my witness, this is the last time I'll mention it, but for Christ's sake, have some balls and ask her out."

"I'm holding you to that," Jack said, knowing that Walt wouldn't let it go until he did act.

The conversation with Walt stuck with him, again. Jack analyzed it over and over before coming to the conclusion that his friend was right. If ever there had been a time for him to act, this was it.

He called Sharon into his office the next Thursday afternoon.

"Can I ask you a question?"

"Of course."

"I got a call from the contractor at the beach last week. They completed the rebuild and I went down last weekend to move everything in."

"That's wonderful," she said.

"The thing is, I'm not the best at the decorating and placement of furniture, what do they call it, Feng Shui?"

"What are you getting at?"

"Every home needs a lady's touch to some degree." He thought he might as well have called Walt and put him on speakerphone to handle the request for him. "And, I was wondering if you didn't have anything going on this weekend, if you might be willing to give me a hand."

That wasn't that hard now was it, you dumb ass.

Just as he said it, the fear set in.

Oh shit, what are you doing?

Here it comes.

"Sure, I'd be happy to help." Sharon wondered if he would open up again, and found herself bordering on excitement.

You've got to be kidding me.

Walt, you fucking bastard. Right again.

Trying his best to appear poised and confident all along, yet failing miserably, Jack stammered, "Excellent. I plan on heading out around four if that's okay with you."

"Thank you for the invitation.. I'm looking forward to it."

As she left his office, shutting the door behind her, Jack felt a sense of pride he hadn't felt since the first time he gathered the strength to ask Stephanie out. He had to make one call before he headed home to pack and plan.

"You can lay off now, it's done." He fought to keep the smile from spreading across his face.

"Congratulations, Jack. Keep it up. Actions breed results." Walt was happy for him; he deserved I

* * *

When Taylor reviewed the disc that Dan brought back from Atlanta, he couldn't believe it was real. How someone had been able to get such a gem was beyond him, but he had it now and that was all that mattered. In his heart, he was hopeful that using it would never be an issue that would present itself. It was time to do some prep work.

Bob Powell was at home in Birmingham reviewing opinions from his territory when the phone rang.

"I think it's time for an update, Bob. If you can get ready, I'll have the plane pick you up next Monday." Taylor got straight to the point.

"Not a problem. When do you need me at the airport?"

"Rick should be there by noon," Taylor replied.

Bob arrived in Dallas and was taken to the Plaza by Rick Garner, the same man who had flown him in from Birmingham. Rick had to fly him back later that day, so it wasn't necessary for him to rent a car this time. Rick pulled his company car to the front of the Plaza, letting Bob out before leaving for a couple of errands before the return trip scheduled for that night.

Taylor had no intention of disclosing his recent acquisition to Bob, but he knew that ultimately Bob would likely be the messenger if its use were to be required. It had been a while since Bob had been called upon by his employer to utilize his skills, and Taylor wanted to ensure he was keeping track with the company's business. Bob entered his office assuming a new problem had arisen.

"Have you been following the situations in Ohio and Illinois?" Taylor asked.

"I've got my finger on the pulse, as always."

"It might be time to pay a visit to Faulk. You know, he's been swaying recently." Taylor was referring to Howard Faulk, a Republican on the Illinois Supreme Court, who had been the swing vote for the last year for the GOP. Faulk had crossed over on several civil cases that didn't involve Insure Pro, but were close enough to give reason for concern. Illinois had followed the Alabama model in '98, with the GOP taking a majority, though not as strong as its southern sister. Likewise, in '04 the Democrats made gains, closing the gap to a four-to-five minority. While all the GOP judges had been consistent in their rulings, Faulk was a renegade, and his backers were getting weary that he had intentions of switching parties in the next election.

"I talked with Howard a week ago as a matter of fact, and he reminded me that he has not ruled against us since he took his seat. He's a good judge, Taylor, and a better politician. From what I can tell, he's taking a page out of Garrett's book, protecting his moderate base for the next cycle." Bob hoped that he had assuaged Taylor's doubts.

"Speaking of Garrett, when was the last time you talked to Jack?"

"It's been a while. This Atlanta thing has been taking a toll on him from what I've been advised. The JIC has started their investigation and it will be some time before they issue a ruling."

"What do you expect them to do?"

"At a minimum I see a public reprimand, though it's possible it could be worse."

"Is removal an option?"

"It's an option, but highly unlikely."

"Do you have any pull with the JIC?"

"I'm close to all the judicial members, but don't know the first thing about the laymen. Why do you ask?"

"Pull some strings when the time comes; we don't need Garrett taking any more shit than he already has from this thing."

"No problem. Just let me know when, and I'll make the call. Ron Thompson is the chairman of the commission – I'll ask him to keep me apprised on the status."

"Keep me informed on it, Bob." Taylor was genuinely interested in the status of the JIC inquiry. He wanted to be sure that no one else had Garrett's attention other than him when it mattered most, and if Bob could pull it off with the JIC, he was all theirs.

Bob Powell knew how to do his job, and he did it very well.

Powell had been elected Chief Justice in 1974, as a Democrat, which was the only way to be elected at the time

Mike Gedgoudas

Within a couple of years he had become maligned with his own party because he viewed himself as a moderate, and moderation was not the rule of the day. His dissenting opinions brought rebuke from his donors, and he quickly fell into line to protect his political career. His writings, though, did not go unnoticed and he was approached by traditionally GOP based groups intent on getting at least some influence on the Court. Bob was determined to change the unilateralism of the Alabama Court, not toward a complete swing to the right, but to middle ground, where be believed the electorate resided. His financial base would have none of it, nor did those who were courting him. He continued exercising judicial restraint in the decisions he reached, both for and against each of the competing factions that were vying for his loyalty.

His middle-of-the-road temperament caught the attention of the National Association of Judges early in his tenure, and three years into his first term he was elected President of the Association. The Association was a non-partisan group formed in the late 60s to promote public confidence and higher ethical standards in the judiciary. Though it initially consisted of only a handful of judges from several states, it had grown to include a membership of more than twenty thousand county, state and federal jurists. Though the position enjoyed no pay, it provided him full access to judges from around the country. His contact list grew exponentially, and Bob used his newfound honor to its full potential. By 1980, he had endorsements from not only his own party, but national interests as well. He even received a reasonably significant sum in contributions from traditionally adverse interests, if for nothing else, to keep some degree of hope alive. The leading campaign contributor from sources other than his usual base happened to be Insure Pro, a growing insurer in the southeast that had already grasped a stronghold in the western part of the country. The executives at Insure Pro viewed their investment much like a futures option in the market. In the event of a shift, they at least had their foot in the door. He won his second term with ease, and continued his moderate approach to judicial decision making.

With his position in the Association, he networked with judges from across the union, discussing recent trends and

120

putting in untold hours campaigning for judicial election reform. The latter of his initiatives would prove to be the nail in his professional coffin. He watched helplessly as his financiers faded away, and he came to realize that he would be without sufficient funds to compete in the 1986 race.

With two years left in his second term, he resigned himself to the conclusion that his judicial career was over. Bob had wanted desperately to re-establish the Court as an independent branch of government, one that was less susceptible to the influence that permeated the executive and legislative arms, but his utopia wasn't shared by a majority of the players. He was battling depression when he received a call from Leo Kirschberg at Insure Pro. Leo had been monitoring Bob's progress on the Court and with the National Association of Judges. It had been Leo's decision to donate to Powell's campaign earlier, and the gesture resulted in a meeting between the two where Leo impressed Bob with his ability to see issues from different perspectives. Bob had previously assumed that corporate execs like Leo were blindly led by the bottom line, no matter what misfortune fell upon the everyday citizen. He concluded that he had been wrong about Leo. The CEO understood that corporate greed did exist and that sometimes the establishment needed to be reminded of its duties to those it served.

When rumors circulated that a third term was unlikely, Leo contacted Bob about the possibility of life after the Court. Leo knew Bob's reputation from his Association involvement was that of a moderator among the judges and their respective power bases. He had become somewhat of a mediator for the judges and their constituencies across the nation, often times persuading one or the other to let a matter go when it was clear that the issue was irrelevant. Leo had suggested that Bob could have a lucrative career on the lobbying side, not as the wining and dining boys did, essentially bribing their way into greener pastures, but as a liaison between industry and the judiciary.

Bob had become disillusioned with the lack of harmony on the higher courts. A change of pace was appealing. He had seen insurers and corporate defendants getting the shaft in petty matters for so long that some time out of the spotlight wouldn't be a bad idea. He announced his departure a year before the primary to allow candidates an opportunity to pursue their goals. His stated reason for leaving the Court was to spend more time with his family and pursue other interests. according to the press release to the media. Within a month, he became an employee, of Insure Pro, although classified as an independent contractor.

He was placed under the general counsel's direction, and was charged with maintaining public relations with judicial and legislative bodies throughout the states. In reality, his job was to follow decisions in the states with elected judgeships and lobby those men and women on behalf of the company. With his bipartisan background, he was welcomed across the board, and he performed well. His friendships with Democrats and Republicans alike, combined with a rational approach to politics, led to Insure Pro's gaining ground in many states where they had previously been ignored.

He had never been terribly fond of Taylor Franklin. Taylor joined Insure Pro only months after Leo had hired Bob, and from the minute he first met him, he took him for an arrogant, over-the-top kind of guy. Taylor hated the opposition, whereas Bob saw them as an opportunity for compromise. He had no choice about whom he reported to though, and the fact that he retained his Alabama residence limited the amount of time he was required to spend with him. Bob also knew that Taylor was very much aware of his ties with Court members in Alabama, a place where the company had taken many a beating, which resulted in Bob's being given wide latitude in dealing with matters arising out of his home state.

The Garrett situation had troubled Bob immensely. He had known Jack Garrett for a long time, and he knew that Jack was a decent man. Why this video had hit the airwaves was beyond him, but he was sure that Jack Garrett would be able to make it through, especially if he intervened.

FIFTEEN

Jack and Sharon arrived in Orange Beach just as the sun was beginning to set over the gulf. When they entered the driveway at his house, Sharon gasped, speechless. She had imagined it much smaller, similar to the vacation homes that were rented to weekend visitors. After visiting his smaller home in the capital, she expected the beach house to be comparable to it.

"Wow, this is beautiful, Jack!" she said as they entered the circular drive then veered toward the garage on the side.

"Thank you. This is my dream home, and I'm thankful every day that I'm fortunate enough to enjoy it – again."

Sharon could not comprehend how much homes like Jack's cost in Montgomery. But, at the beach! She knew this was not a cheap purchase. Jack hadn't told her much about his career before the bench, so she had no idea about his financial status. Not that it mattered to her, but anyone arriving here must have let some of those thoughts creep in.

"Please forgive the mess," Jack said, as he parked his Chevy Tahoe in the garage and showed her inside.

The interior was as exquisite as the outside of the house, except for the furniture, which was sitting in the middle of the living room, waiting for someone to organize it.

"I told you I needed a woman's touch," Jack said, as they walked in.

Sharon, assuming that he needed help hanging pictures in the right places, organizing linens and the like, hadn't expected that he needed help with everything. As he brought their luggage into the house, she walked around, giving herself a tour. It was the kind of place that she dreamed of living in as a young girl – with high ceilings, lots of windows, a large deck overlooking a spacious yard and the second floor balcony with a great view of the water.

"Well. I'd say we've got quite a lot of work to do," she said, still admiring the home.

"We'll have plenty of time to get this place straightened out," Jack replied. "How about you make yourself at home and relax for a while. I need to run to the grocery store and pick up some things."

"I'd be happy to go with you."

"You take it easy, you're my guest. I'll be back in thirty minutes."

"All right then, do you mind if I look around?"

"By all means. I'd love to hear any ideas you have." As soon as Jack left to get provisions, Sharon began walking through the house, making mental notes.

After he returned and stored the staples, he started dinner, no special affair tonight, just frozen pizza. They had decided on the drive down, that pizza would be quick and easy. After dinner they retired to the upstairs balcony with a bottle of cabernet, listening to the waves, and resumed where they had left off at his house before the storm.

Jack asked if there was anything she wanted to know about him, trying to invite her into his life a little more.

"Anything?" she asked.

"Consider me an open book."

She immediately hit on the only two topics he had hoped to avoid, Stephanie and the Atlanta problem. Knowing that the only way to get her more receptive to him was to truly open up, he told her first about his failed marriage. He had loved Stephanie deeply. Everything he had accomplished in his early career, he had done so that she could live a comfortable life. When she left, it came as a complete surprise to him, and though he had gotten over her long ago, he still struggled with the humiliation of having been left alone. He had not dated since her departure, and when Sharon had come to his place during the storm, he informed her, it was the closest thing to companionship he had experienced since Stephanie had been there.

"Does that make you feel like you couldn't do it again?" she asked, wondering if the wounds were so deep that he wouldn't put himself on the line again, out of self-preservation to avoid another heartbreak.

"For a long time, I had resigned myself to being alone," he said, "I just assumed that that was what God had in store for me. But I came to realize that maybe God doesn't decide whether you should or shouldn't have someone in your life. He puts people out there, and you have to make a decision as to whether you want to take that chance or not."

Sharon's divorce had been amicable; still she agreed with Jack's attitude on the subject. But divorce had left her with feelings of inadequacy. She figured that if she couldn't make it work before, why would a second effort be any different? Maybe there had been something wrong with her that had made her husband decide to leave, even though he had assured her the problem was with him.

Jack felt the burden lifting off his mind as they continued the conversation. Other than Walt, he had not talked to anyone about Stephanie since she left. The female perspective of the therapy Sharon was unknowingly providing was what he had needed for a long time. Sharon, too, was getting some therapy of her own, as she discussed her life story with him. They were learning more about each other than either had ever imagined, and were finally beginning to see the real inner person. Each of them was equally interested and impressed with the other's history.

When it came to the night in Atlanta, Sharon sensed Jack's retreat. It took some time to assure him that she was on his side.

"Have you seen it?" she asked, referring to the video.

"I didn't see any need to. I was told that it did exist, and that was all I needed to hear."

"What happened?"

"If I knew the answer to that, I assure you I'd tell you. The whole thing is strange, Sharon. I don't have the first memory of anything that happened that night, other than sitting in the lounge talking with a woman who had introduced herself and seemed nice enough."

"Would you know her if you saw her?"

"Not at all. It's a fog to me. It reminded me of the feeling you have after waking from anesthesia for surgery, when there is just nothing, no sense of time having elapsed, no memory of the procedure. It's just strange."

"Why do you think it came out in the media?"

"Whoever did it must have been paid. How much, I don't know, by whom I don't know, for what reason, I don't know. It seems that 'I don't know' is the answer to every question that's presented. But if I ever do find out..." He paused. It was clear that even the thought about it made him even angrier.

"If?"

"I'm as far from violent as they come, but I have imagined the possibility of confronting whoever did this and knocking his teeth out."

Sharon laughed, "Yeah, I can see you doing that."

She managed to pull a smile from him as well. "More of a fantasy, I suppose, but you know what I mean."

"You tell me if you find out, and I'll punch him for you. It's not becoming of a chief justice to engage in a brawl."

"But it is for a staff attorney?"

After more laughter, they both realized that they had transformed a conversation about the dreaded subject into a lighthearted, funny dialogue. They left the heavy topics, moving on to various other subjects and enjoyed each other's company for several hours before bedtime.

Over the weekend, Sharon helped him arrange the house into a warm, comfortable atmosphere. They enjoyed togetherness, and talked, and ate and listened.

When they returned home, Jack helped bring her bags to the door, and thanked her for coming with him, for helping with the house and for the talks. Sharon leaned in. Jack was as nervous as ever, wondering if she was making a move, or if he needed to. She put her arms around his waist, turning her head away from him, and hugged. "Thank you for inviting me. I had a great time."

It was less than romantic, but it was kind and warm, and he appreciated it nonetheless. From that point, things would begin to be different between them. Layers of insulation had begun to melt away and a true friendship was forming.

* * *

Buck Padgett finally received what he had been waiting for. The defendant, in accordance with the Court's scheduling order, provided Buck with their expert information. He had never heard of Forensic Engineering before, but that was no surprise as there were thousands of engineering firms in the country, some of which provided expert testimony in civil lawsuits, most of which did not. The opinions held by Forensic Engineering on behalf of Insure Pro, as set forth in their submission, were brief and didn't provide anything more than what was required under the rules of civil procedure, standard protocol for these cases. Expounding on them was a matter that would be explored when depositions were taken. Roger Stoltz was listed as the individual who would be testifying on behalf of the defendant. He would opine that the damage sustained at the Whisenhunt beach home was caused either by flooding, from Peter's surge, as supported by information garnered from the National Weather Center and readings obtained locally through several sources, and/or as a result of flaws in the design, engineering and/or construction of the house itself – either of which were valid reasons for precluding coverage under the policy that the family had purchased.

Buck expected the opinions would be so, as they were already set forth in the denial letter his client received from the company months after the storm had passed. What he was waiting on was an identification of the group that they would use to argue those reasons.

His experts had already formulated their opinions, conducted the site inspection and completed the necessary research that they would rely upon. There was nothing they would say regarding the opposition's testimony; that would be a matter left for Buck to handle through cross examination. What he needed now was to find out who Roger Stoltz and Forensic Engineering were, and why they had been chosen by Insure Pro.

Discovering the true identity of the adversary was not a novel idea; it was routinely used in these cases. Typically, the opposing party would seek to obtain copies of depositions previously given by the expert to try and determine a pattern of testimony, as well as to portray them as being biased or one-sided. Such was the case usually, as most experts who testified for plaintiffs had done so significantly more often, if not exclusively so, than for defendants. The converse was also true.

Buck flipped through the defense's report, skimming through the details, then picked up the phone and called Herman. It was time to get to know Roger Stoltz and his company.

"Chief, can you come up for a sec?" Buck said when Herman answered.

"Be right there," he replied.

When he arrived in Buck's office, he glanced at the open folder on Buck's desk. "News from Insure Pro?" he asked. "Been waitin' on that."

"Insure Pro is using a group out of Irving called Forensic Engineering, headed up by a Roger Stoltz" Buck said handing him a paper from the folder. See what you can dig up on them."

"I'll get on it," was all Herman said, as he took a copy of the paperwork from Buck and left.

Herman Cunningham had been working for Buck Padgett for ten years as his lead investigator. He retired as Chief of Police from the Mobile Police Department before coming to work for Buck. Herman had become the youngest and only African American Chief of Police in the department's history. He made his way through the ranks, working four years as a patrol officer, then two in homicide before being appointed as Chief. He'd amassed many contacts during his tenure that ultimately proved beneficial to his subsequent career. The truth was that most investigators in law firms were former cops, thanks in large part to their contacts in the field.

Like many officers, Herman had moonlighted for attorneys during his time on the force, all of it for Buck Padgett. The department's policy didn't expressly forbid such a situation, but it certainly didn't condone it either. Fact was that officer's pay was not commensurate with the requirements of the job, and most needed to supplement their salary just to make ends meet. Herman initially worked recruiting cases for Padgett, which he still did, but after retiring from the department, he was utilized as a true investigator, obtaining information that most people could not. Many former cops still had access to the NCIC, the National Criminal Index Computer, which could provide valuable personal information as well as background data and histories of anyone. Good investigators found a way to obtain information that no mere mortal could have imagined, the reasons for which remained their secret.

The Chief wasn't a good investigator...he was a great one.

As soon as he got back to his office, Chief was on the phone, working his magic.

* * *

The litigation committee at Insure Pro was scheduled to have its first assembly to discuss the Hurricane Peter litigation. By the end of the summer, a total of only twenty lawsuits had been filed. Of those, eighty percent had been filed by small town lawyers who presented no appreciable threat to the company. More would surely come, but the initial numbers had been promising.

The committee consisted of Taylor, Hugh Capelli, two of Hugh's divisional managers, and Leo Kirschberg, who would sit in for a while to get a feel for the situation. Les Vance and Luther Abercrombie would come in from Birmingham, bringing two of their associates who would perform much of the grunt work on the cases. For the associates, it was a treat to be invited; their superiors paid their way, treating them to dinners at the best restaurants in Dallas. It was a small group and Taylor intended that it remain that way throughout the litigation. Too many people not only extended the meetings for far too long, but also opened unnecessary opportunities for leaks of privileged information, a risk that was never worth taking.

The meeting was held at the Plaza in the first floor main conference room. The Colvin Room, named after Leo's predecessor, Bernard Colvin, was less opulent than the other offices that inhabited the Plaza. Few meetings were held there, except for the periodic litigation updates, and since there was no need to use the space to impress anyone, it was designed for utility. A large oval-shaped conference table with a black marble top was centered in the middle of the room, surrounded by twenty pivoting leather-clad chairs, none of which emitted luxury. The floor-to-ceiling windows lining the rear wall peered out to the wooded perimeter of the compound. No artwork lined the walls. This was a place for business, nothing else.

Taylor began the meeting with a request to Les to update the group on the status of the Whisenhunt case, as well as a brief recitation of the status of the other cases that were pending.

"We've obtained the expert information from the plaintiffs, and have provided ours to them," he said. "Discovery is ongoing, but we expect to begin expert depositions within the next month or so. Other than that, the process is working its way through."

"Tell me the projected numbers on a negative result," Leo chimed in, directing his query to Les Vance.

"With the engineer's testimony, worst case scenario would be payment of the policy limits for the structure and the personal property."

"You don't see an opening for other damages?" Leo continued, fully aware of the fact that Buck Padgett had alleged the company was guilty of bad faith in their dealings with the Whisenhunts.

"I don't see how they could get there with what we have, sir."

Taylor sat back and enjoyed the dialogue. It was his plan that had been put into action, and the trial team was proving to Leo that his genius was going to pay off for the company. Even though Leo had not been apprised of Taylor's plan, as litigation strategy had been left to the general counsel's discretion anyway, Taylor's confidence grew as the discussion continued.

"If that's all we are looking at, then are there any further issues I need to be aware of?" Leo asked.

"No sir," Taylor responded.

Leo Kirschberg's role at Insure Pro had become largely that of a figurehead. He had been suffering from early stages of Parkinson's disease for several years, and his time at the office had been significantly curtailed. Though many companies would have named a successor at this point, Insure Pro's market share had continued to grow under this reign, and their stock value was higher than ever. While the Board of Governors was aware of his health situation, nothing indicated that a change was in order at this point.

"Thank you, gentlemen," Leo said, as he rose from his seat at the head of the table and left the room.

"Mr. Franklin, do we have any other experts we intend to list for trial purposes?" Les asked, after Leo had left the room.

"No need, Les. Roger has it covered." Taylor showed his displeasure that Les would second-guess him.

"With all due respect, wouldn't it be wise to have a secondary firm on hand, just to corroborate Roger's position?"

"Why insinuate that we aren't confident with our retained experts, Les? Putting another one in the mix only opens the door to conflicting testimony." Taylor was perturbed that Les would be so bold in front of his staff.

Les had never used Roger Stoltz on behalf of this client before, and was simply doing his job in asking the reasonable question he had. He was, after all, lead counsel in the case. Taylor put an end to the discussion quickly. "Les, if you want another engineer to testify, so be it, but hire him yourself. We're not paying for it because it's unnecessary."

There was no rebuttal. Insure Pro was their client and, if they chose not to follow the advice of their counsel, that was their decision. Gibson Vance was certainly not going to foot the bill for an expert that the client expressly indicated was unwanted.

After a brief discussion of the other pending cases and their status, the meeting was adjourned. Les, Luther, and the crew from Alabama left the Plaza to return to their hotel near the airport, and Taylor dismissed the others, returning to his office.

Taylor knew that Insure Pro was in the driver's seat with the Whisenhunt case. If things worked out as they should, he would be next in line for Leo's job.

* * *

Jack Garrett had never been happier, at least not since the days with Stephanie. After returning from the beach with Sharon, work had become fun again. He and Sharon had eaten dinner together on several occasions, discussing recent appeals, Jack's standard rationale to gain her company, but invariably they would return to discussing their personal interests and lives. Sharon welcomed the invitations, but wondered if Jack was simply trying to be friendly, or if there would be more to it. The thought of a relationship with an employee had initially troubled Jack, but after further reflection, it was apparent that Sharon was not a traditional employee. Staff attorneys had the right and ability to work for whomever they wished, and many, especially Sharon, were coveted by each justice on the Court.

Furthermore, Jack had not harassed her in any way. The problem, as Jack saw it, was that he couldn't make his desires known, for fear of crossing the line. Sharon would have to be the instigator, and he questioned whether that would ever happen.

Although he badly wanted to express his true intentions, he had resigned himself to wait it out, for now.

* * *

After Chief had left Buck's office to begin the investigation of Forensic Engineering, Buck called his associate in for a brief meeting. Additional questions would need to be directed to the defendant in the Whisenhunt case, all pertaining to their expert, but he would wait on the initial report from Chief before they began. It would be a short wait.

Herman called Buck the next morning from his home office, where most of his work was performed.

"From the looks of it, these guys are career experts, sir," he reported. "They've been involved in more than two hundred cases, mostly in Texas, over the last two years – likely more elsewhere."

"On whose behalf?" Buck asked.

"Still working on that, although I can only suppose it's largely defense."

"Keep working on it and give me updates with any additional information you get your hands on."

Buck notified his associate of exactly what he wanted from Insure Pro and Forensic Engineering, as he sat silently taking notes. By the next day, copies were in the mail to Les Vance and Roger Stoltz.

* * *

Taylor received a copy of the plaintiff's additional discovery requests by way of his fax machine, from Les. The questions were typically asked during deposition, but arguing such matter in Court would prove worthless.

Buck had requested that Insure Pro provide a list of all cases in which Roger's company had testified for them as a defendant. The request was accompanied by subpoenas to Forensic Engineering for copies of their bank statements, articles of incorporation, list of officers and directors, and a breakdown of the fees, which the company had received over the past five years, including a list of the sources of those fees.

Taylor called Les immediately. "What the fuck is this?"

"Padgett knows what he's doing," Les said.

"File an objection. He's not entitled to any of this."

"If you want me to file an objection, I will, but Willingham is going to let them have it."

"Did I stutter?" Taylor squawked back.

"We'll file it tomorrow," Les said, not appreciating Taylor's demeaning attitude. If he wanted an objection filed, Les was more than happy to placate him. After all, it simply meant more time billed to the client. But Les knew better than to request to have oral argument before the Court on such an issue. It would only serve to piss off the judge who would ultimately hear the case.

Gibson Vance filed Taylor's objection to the requested information, without the usual request for oral argument. Judge Hardeman overruled it immediately.

Les took a degree of satisfaction in relaying the message of the judge's decision to Taylor, hoping that perhaps now he would listen to the advice of his appointed counsel.

"Appeal it," was Taylor's first response when Les called with the news.

"If you want me to appeal it, fine. It'll prolong the trial for another two or three months, and by the time the case gets to the Supremes, they will be so thoroughly disgusted with us that they won't even bother to listen to our valid arguments." Les knew he had the upper hand now, and he was sick and tired of Taylor spouting off at the mouth just because he was the client and had a law degree. Franklin knew nothing of how the system worked in Alabama, and he had better quit letting his temper control the defense's game plan.

"How long do we have to respond?" Taylor finally asked, still steaming at Buck Padgett and Les Vance.

"Thirty days." *The arrogant bastard doesn't even know the rules of procedure in Alabama.*

"I'll get you the response, but send it to him in forty days."

"Whatever you say." Les knew the extra ten days meant nothing other than a meaningless victory for Taylor in the argument they had just finished.

* * *

Roger called Taylor as soon as the subpoenas arrived at his office, courtesy of the local sheriff's department. "What the hell am I supposed to do with these?" he asked.

"Get the goddamned information together," Taylor yelled.

"But the bank statements, for Christ's sake?"

"Just get it, and don't worry about it. Everything will be fine."

"Taylor, I don't like the smell of this at all." Roger's tone reflected his nervousness.

"I said, just get it together. Call me when you have it and I'll come over and make sure we send what we need to. Understood?"

"Yes sir."

Roger called Taylor two days later, informing him that he had accumulated the documents required by the subpoena. Roger hadn't been this stressed about anything since the Houston case that led to his dismissal from Allied Engineering.

Taylor Franklin made the trip to Irving to review the submissions. He didn't know what Buck had up his sleeve, but there was no question that he was a thorough lawyer, unlike the other punks who had jumped on the Hurricane Peter bandwagon.

SIXTEEN

By early September, Buck received the responses to the subpoenas and additional discovery to Insure Pro. The insurer's responses were vague, as expected, but that was what he had Chief for. Roger had given him more than he thought he'd receive.

According to Insure Pro, Forensic Engineering had testified, or been listed as an expert for them, in a total of one hundred seventy-five cases over the last three years. No list of actual case names was provided, as they asserted that it would be overly time-consuming and burdensome on the company to search their records for such information, and there was no database containing the requested lists. They did, however, inform Buck of the counties in Texas where the majority of the cases had been filed. Likewise, there had been no accounting of the amount of monies paid to Roger's company over the past five years, although Insure Pro did state that they paid hourly rates, which were consistent with other professionals in the country – approximately one hundred dollars per hour for research and investigation, and two hundred per hour for testimony.

Roger sent the corporate records as filed in the Texas Secretary of State's Office, along with the articles of incorporation. Bank statements for the past several years, all from First Federal Bank & Trust, were also sent. Buck had what he needed to get Herman started on his final push to discover more about Roger Stoltz and company.

He got Chief on the phone. "Do you have any contacts with any banks in Texas?"

"A few. What do you need?"

"Make some calls and see what you can dig up on Roger Stoltz, Taylor Franklin and Jerry Shanks. Then get me a list of all corporations or other business entities out of Texas with any of their names listed as officers or directors, and cross reference any addresses as well\. There could be other names used with the same addresses."

"I'll get on it, but who the hell is Jerry Shanks? I haven't heard the name before."

"Me neither, but he was listed on the articles of incorporation of Forensic Engineering."

As soon as the conversation was over, Chief got to work on the Whisenhunt expert file. Buck was going to get answers sooner than he thought – and with them, many more questions.

* * *

Jack received the call at midnight. At first he thought it was a prank call; there was nothing but uncontrollable sobbing, with an occasional coherent word thrown in. "My mom, Jack, my mom," he finally heard. "She's gone. What am I going to do?" Sharon's voice was strained and she was obviously in shock.

"Gone, what do you mean, gone?" was all he could think to say.

"She's dead," Sharon finally said. "The nursing home just called. They said mom passed away this morning."

Jack was speechless. The woman he wanted so badly had just received the worst news most children can hear during their lives, and he had no clue what to say. He was racking his brain, knowing full well the magnitude of what had happened to her. He finally mustered, "I'm so sorry. What can I do?"

"I don't know, Jack, I don't know what to do."

"I'll be there in twenty minutes," he said.

Jack changed into some decent clothes and headed for Sharon's house, still trying to think of what to say to her when he arrived. As she opened the door, still sobbing, he opened his arms, inviting an embrace. "I'm so sorry," he said, as she fell into him.

Sharon cried in Jack's arms for what seemed like an hour to him. When she was able to compose herself, he moved her to the sofa, holding both of her hands in his.

"You tell me what you need. Anything at all, just tell me." He felt her pain, and wanted desperately to help.

"I don't know," she repeated over and over.

During the next hour, Sharon began to regain her composure, and she told Jack about her mother. She had been in a nursing home for two years, yet Sharon had failed to mention anything about her in their previous conversations. Her mom had been diagnosed with COPD, chronic obstructive pulmonary disease, fifteen years earlier. A chronic smoker for fifty years, it was no surprise when she was diagnosed. Sharon visited her weekly; her mother's health had begun to deteriorate over the last two months. Hospice had been called in to work with pain management, and Sharon was fully aware of the gravity of the situation. Though she knew her mother was nearing the end, she still held hope that she could hold on for a while longer.

Jack listened, and held her while she grieved. He didn't know what else to do. As she calmed down further, Jack gained her attention and told her that he would make sure everything was taken care of. Sharon was able to tell him about the pre-arranged funeral plans, and Jack made note of what he needed to do.

He stayed with her for several hours before she insisted that she would be fine. He returned to his house, where he began planning the funeral of a woman he had never met.

Constance Fielding was laid to rest the following weekend in Montgomery. Jack attended the service with Sharon and was surprised at how few people had attended. There were several friends, some of whom had been transported by the nursing home but, other than Sharon and her sons, it was a small crowd. It was the first time he had met her children, and the introduction was brief, with a casual greeting before the service began. There was no wake, or gathering, after the ceremony, and the family had to return to their respective homes, as life's obligations kept on – without their mother.

Jack took Sharon back to her house, dropping her off at her front door. She was worn out from the last several days, and simply hugged him and thanked him for all he had done. He watched her walk in and shut the door behind her then returned to his car. It had been almost as tiring for him as it had been for Sharon, and when he arrived home he had nothing left in him.

Jack went straight to bed, hoping that Sharon would be able to get some rest as well.

* * *

When Buck Padgett had received what he needed, he sent Les Vance a notice to take the deposition of Roger Stoltz. He was less concerned with what Roger had to say about the Whisenhunt's beach home than he was about who Forensic Engineering really was. He couldn't wait to get his claws into Roger.

Les called Taylor to inform him of the deposition notice and to get dates when Roger would be available for his testimony.

"Aren't we going to take their experts' testimony first?" Taylor asked.

"Buck has noticed Roger's deposition first. The rules provide that he gets to go first in that case. But yes, I am going to schedule the deposition of their folks as well."

"When does Buck want to get this done?"

"He has requested the first of October; can we get Roger in town by then?"

"Fine, I will bring him." Taylor had participated in many depositions with Roger Stoltz, and had previously prepared him for testimony. Other than going over minor details on this specific case, Roger was already prepared to testify, due to his years of experience.

Taylor Franklin and Roger Stoltz arrived in Birmingham on October first, courtesy of Insure Pro's Gulfstream IV private jet. They were taken to Gibson Vance from the airport for a brief meeting with Les and Luther Abercrombie. The deposition was scheduled for the next day at Gibson Vance, beginning at nine in the morning.

* * *

Buck Padgett arrived in Birmingham the afternoon before the deposition, in order to settle in and review the documents he would be using. He had brought with him an associate who was familiar with the documents and would assist him with the managing and retrieval of the volumes of files Buck had accumulated thus far in the case. He was up until midnight going over everything multiple times. Buck was a perfectionist and couldn't imagine preparing for a case any differently. His method had, after all, resulted in making him a very rich man with a high winning percentage.

They arrived at Gibson Vance shortly before the designated time for the deposition and were led into the main conference room. The main conference room at Gibson, Vance, Burson & Todd was located on the thirty-fifth floor of the Bank One Building in downtown Birmingham. Compared to other major financial and medical areas' skylines, the skyline of the largest city in the State was quite small. But there was no shortage of lawyers and doctors in the Steel City, a name long held and long ago misplaced for Birmingham.

In the 1940s and 50s, Birmingham was second only to Pittsburg in steel production. Certainly the war effort helped the nickname along. But today, the neighborhoods that previously housed the upper classes and high-level workers in the steel industry had become crime ridden. Most who worked downtown wouldn't dream of living in the area. Despite the city's efforts at revitalization, some older downtown buildings having been reconstructed into loft apartments, much of the population lived miles to the south.

The steel industry gave way, over the past several decades, to banking and medicine. Birmingham had become a banking hub almost on a par with Charlotte, especially after Wachovia Bank came to town and bought the once largest Alabama-based national bank, SouthTrust. The evolution of the University of Alabama at Birmingham, UAB, along with its medical school and research departments, had also changed the landscape of the city. Doctors and scientists from across the globe were calling B'ham home now.

The main conference room at Gibson Vance consisted of a large oval-shaped mahogany table, with twenty black Corinthian leather-backed chairs seated neatly around it. All placed squarely with the armrests within an inch of the table. The artwork was limited, for a room this size, but expense was not spared.

Two original Dali's adorned the opposite end walls surrounding the large table, the results of Les Vance's New York trip several years ago. The first, on the north end of the room, was Mercury and Argos," created by Dali in 1981. The south end was framed with "Topological Study for 'Exploded Head," created around 1982. Although the pieces hardly complemented one another, Melanie had insisted that they be placed in the main conference room. The funds used to purchase the artwork were a result of a rather successful excursion to Las Vegas for Mr. and Mrs. Vance. Although Les was as much an art aficionado as Stalin was a humanitarian, he had no choice but to allow Melanie free reign when it came to this dispute. He knew his place and there was no use in stirring up old issues.

Gibson Vance represented all the names when it came to litigation in Alabama. They, along with a few other select firms, were counsel for every major banking, insurance, manufacturing, automotive and corporate entity. They also ran the PR campaigns for most of the conservative candidates. Everyone who knew anything about 'down south' politics knew that a third of the last decade's high level political offices were held by former Gibson Vance partners. It had been training grounds for the next generation's leaders since Horace Gibson founded the firm in 1956. It was also one of the few remaining firms that kept its old name virtually intact, while most other firms had such high turnover that stationery needed to be reprinted every six months.

When Buck entered the overpriced and awfully decorated room, the defense team was already present, as was the court reporter, who would take down every word said by anyone during the proceeding. Introductions were made, and all the lawyers smiled and shook hands as though they were long time friends getting back together. A little small talk amongst them was the customary ritual before they sat down and became enemies again. Buck always thought the whole procedure was rather nauseating, as did Taylor, but breaking the tradition was something none of them wanted to do, almost as if it would somehow jinx the outcome.

Buck began the deposition with standard questions – all directed to Roger, about his background, education and job history, etc. It was a tedious process that ate up almost an hour, most of which would ultimately prove to be of no value. After he was satisfied that he'd gone far enough, he was ready to begin the inquisition.

140

"Tell me what your opinions are as to the cause of the damage to Mr. Whisenhunt's home, please sir," he started.

"My opinions are that the residence in question was destroyed as a result of the surge of water that was associated with the hurricane, primarily. As a second point, I believe that there was inadequate construction and design from an engineering standpoint that could have contributed to the loss, which would have occurred in conjunction with the surge." Roger had his testimony down, and he knew that he was to provide simple, brief answers, and say nothing more. It was up to the lawyer to question him further; volunteering information was strictly forbidden.

"What do you base these opinions on, Mr. Stoltz?"

"I base them on my site inspection, my training as an engineer, and my review of data regarding the storm itself."

"What data did you review?"

"The National Weather Service had surge measurements obtained throughout the gulf coast area, and according to the data from a location within one hundred feet of the residence, the surge had measured approximately twenty feet, which would have brought water almost to the roof. The rapid influx of the water coming in, and later when it receded, was what took the structure off its foundation."

"I see, and at how many structures did you conduct a site inspection, sir?"

"My team of engineers and I performed somewhere in the neighborhood of three thousand, give or take. I don't have the exact numbers."

"How did you know where to go for these inspections?"

"We went where we were asked to go by our client, Insure Pro."

"Certainly you have some kind of list or database which would reflect the properties you visited, don't you?"

"Yes, sir, but I didn't personally visit them all. Other members of our company were present as well, and I personally supervised the processing of the data that was compiled on each one, but I can't tell you I remember them all from memory."

"The Whisenhunt property was located at 1664 Pecan Drive, correct?"

"Yes sir, I believe so."

"Did you conduct a site inspection at 1660 Pecan Drive?"

Roger took a minute to look through the documents they had brought to the deposition. As he was reviewing them, Taylor and Les were frantically flipping through their files, trying to find anything on 1660, and making notes about the question that was asked. After several minutes, he finally answered the question, "No sir."

"And tell us, please sir, why you did not conduct a site inspection at 1660 Pecan Drive."

"I was not asked to do so."

"So you know nothing about that property – who owns it, who insures it, nothing?"

"I do not."

Buck asked for a break, as they had been going for well over two hours and he needed to use the restroom and prepare for the rest of the testimony. Everyone agreed. After Buck left the conference room, Les asked Taylor about the 1660 address. Taylor had no idea, but was sending a message to Hugh Capelli to investigate the address and get him the information as soon as possible. When the break was over, Buck resumed his questioning of Roger Stoltz.

"Tell me who Jerry Shanks is, please sir."

Les looked at Taylor with utter astonishment on his face, tapped him on his leg and leaned in whispering, "What the hell is he doing? He didn't ask one question about the opinions other than what they were. He's not even cross-examining him."

Taylor was equally as dumbfounded. "I have no idea, maybe he's going to come back to it."

Taylor could tell that Les was straining to make sense of the situation; then Les simply whispered back, "I don't think he is, and I've got a bad feeling about this."

"Jerry Shanks is my business partner," Roger replied.

"Is he an engineer?"

"No sir, he provided some of the capital for our start up, and he has an investment interest in the company."

"How did you meet him, please sir?"

"Mr. Franklin introduced me." Roger went on to tell Buck that he had performed some consulting work for Taylor and was interested in starting his own firm, but lacked the funds necessary to get started. Taylor had introduced him to Jerry Shanks. Jerry was interested in investing in his company and would provide capital in exchange for holding an interest in the fees generated. He would retain his interest in the company until a stated return on his investment had been received. Roger had been apprised that these questions would likely be asked and he was ready for them.

"You did not know of him before Mr. Franklin introduced you?"

"No sir."

"Have you ever heard of Fairway Investment Group, LLC?"

"Yes sir, that is Jerry Shanks' investment company."

"And you've received money from Fairway, have you not?"

"The start-up capital initially, and if we have a cash flow issue, Jerry will ensure that we can meet our obligations until fees are received to repay the advance."

"How about Harbor Investments, LLC, or Lightning Funding, LLC?"

"I've never heard of either of them, sir."

Taylor interrupted the testimony, instructing the court reporter to go off the record, "Mr. Padgett, where are you going with this line of questioning? You are getting out of line now, sir." Taylor was visibly upset, and had begun to tremble as his irritation grew. "I need a recess," he said as he rose from the table. Les Vance followed him out of the conference room as Taylor began walking to Les' office.

"What's going on, Taylor?" Les was just as confused about the questioning as Roger had been.

"He's prying into my personal business and I don't appreciate it one goddamned bit." Taylor was pacing back and forth in Les' office, refusing to look at anything but the floor.

"Who are these companies, Taylor?" Les needed some idea of what was going on.

"Stop this deposition now; I'm not letting him go any further with it."

"Are you going to explain this to me or am I being kept out of the loop on something?" Les asked.

"Get Padgett in here. I want to know where he's going with this, but I am not letting him run over me voluntarily."

Les made his way back to the main conference room where Buck was sitting in his seat, rifling through his paperwork. "Buck, can I have a minute, please?"

"Sure." Buck followed him back to his office where Taylor paced back and forth. As they entered, Taylor turned to face Buck. "I want to know where you're going with this line of questioning."

"I believe you know already, sir." Buck couldn't hold back the slight grin that was forming on his face.

"Then this deposition is over."

"I beg to differ, sir. I am entitled to ask these questions and, if you're as smart as you think you are, then you know damn well that I can."

"Then you'll have to do it with a court order. Consider the deposition cancelled. You may leave, sir."

"As you wish." Buck was satisfied that he had Taylor on the ropes, and he was going to pound away. It would just take a little longer than he expected.

After Buck had gathered his files and left the offices of Gibson Vance, Les sat at his desk, wondering what had just happened. "You've got to tell me what this is all about." He was getting angry at his client's refusal to cooperate with him.

"I don't give a shit what he does. You fight it to the end, do you understand?"

"But I at least need to know what I'm fighting against," Les replied.

"I am the client, Les, and it's none of your business; it's a personal matter. If you can't handle this litigation, tell me now, and we will be happy to find other counsel in Alabama that would be more than happy to have our business."

"We can handle this case, Taylor, but…"

"Then do as you are instructed, and quit asking questions that are of no importance to you," Taylor shot back before Les could prod further. "I have a plane to catch now." Taylor returned to the conference room and grabbed his files. Roger Stoltz was still sitting at the table, looking bewildered. He had just seen the plaintiff's lawyer get his files and hop on the elevator. "Roger, get your shit. We are done for the day."

Taylor Franklin led his expert out of the offices of Gibson Vance to the limo awaiting them for the return to the airport. Roger knew better than to ask anything of Taylor at this point. Within an hour they were in the air, on their way back to Dallas.

As soon as they had left the building, Les dictated a letter to the client, confirming that the deposition had been postponed, or canceled – which he was not sure – at the client's request, along with a recitation of the fact that he had been instructed to oppose any attempts to voluntarily provide the information sought by Buck Padgett. It was written to cover his ass more than anything, as his client refused to discuss details of the situation with him.

Les began to wonder whether Insure Pro was actually worth keeping as a client, given the actions of their general counsel, but after reviewing the annual fees paid by the company, he figured he couldn't afford to lose the business. If they were going to lose this case, it would be someone else's fault, certainly not that of him or his firm.

* * *

Three days after Taylor had stormed out of the conference room, taking Roger Stoltz with him, Les received the subpoenas from Buck Padgett. They were directed at several different entities, but all requested that the same documents be provided. Requests for all bank statements and deposits, as well as articles of incorporation and lists of all officers, were directed to Lightning Funding, LLC, Harbor Investments, LLC, Fairway Investment Group, LLC and Forensic Engineering, LLC. The last subpoena was directed to First Federal Bank & Trust, and requested all financial documents, statements, etc. in their possession regarding the named companies.

His confusion was growing at a furious pace.

What the fuck are they doing?

He called Taylor to inform him of the subpoenas.

"I said fight it, or do I need to start finding someone who will?" was all he said in response to the news.

"We'll file the objections immediately."

Before he ended the call, Taylor chimed, "Good. Then we have an understanding."

145

Les Vance filed the mandated objections the following morning, asserting that the information they sought was unreasonable, irrelevant, immaterial, confidential and every other legal term that came to mind. The objections would serve to keep the subpoenas from being issued by the Court until a hearing was held. A call to the judge's office in Baldwin County was all that was required to get a hearing date on the matter. It was scheduled for two weeks later.

Buck anticipated that the insurer would fight his subpoenas, and was encouraged to see that the judge had set the matter for hearing so quickly. He wanted badly for Taylor to be present at the hearing so that he could get an earful from the presiding judge over their waste of the court's time in such a matter. Unfortunately for Buck, Mr. Franklin would not show.

The Baldwin County Courthouse was located in the center of the town of Bay Minette, just off of D'Olive Street. A one-way-street worked its way around the courthouse, directing traffic on U.S. Highway 31 to the north, with a matching one-way for southbound traffic on the other side of the building. Like most of the smaller counties in the state, the Courthouse was the largest structure in the town, centrally located for convenience of the residents. Bay Minette had been the county seat for over a century, since a group of local men who had wanted the seat moved from the city of Daphne, further south, organized a coup of sorts to relocate the courthouse. Several factions opposed, the group so they created a murder that never happened and reported it to the authorities. As the police were chasing a mythical killer, the group traveled the fifteen miles to Daphne, removed all the records from the existing courthouse and transferred them to Bay Minette.

The courthouse had been renovated in the mid-nineties to keep pace with the electronic age, and to remove the asbestos that had been used in the prior building. The exterior of the building was substantially more modern than before, with light tan colored walls constructed of synthetic stucco. The two-story structure had a greenish tinged metal roof, and the renovators had built a clock tower over the entrance, standing ten feet above the second floor. A clock was inset on the north and south sides of the tower, giving travelers and locals the correct time of day.

Courtroom 1 was located on the first floor on the north end of the building. Before the renovation, it had been decided that the old feel and appearance of the courtrooms would be maintained during the reconstruction, and the builder had done a remarkable job in doing so. Courtroom 1 belonged to the presiding judge in the county, James Willingham, who had been on the bench for three decades, a tenure that approached the longest running streak in the state, given the fact that even circuit court judges were elected as well. The courtroom had been rebuilt as a tribute to the old style in Alabama – the judge's bench was the focal point in the room, centered on the rear wall when walking into the room. At his side, on the right, was a seat for his judicial assistant and on his left was the witness stand. The jury box was positioned on the wall to the left of the judge and had a swinging door that provided access to it, with two rows of seven pivoting chairs for jurors to sit in. The rear row was elevated a couple of feet to allow those occupying that row to see over the first row. A three-foot wooden wall separated the jurors from counsel's tables. There were two tables located immediately in front of the bench, the one closest to the jury box reserved for the plaintiff, and the table on the right side for the defendant.

Behind the area designated for the litigants, jurors and judge were wooden pews, two rows and eight deep, with an aisle separating them that led to the jury room, where jurors would assemble before the proceedings began, and, if the case was submitted to them, ultimately decide the outcome. Stairs outside the courtroom led to a mezzanine-level balcony on three sides, overlooking the action from above. The balcony level had stadium seating of wooden pews, three rows deep on each side. Upon first entering Courtroom 1, it wasn't difficult to imagine that Atticus Finch himself had argued the fate of Tom Robinson in this very courtroom.

* * *

Buck Padgett had argued all three of his largest cases in this very courtroom, and every time he entered it he felt at peace, as though this was his second home. Being a native of Bay Minette, Buck was always known to walk the halls, talking to the locals whom he had known his whole life. He would also pop in on several of the other offices in the courthouse, usually to flirt a bit with the women, making them feel extra special. It also helped when it came time to renew his license or car tags, as Buck never had to wait in line. He was on a first name basis with every secretary of every judge, as well as their judicial assistants and law clerks, which made scheduling a rather simple matter. Buck Padgett was always given priority in the Baldwin County Courthouse, a leisure only a handful of local practitioners enjoyed.

The hearing was scheduled to begin at eleven in the morning, and Buck had arrived at the courthouse an hour early to make his rounds. With his office in Mobile, he only made his way back to his home county when business called, and he ensured that every trip to Bay Minette was utilized to its fullest. After shooting the bull with a couple of the other judges who were in their chambers, he made his way to Judge Willingham's office, where he chatted with his secretary, Denise, for a couple of minutes before asking if James was in. Denise rang the Judge in his chambers and notified him that Buck was in.

"Send him in," was all he said before placing the receiver down.

Buck walked in his chambers, plopping his file down on one of the two empty chairs fronting the judge's desk, and extended his hand, "Good morning, Your Honor, I hope all is well with Clara?" he asked, referring to the judge's wife of forty years.

"She's been just fine, Buck, and you?"

"Never better."

"What do we have here today, my friend?" Willingham asked.

"Just a routine discovery squabble." Buck knew Judge Willingham was not asking to hear his argument or any details of the pending matter, and he was always careful not to speak ex parte about a pending case.

"Are the others here yet?"

"They weren't when I got here, but I assume they should be here shortly." Willingham asked Denise to call him when the other lawyers arrived, then he and Buck sat discussing the local gossip while they waited.

At five minutes of eleven, Denise rang in to let the judge know that everyone was present. "Where do you want them, Your Honor?"

"Put them in the courtroom, please."

Denise directed Les Vance and Luther Abercrombie to the courtroom and told them the judge would be with them shortly. They took their place at the table to the judge's left. Several minutes later, Judge Willingham emerged from his chambers, with Buck Padgett following behind.

Shit. This is not going to be good. Les and Luther both thought simultaneously, after seeing the judge on this case walk out of his office chuckling with plaintiff's counsel. They knew better than to question anything, and simply greeted the judge.

"Good morning, Your Honor," they took turns saying, each stretching out a hand. A brief 'hello' to Buck and a handshake, and they were back at their table. Buck took his place nearest the empty jury box.

"What are we here about today, gentlemen?" Willingham asked, looking directly at Buck. Judge Willingham had not had an opportunity to review the objection filed by Les, or at least hadn't bothered to do so yet.

"I've issued some subpoenas regarding their expert testimony, Judge. We began the deposition of this expert a couple of weeks ago, and I was asked to leave before I was able to conclude my examination. So, I prepared subpoenas to gather the information that I sought from the expert."

"What say you?" Willingham asked the Gibson Vance team.

"Your Honor, plaintiff's counsel is trying to subpoena records regarding companies that are not involved in this lawsuit, up to and including bank statements. They are irrelevant to this case, and contain privileged information," Les replied.

"What do you say, Buck?"

"These companies that they reference – it is our belief that they are all intertwined with the company of the expert they intend to use, and I believe that they all lead back to the defendant in this case, which may form the basis for precluding any such testimony. This is discovery, Judge, and I am just trying my best to represent my client. As for the confidential or privilege claims, I would be more than happy to agree to a protective order so that any information I receive will be used only for purposes of this case."

"Sounds reasonable to me," Willingham said, looking back at Les. "Why wouldn't he be entitled to get this with an agreement that it not be disclosed to anyone outside of this case? I mean, if nothing turns up, I won't allow it to come in at trial."

It was the first Les had heard of any connections between Roger Stoltz and Insure Pro other than simply being an expert, since Taylor refused to discuss it with him, and he was trying to comprehend what he was hearing. "Your Honor, it's just not relevant," was all he could utter.

"I just said it may be, it may not be, but for purposes of discovery, he's entitled to it." Willingham's tone became stern.

Les had practiced law long enough to know when a matter had been decided by a judge, and arguing further would serve no purpose other than to discredit future arguments before the court. "I understand, Your Honor; may I request that we draft the protective order?"

"I have a standard one that I use, Mr. Vance; I'll just include it with the order. Mr. Padgett, you may issue the subpoenas."

"Thank you, Your Honor," Buck replied.

Buck stood from his seat and offered his hand to Les again, which he accepted. "I guess that's it."

Les and Luther picked up their files and left Courtroom 1 for the three hour drive back to Birmingham. During the return trip they tried to decipher what was going on with their client, but they came up empty. Les knew that they were powerless to review or cull through the documents Buck Padgett was subpoenaing, as the banks and companies would respond directly to him. They would be entitled to copies of everything he got, but they would get it all after he did. Les liked this case less by the day.

SEVENTEEN

By mid-November, Buck had the documents he had requested from the subpoenas. He called in his legal research and writing associate, who was primarily responsible for writing appeals briefs and other trial briefs for the various courts in which they had cases pending. Buck gave his associate the series of events in the Whisenhunt expert file that would be the subject of the next filing and dismissed her with instructions to have the brief on his desk within three days. She hurried away to begin researching the issue presented.

Buck figured he would be back in Baldwin County and Courtroom 1 within a month, maybe less.

* * *

Bob Powell arrived in Montgomery on November 20th for his scheduled meeting with the members of the Judicial Inquiry Commission. It was an honor extended to a rare few people, and, in virtually every case, was done so out of respect for the visitor and his or her position or reputation in the judicial community. Bob had called Ron Jackson, the senior member of the Commission, and requested that he be allowed to speak before the panel prior to a ruling in the Jackson Garrett inquiry. Ron had been a circuit court judge when Powell was on the High Court, and held Bob in the highest of regard.

Bob met with the group in a conference room in the Judicial Annex, located across the street from the Supreme Court. He was already aware of the nature of the complaint against Jack, but he

151

was not apprised of who had filed it. The identity of the complainant was kept sealed with the commission to protect the complainant from unwarranted retaliation. Complainants could range from litigants who would have appeared before the judge, to staff members, rival judges, competing candidates, pretty much anyone, and Bob knew they would not divulge the identity, even for him. The identity was not relevant to his task at any rate.

Bob took his seat at the table and waited for Ron to begin.

"Mr. Powell, the members of the Commission have agreed to allow you to address them, at your request, regarding the Garrett complaint. We are willing to consider anything you have that may be of importance."

"Thank you, Your Honor," Bob began. "As you all know, I am not only a colleague of Jack Garrett's, I consider myself a friend as well. I have known Jack for his entire career as a public servant to the people of this state, and I hold nothing but the utmost respect for him. I realize the nature of the charges that have been brought, and I assure you that I am aware of the gravity of the situation. I know for a fact that Jack is not only embarrassed by what has happened, but that he is also truly sorry for his actions." Bob was winging it, as he hadn't discussed the details of the case with Jack at all, and certainly hadn't heard an apology from him for it. "It would seem to me that Jack is guilty, if anything, of using poor judgment in his personal life, but such a matter does not rise to the level of judicial misconduct for which this body should impose sanctions, reprimand or dismissal. I firmly believe that, if this Commission were to impose even the smallest penalty available, it would mean a certain end to his career as a jurist, something that the facts simply do not warrant. I can only imagine that such a result would only open the floodgates to a multitude of complaints against judges across this state for even the most menial of charges, in hopes of gaining political clout. Should any of you have specific questions of me, I will be happy to entertain them, and I thank each and every one of you for allowing me to appear before you in this matter." Bob sat back in his chair, crossing his legs, and folding his hands together.

"Does any member of the panel have any questions of Mr. Powell?" Ron asked.

Bob scanned the room, eyeing each member of the Commission, just as he had during his argument on behalf of Jack Garrett. There was no response from any member.

"On behalf of the Commission, we would all like to thank you for your time, sir," Ron said as he rose from his seat at the head of the table. "Meeting adjourned."

Bob left the Judicial Annex and began the hour-long drive home. From what he could tell, the panel had been receptive to his argument, and he knew he had done all he could do to save Jack Garrett's career. He could only hope it was enough.

* * *

When Les Vance returned from the Thanksgiving holiday, he had a package from Padgett & Keeler. *Here we go again.*

Buck Padgett had filed a Motion to Preclude Expert Testimony in the Whisenhunt case, and Judge Willingham had set the motion for a hearing and oral argument on December 12th. Les skimmed through the motion, not studying it fully, just trying to get the basic points that Buck was asserting to prevent Roger Stoltz from testifying in the case. He would have little time to respond, and the written response would not be as important as the argument in front of Willingham anyway. He read it three times, each time becoming more and more agitated at Taylor Franklin for keeping him in the dark for so long. Les had received the subpoenaed documents within days of Buck Padgett, and had already figured out where he was going with the expert issue; it was just a matter of waiting for the trial lawyer to file his motion.

The issue regarding Roger Stoltz was pivotal for Insure Pro in this litigation. If Willingham precluded his testimony, there was no defense and, with a trial date set in February, there would be no time to get a new expert on the case. Even if they could hire a replacement, the site investigation would be compromised due to the significant delay, and Willingham would probably prevent any of Stoltz' work from being used by the new engineer. With no factual defense supported by expert testimony, Willingham would probably rule, by himself, in favor of the Whisenhunt's on the benefits due under the policy, without letting it go to a jury, which would open the door to a claim of bad faith on the part of Insure Pro. The Whisenhunts alone could get millions in punitive damages, setting the stage for the remaining claims. The numbers could be devastating.

Les called Taylor. "Padgett's filed a motion to preclude on Roger."

"I knew that motherfucker was going to go there," Taylor said. "You realize what would happen if Roger isn't allowed to testify?"

"It would eliminate our defense," Les responded.

"You will fight this to the end, do you understand? If Willingham precludes, take it up. We cannot lose on this, Les."

"Do you want to come to the hearing?"

"With my name spread across this shit, I think it's best that I stay away for now. In light of these developments, I will take a back seat; I don't want to piss off Willingham in any manner."

"I'll call you after the hearing then." Les was encouraged to hear that Taylor was standing down from his participation in the case, and hoped he would back out altogether, but for now, his whole case was resting in the hands of Judge James Willingham, and that did not bode well for him.

* * *

Jack gave Sharon some space after her mother died. He didn't want to, but he knew that she needed time to grieve, and he simply didn't know how to help her through it. He finally decided that if he was going to keep her in his life, he needed to make the effort; he couldn't wait on her. She had been keeping to herself at work, doing her job perfectly, as always, but solitarily. He called her early on a Friday evening, "Do you feel like some company?"

"I was beginning to wonder if you would ever call again," Sharon said. The most welcome words Jack could have ever heard.

"I'm sorry, Sharon, I just thought you needed some time and I didn't want to intrude." He hoped she accepted his explanation.

"No apologies are necessary. I'd love to get out of this house, though."

"Give me a half hour, does that work?"

"Sure, I'll see you then." Jack changed clothes as fast as he could and started off for Sharon's, chastising himself for having been wrong about stepping back, but grateful nonetheless that he hadn't completely screwed himself.

He took her to dinner at Fawn's Grill, a quaint little restaurant downtown, known for its fine cuisine. It catered to the political crowd and was a favorite of legislators when session was in. With the legislature on break, Fawn's was not too crowded and they got a table by themselves in a corner. They talked about her mother for a while, and it was clear to Jack that she was getting through things better than he would have expected. She asked about him, and how well he was holding up with the pending complaint against him with the JIC.

"Have you gotten any indication when a ruling may come down?" she asked.

"They don't really keep me in the loop on it, you know, but I can only assume that they have to be fairly close to a decision."

"Any idea what they might do?"

"None whatsoever." Her question had gotten him thinking again about the possibilities. Jack occasionally went over the different scenarios in his head – a public reprimand, the least severe of punishments, would likely mean certain doom come time for the next election, as his opponent would litter the airways with reminders to the public of his poor decisions; if the JIC decided to be harsher, he could likely lose his seat immediately. Nothing short of a closing of the case with no action taken could help his career survive, and, though he had told himself many times that returning to private practice might not be so bad, in his heart he didn't want to leave the bench.

"I'm sure everything will work out for the best," she said.

"I don't know, dear, I hope so, but I just don't have the warm fuzzies about it."

They talked generally over dinner, exchanging stories about past cases, getting into nothing terribly personal. They both had significant personal matters they were dealing with, and each wanted to get back to a place where those issues weren't in the foreground. After dinner he drove her home, dropping her off at the front door again. "Thanks for getting me out, I really needed it," she said.

"It's my pleasure. Anytime you need to get away, just let me know."

She gave him a brief hug, then disappeared into the house, leaving him to return home. Despite her best efforts to ease his mind about the JIC matter, it was all he could think about on the way home. He needed something to get his mind off it.

He wouldn't get it.

Shortly after he arrived back at his house, he received a phone call from an old friend. "Jack, Bob Powell, how are you doing, my friend?"

"I'm hanging in there, Bob, how have you been?"

"Very well, thank you. Have you got a minute to talk?"

"Sure. What can I do for you?"

"Well, it's not what you can do for me, but I need to tell you about something and ask your thoughts," Bob replied. Powell had a job to do, and he didn't like the fact that he had to lie to his friend about what had already transpired, but it was a necessary evil in order to accomplish the goal of his task.

"I'm listening."

"I received a call from a member of the JIC regarding your case, and they have asked if I would be willing to appear before them regarding the matter. As you know, they tend to lend an ear to various people on cases before them, and I can only assume that, due to my tenure on the Association, they would like some input from me. You know I'm on your side here, but I wanted to make sure that I had your blessings before I went."

"Do you have any idea what they're thinking?" Jack asked.

"I was not advised, nor do I expect to be; that's not the way they work. But I don't see how their request for me to speak to them, or my doing so, if you approve, could be harmful in any way."

"If you think it will help, by all means, you have my permission. I just want this thing over with."

"I will do everything I can, and if I get any word on it, you'll be the first to know."

Jack thanked him for the offer as they hung up, but Bob's call didn't make him feel any better about the situation.

EIGHTEEN

James Willingham had been a circuit court judge for almost thirty years, winning each election as a Democrat. Circuit judgeships were significantly less susceptible to political swings than statewide elections, mainly because only the voters in the county in which the race was held could vote. Name recognition became everything, and James Willingham was known and respected by everyone in the community. In more than half of his victories he was unopposed.

Although elected as a Democrat, Willingham was known to be a fair judge, certainly not a rubber stamp for one side or the other. He had profound respect for the Constitution, and specifically, the right to trial by jury, and he would always err on the side of allowing a jury to decide the case over ruling on the merits of it himself. Though many defense lawyers portrayed this ideology as plaintiff-oriented, such was not the case. Willingham would give a fair trial to both parties, and when the jury ruled, he accepted their verdict as what it was…the voice of the people. Over his thirty years he had only set aside a jury's verdict on a handful of occasions and had rarely been reversed on appeal, giving more credibility to his judicial philosophy. He was a large man with gray hair and a thunderous voice that he raised only when absolutely necessary to maintain order in his courtroom. He spoke pleasantly when addressing counsel, mindful never to let a jury assume he had an opinion on the merits of the case being tried. Most lawyers who had had the pleasure of trying a case before him, plaintiff and defense alike, respected him.

He called the motion docket on December 12th and the Whisenhunt case had been placed as the first one to be heard, another considerate gesture to Buck Padgett. Both sides had their attorneys present, with the exception of Taylor Franklin, who had other business in Texas and was unable to attend, according to Les Vance.

"Mr. Padgett, I believe that this is your motion, is it not?"

"It is, Your Honor. May it please the Court, I will proceed with argument?"

"You may."

"Your Honor, as you are aware, we have filed a motion seeking to preclude the defendant from using Roger Stoltz and Forensic Engineering, LLC as an expert in this case. The basis of my motion is quite simple; it is our position that, for all intents and purposes, Roger Stoltz and his company are one and the same as Insure Pro, the defendant."

Les glanced over at Luther Abercrombie, assuming from what he had read that this was going to be Buck's argument. *Why in the hell did I let Taylor get me into this shit hole?*

Buck proceeded with his explanation to Judge Willingham by outlining the companies that led down the "food chain" from Insure Pro to Forensic Engineering. "According to court records, Roger Stoltz first testified for Insure Pro in 2000 and since then he had rendered expert opinions on their behalf in almost two hundred cases. As a matter of fact, Insure Pro had not used a structural engineering firm other than his since 2001. The firm had raked in an average of twenty thousand dollars per case, with a total fee income of four million dollars over the last six years, all in checks for their fees paid by the client, Insure Pro. Based upon the subpoenaed documents, Forensic Engineering has been listed as experts in a grand total of fifteen cases over the last five years, so there was no question that virtually all of their business had come from Insure Pro. The problem was the company's overhead – there were seven engineers and fourteen support staff, along with the office building and insurance and benefits to account for. With even the most conservative estimates, the company's overhead would have exceeded six million dollars during that time frame – a losing proposition. Nevertheless, according to their last bank statement, at month's end there was over two hundred grand in their operating account. The building they occupied was owned by Jerry Shanks, one of the main incorporators and investors, who had retired from Insure Pro as a claims manager with a pension of around fifty grand a year."

"Your Honor, these details are all very interesting, but none are relevant to this case," Les interrupted.

"You will speak when it is your turn," Willingham snapped back, pointing Les back into his chair. "Please proceed," he said to Buck.

"According to the documents we received, Lightning Funding, LLC was formed in 2001. Taylor Franklin, Insure Pro's general counsel and vice president, was the sole incorporator and the business was described as a financial funding source for litigators in the south and east. Start up capital was approximately five million dollars, none of which Franklin personally had. A grant was given by Insure Pro to the company to begin operations. Apparently, Lightning Funding did very little business, other than to send money to another company, Harbor Investments, LLC, also incorporated in 2001. Harbor's officers were listed as Jerry Shanks, a retired Insure Pro claims guy, and Deanna Franklin, Taylor Franklin's wife. Their business description was identical to that of Lightning Funding, and they got in the habit of doing nothing other than sending funds to a company called Fairway Investment Group, LLC, which of course was formed in 2001 as well, and by none other than Jerry Shanks. The trend continued with Fairway operating as nothing more than a conduit to funnel cash into Forensic Engineering, LLC, to the tune of more than ten million dollars over the past five years. Of even more interest is the fact that all of these companies were incorporated within two weeks of each other." Buck paused for a moment to allow his factual recitation to sink in with the Judge.

"Your Honor, the evidence reveals that Forensic Engineering is nothing more than an arm of Insure Pro, and that they have gone to great lengths to hide that fact from the Court and ultimately this jury. As the Court is aware, a party may not act as its own expert witness in a case. For that reason, I ask that you preclude Roger Stoltz, or any other member of his so-called expert firm, from testifying in this case." Buck took his seat confidently.

Les Vance had been angry at Taylor in the past, but nothing approached the contempt he had for him now. Had he been apprised of this scheme when he inquired about it, he might have had enough time to prepare a more persuasive argument. But Les was a great lawyer, as he had reminded himself on many an occasion, and surely he could muster a reasonable explanation for Judge Willingham.

"Your Honor, may I respond?" He understood that deference to the judge was expected at this point.

"You may."

"I realize that Mr. Padgett's fantasy about some great conspiracy is interesting to the ear, but the reality of the matter is that neither Mr. Stoltz, nor his firm, is an employee of my client. Where their funds are obtained has no real relevance to the issues in this case, and it simply appears that the plaintiff is grasping at anything they can because they cannot refute the testimony of our expert. Even if you assume that my client provided additional funds, which I certainly do not concede, at most the Court could allow Mr. Padgett to argue just as he has here today, and let the jury consider all the evidence and render a verdict. After all, isn't that what we all want?" Les had done his homework on Judge Willingham, and prayed this appeal to his belief system would prevail.

"I believe that I understand the position of the parties," Willingham began, "and to be honest with you, Mr. Vance, I am troubled by the appearance of deception that your client has perpetrated. I will take this matter under advisement, and will forward an order within the next day or so."

James Willingham rose from the bench, retreating to his chambers, as the lawyers gathered their belongings and left Courtroom 1. Les would sweat the wait substantially more than Buck, and, as they left the courthouse, both of them knew it.

Two days after the hearing, Buck Padgett and Les Vance received a faxed copy from the chambers of Judge James Willingham:

This cause came before the Court on Plaintiff's Motion to Preclude Expert Testimony, the Court having reviewed the briefs of the parties and heard argument on same, it is hereby ORDERED, ADJUDGED and DECREED that said motion is due to be, and is hereby GRANTED. Defendant is hereby precluded from calling Roger Stoltz or any member of his company, Forensic Engineering, LLC, as a witness in this cause for purposes of providing expert opinions as to the cause of the damage to the structure made the basis of this suit.

The order was signed and dated in the usual fashion by Willingham.

As soon as Les received the Order, he contacted his appellate brief specialist at Gibson Vance. He had already been given instructions from Taylor that an adverse ruling would be appealed, and he knew that if there was any chance for victory, Willingham's decision would have to be reversed by the Supreme Court.

* * *

Gibson Vance prepared the Writ of Mandamus, an appeal of a trial judge's ruling on an issue before trial, to the Alabama Supreme Court. The writ requested that the Supreme Court order Judge Willingham to reverse his opinion with respect to Roger's testimony. In the event the High Court agreed, Willingham would have no choice but to abide by their instructions. The primary argument was the one advanced by Les at the hearing – that Buck could argue as he wished, but that precluding the expert was an abuse of Willingham's discretion.

Les forwarded a copy of the final draft to Taylor Franklin.

Taylor sent a cursory reply, stating that it looked fine, although Taylor knew that the brief was not what would carry Insure Pro into the next round with their expert intact. He realized that timing was everything and picked up the phone and called Les.

"Hold off on filing the writ until I say so," he told Les.

"We have it ready to go; are you sure you want to wait?"

"I'll let you know when to file," Taylor replied.

He had one more call to make.

* * *

"Hello."

"Bob, we need for the JIC matter to come to a close," Taylor told Powell.

"I'll make the call," Bob said. Bob was completely unaware of the status of the Whisenhunt case, and Taylor was telling him only as much as he thought he needed to know.

"Let me know when it will be ready." Taylor said.

Bob called Ron Jackson to inquire as to the status of the Garrett complaint.

"You know I was with you from the beginning, Bob, and I've managed to convince the panel that this is not a matter for our intervention," Ron said.

"When will the decision be ready?"

"I can prepare a statement today if you like."

"Let's get through the holidays first. Middle of January would be best for me, and I want to be able to break the news."

Ron agreed to the request, asking Bob to call him when he was ready for the final report.

Bob relayed to Taylor that it was their call as to when Jack Garrett received the news of his fate.

Everything was going according to schedule, except for Judge Willingham.

* * *

Jack didn't want to be alone for Christmas, not again. He called Sharon to see if she had any plans of her own.

Her pride and joy, Keith, who was not married and had no children, was coming for Christmas Eve and Day, but she welcomed Jack to join them at her house. He wasn't sure whether it would be proper for him to intrude, but she had assured him that he was more than welcome. After mulling it over for a good five minutes, he determined that he would enjoy the season with them. After all, over a decade of solitary confinement during the most wonderful time of the year was more than enough punishment for one man to endure.

Jack's Christmas was the best he'd had in years. He was surprised at how well he and Keith had hit it off, much to his delight. He could only have imagined that meeting Sharon's son would have been like meeting a younger man who was skeptical of a stranger being even tangentially involved with his mother. Keith was in his mid-twenties, an entrepreneur and a good soul, from what he could tell. The two talked at length, sharing stories about their lives and careers, and Jack was impressed with his maturity. He thought, many times, that Keith could have been his own son, and a perfect one at that, had he made the decision to have children himself.

Sharon cooked Christmas dinner for the three of them – turkey and dressing, cranberry sauce, green beans, mashed sweet potatoes and tossed salad, the southern staple for this time of year. It was the first time he had an opportunity to evaluate her culinary skills and he found that she was quite gifted.

Jack had brought a present for each of them, having been informed early enough that he was invited to the family gathering. Not knowing anything about Keith made it difficult, so he went with all he knew about him from Sharon's brief description about her youngest boy. After Christmas dinner, he presented him with a leather bound book outlining the history of jujitsu, his chosen discipline in the martial arts. "I suppose you may already have one?" Jack asked, assumedly.

"Not at all, Jack, this really wasn't necessary," Keith replied.

Sharon proved no easier to shop for. He settled on giving her a homemade gift certificate, entitling her to the keys to his beach home for a weekend, just to get away. He made it explicitly clear that he had no intention of joining her when she chose to exercise the option, as it was for her exclusively. She was thrilled at the gesture, and Keith jokingly suggested that he would be a perfect date for her.

Sharon and her son apologized for not having a gift for Jack, but he would have none of it. "Allowing me to be a part of your Christmas is the best gift I could have ever received," he said, putting an end to the discussion.

They spent the rest of the day lounging around Sharon's home, watching the football game in the afternoon and enjoying the moment. By dusk, Jack decided he would give mother and son some time together and falsely told them that he was exhausted and ready to get some sleep.

As he made his way home, he felt true happiness.

* * *

Ordinarily, Taylor would have enjoyed the Christmas season just as he always did, as Christmas was his favorite holiday, but this year was different, and Dee could tell that he was deeply preoccupied. She could see that his mind was elsewhere, but appreciated that he needed his space this year. He was thankful that she knew him well enough to allow him to focus on what paid the bills, and he loved her all the more for it as well.

He let the post-holiday funk wash away, and called Bob Powell. "It's time to get the ball rolling," he said.

After his brief conversation with the former chief justice, he called Les Vance. "File the writ of mandamus, Les; we should have everything in place by the time it's assigned."

Taylor knew that when the writ was filed, it would be assigned within a day or so, and that the process of coming to a decision would last for a week or better…plenty of time for Bob to do what he was paid to do.

* * *

Bob called Ron Jackson the day following Taylor's call. "Ron, how soon can the official report be released?"

"I've already prepared it, Bob, just waiting on your call."

"I'd like to tell Jack myself, if you have no objection."

"Just let me know what you want me to do," Ron replied.

"Let me get in touch with Jack and see when I can meet with him. I'll call you when I get the arrangements made."

Jack was at home in Montgomery still reminiscing the holidays, when Bob called.

"Jack, Bob Powell," he said, as Jack answered the phone.

"How was your holiday, my friend?" Jack replied.

"Susan and I had a wonderful time, Katie and Jeff brought the grandkids this year, and it was perfect."

"So, have you heard from the JIC? I assume that's what you're calling about."

"I got a call this morning, and apparently there is quite a bit of dissention in the panel, but I've been told that a final decision is due in three days. They have agreed to present it to me, I guess because they know our history, and none of them want any potential repercussions on an individual basis. Will you be around?"

"I'll be at the coast this weekend. What do you mean, repercussions?"

"It's always best to prepare yourself for the worst in these matters, Jack; you know that as well as I do."

164

"I'm not sure how I'm supposed to take that," Jack replied.

"I'm not insinuating anything; I just feel like they are having a hard time with this. At any rate, that's what I've been told. Listen, I'll be happy to come down and see you this weekend. I haven't seen the new place anyway."

"If you think that's best, as you wish, Bob."

"I'll see you soon then." Bob was growing less and less fond of the requirements of his position, and the continued misleading of Jack Garrett was unnerving to him. He had prided himself on his honesty for his whole life, and the transformation that Insure Pro was forcing on his ideals was beginning to get under his skin.

* * *

Jack had actually planned on heading to Orange Beach for the weekend, as he needed to check on the house, and the yard was likely in need of some tending to as well. Bob's call had destroyed the elation that had been his after the holidays. Within minutes, he felt his world caving in on him. He was certain that he had lost his job and, with it, any possibility of Sharon. When she found out that he was no longer chief justice, she would lose all respect for him. He would be alone.

Alone.

Alone.

Alone.

He couldn't stop the influx of negativity. He had worked so hard for so long to get where he was in life; he had taken the chance with Sharon; dealt with the adversity of the inquiry, and now he was about to lose everything. The pessimism was relentless and it worked its way deeper into his being with each thought.

He left a day early for Orange Beach because he had to get away from the capital. When he reached Foley, less than an hour from his paradise, he stopped at a pawn shop. As he walked in, he scanned the glass case located near the cash register. The clerk saw him evaluating the merchandise. "What are you looking for, sir?"

"A gun. Anything, I suppose, will do."

"I guess that all depends on what you need it for."

"Personal protection, I guess, nothing expensive," Jack replied.

"I've got this .38," the clerk said, pointing to the pistol in the case next to Jack. "It'll do the job as well as any, and it's on sale."

"I'll take it." Jack paid for the first gun he had ever owned in cash, at a pawn shop in Foley, Alabama.

When he pulled into the garage in Orange Beach he sat in his Tahoe for twenty minutes, staring at the firearm he had purchased less than an hour ago. He finally entered the house and immediately went to his study where he placed it into the drawer of his desk. He needed sleep but, no matter how hard he tried, it would not come. After half a bottle of whiskey, he managed to doze off.

NINETEEN

Jack thought he would sleep like a baby after Bob left, having informed him that the JIC was taking no action. The weight of the world had been lifted off his shoulders, and as far as he was concerned, he had been vindicated. Instead, he felt only shame.

What in God's name were you thinking?

For the first, and only time in his life, Jack Garrett, Chief Justice of the Alabama Supreme Court, contemplated suicide.

The easy way out. He was sick to his stomach.

He wouldn't sleep tonight either.

When he got up the following morning, he walked upstairs to the balcony overlooking the Gulf of Mexico and had his coffee. As he peered out on the calm surf, he revisited all of the things that were important to him now, the same things that had prompted him to consider the coward's exit. He heard nothing – the birds chirping, the wind whipping through the palm trees, not even the occasional car speeding along the front beach road registered in his head. He had taken himself to the brink of lunacy, and survived, for a reason. He remembered then what Walt had told him.

Only one go-around on this big spinning ball we live on.

Look at every situation as an opportunity .Even the less pleasant ones. Don't wake up at eighty wishing...

Walt was right, about a lot of things. Most important, he was right about Jack. Jack was like Walt, deep down, at his core. It just took a trip to the edge to make him realize it. From this moment on, Jack was going to live his life with no regrets.

Only one go-around.

On his way back to the capital, he stopped by the pawn shop he had patronized only a couple of days ago, and pawned the .38.

* * *

The Writ of Mandamus was randomly assigned to Justice Christian Mathis, a GOP-backed jurist who was part of the Republican revolution that had taken over the Court years ago. Mathis assigned the matter to his senior staff attorney, Judson Wallis, a capable researcher, although Chris instructed him to give his boss daily updates on the status of the proposed opinion.

Wallis was well aware of Mathis' political ideology, and focused his research on finding a valid explanation as to why James Willingham had failed to serve justice in his ruling in the Whisenhunt case. After several days of reviewing case law and the Rules of Civil Procedure, he came to the only conclusion that existed – Willingham must have abused his discretion in precluding the testimony of Roger Stoltz.

Trial judges were given wide latitude in rulings on discovery matters and admissibility of a given witness's testimony, and their decisions generally were upheld on review. However, the law also was clear that if a motion was filed against an adverse party, the trial judge should view his ultimate ruling, and any circumstances surrounding the motion, in a light most favorable to the party against whom the motion was filed – in this case, Insure Pro. Judd understood from his review of the law that it was encouraged that the jury should be able to hear all relevant facts from both sides, then be allowed to render a decision, and that precluding any testimony was looked down upon if there was any valid legal basis for its admission.

The opinion that was written essentially tracked the argument that Les Vance had asserted before Judge Willingham at the hearing. Insure Pro would be allowed to put Roger Stoltz on the stand and his testimony should not have been precluded. The concession to Buck Padgett was that he would be allowed to argue Roger's funding and the alleged scheme by Insure Pro, at least to the extent he could produce valid evidence to support it.

The opinion was circulated to the other justices for review. The first Democrat to receive the opinion was Elizabeth Callahan, who hailed from Mobile, only a short drive from Baldwin County. Beth had tried her share of cases in front of James Willingham, and considered him a mentor early in her career as a lawyer. She read the opinion by Chris Mathis and informed her staff attorney that she wanted a contrary opinion drafted. After her review of the briefs she concluded that Insure Pro had attempted to deceive the Court and the Whisenhunts as to the true identity of their expert. Such conduct should not be rewarded by allowing them to use Roger as an expert.

Within two days the opinion supporting Judge Willingham was finalized and submitted to the other members of the Court. Each justice had an opportunity to review both opinions and decide which one he agreed with, and, if so inclined, whether to add anything to one of the opinions in joining the author. Rarely were concurring opinions written in mandamus cases, and this would be no exception to the rule.

Judge Willingham was the first to receive a copy of the Order from the Court regarding the mandamus petition that was filed on him, as was standard procedure. Due to time constraints with the pending trial of the Whisenhunt case in light of the appeal of his order precluding the defendant's expert, Willingham had postponed the trial to the middle of April to give the parties time to adjust their trial preparations in accordance with the Supreme Court's ruling.

It was not a huge surprise to him when he received the Supreme Court opinion ruling five to four, agreeing with Insure Pro. They should be allowed to use Roger Stoltz.

Willingham had been reversed The trial judge was well aware that the Republicans still held a majority on the Court, slim as it may have been, and that the defendant in his case was a part of their constituency, so he felt no shame in being overturned. He did what he deemed just and legally sound when he ruled on Buck's motion. They disagreed with him. End of story. The trial would go on.

* * *

Buck Padgett's copy was faxed to his office later the same day. It came as no surprise to him either, as he knew how strong the industry's hold was on the Court's remaining GOP members. Though there was a slight bit of disappointment, he would not let it dampen his spirits about the case, and now he could look forward to getting his hands on Roger Stoltz in front of a jury, where he could decimate him. He still held out hope of getting Willingham to rule in his favor during the trial as well.

He hoped that Chief was having some success in his investigations in south Baldwin County, because, if he was, the bad faith claim was still very much alive.

* * *

Taylor Franklin had scheduled a meeting in Birmingham with Les to discuss the Hurricane Peter litigation, pending the ruling on Willingham's order. They now had a total of ninety-two cases pending against the company, the majority of which were in Baldwin County. With Whisenhunt as the test case, he needed to be there in person to review the files with Les and his team.

He was en route when Les Vance received a copy of the Order from the clerk at the Supreme Court. Les was very much surprised when the order came through, as he had anticipated Willingham would be upheld, given the strong presumption that his rulings were correct under the law. He still had a great deal of skepticism about Roger and the shady corporate scheme that had been created, but they had been given the green light to use him, and there was no turning back now. If he could just get the case submitted to the jury, he won.

Les sent for Taylor at the Birmingham International Airport and looked forward to disclosing their victory to him. It showed further evidence of his, and his firm's, legal superiority in the Alabama courts. Taylor arrived at Gibson Vance shortly after three pm, unaware that the decision had come down, and Les wasn't going to tell him over the phone either. The news would be better delivered to his face. According to Les, the decision was not likely to be issued until the next week or so anyway.

Taylor entered the lobby and notified the receptionist that he was there to see Les, which she already knew. Les approached from the corner. "Nice flight?" he asked.

"Same old shit; are we ready to get started?" Taylor was not in for chit chat; he wanted to get the review underway and get out of Alabama as soon as possible.

We should go to the conference room then," Les said.

Taylor made his way in, while Les detoured by his office to retrieve his files. When Les entered the conference room, Taylor was sitting at the head of the table, his back to the door, studying the Dali hanging on the wall. "I have some rather good news in the Whisenhunt case," Les started.

"They're already back?" Taylor asked, with a look of complete surprise on his face. "You said it wouldn't be for another week or so."

"The opinion was faxed to me shortly before you arrived." Les flipped his copy of the decision across the table, spinning it toward Taylor. "The writ was granted, five to four."

"Fucking beautiful," Taylor said, as he began to read through it. He read the highlights of the main opinion then turned to the final page, "You've got to be fucking kidding me!"

Les was taken aback.

"What?" he jumped in.

"Garrett dissented, that son of a bitch!"

Les hadn't bothered to read through the signatures that followed the opinion; he had been too blinded by the ecstasy of the victory to notice.

"We're going to have to postpone the review, Les; I've got some things I need to deal with," Taylor said as he stood from his seat. "Make me a copy of this," he ordered, referring to the opinion on the writ. He took out his cell phone and called Rick, instructing him to call and put in an early flight plan to return to Dallas. "I apologize, Les, but we'll have to do this later." Taylor left Gibson Vance after being there for only fifteen minutes.

Les was dumbfounded. It was getting to be a habit with Taylor – leaving Les with more unanswered questions as to what was going on. His excitement at having just won the most important part of the Whisenhunt case began to wane.

* * *

Jack Garrett was the lone Republican dissenter from the majority opinion in the Whisenhunt writ. Had it not been for one Democrat, James Stanley, who crossed over to join the GOP to comprise a majority, Willingham's order precluding Roger Stoltz from testifying would have been upheld. When Jack received the two opinions that were circulated, he skimmed them both, before handing them to Sharon. "Tell me what you think," he said, "I'm going with your gut on this one."

Mike Gedgoudas

Sharon Waters had actually been the guilty party. Jack didn't deem it necessary to follow up on the outcome of the High Court's decision. He was living his life with no regrets from now on, and if Sharon felt that the expert shouldn't be allowed to testify, he had no qualms penning his name to her decision.

Taylor's program targeting Alabama's highest court had worked, just not as he had anticipated. Jack's retreat to join the opposition had come dangerously close to costing Insure Pro Roger's testimony, but for James Stanley, and his wretched past.

Shortly after the writ was filed, Justice Stanley received a call at home from an anonymous caller who identified himself only as Mr. Dowdell. Jim's wife answered the call and handed the phone to her husband. "Your Honor," the caller began courteously, "may I have a minute of your time?"

"Who may I ask is this?" Judge Stanley inquired, knowing that his home number was non-published.

"Your Honor, there is a matter coming before the Court, I am sure you are aware of it – out of Baldwin County. We have a mutual interest in this matter, sir, and it appears that the trial judge has overstepped his bounds in a certain matter." The caller got straight to the point, having failed to answer Judge Stanley's question.

"If you don't tell me who this is, then this conversation is over, sir." Confusion was pouring into the judge's head.

"You may wish to hear me out before you threaten any further, Mr. Stanley," the voice shot back. "Surely you remember a young man you had occasion to meet in California some years ago?"

Jim left the presence of his wife, walking outside to finish the discussion. "What are you talking about?" he asked the caller.

"I see you do remember, Your Honor. I am sure we both can agree that such nasty past transgressions need not be brought to light at this time. Especially considering your position in the community and your family."

"What exactly are you asking me to do, sir?"

"Let the trial proceed. I ask nothing more of you. But should you find it necessary to let this rogue judge's ruling stand, well – you will have decided your own fate."

"If you have nothing further, sir, I have dinner waiting," Jim replied, putting an end to the dialogue.

"That is all. Have a good evening, sir."

When he walked back into the house, Jim told his wife that another lobbyist was calling, asking questions that she never had any interest in listening to. The truth of the matter was too painful for Jim to discuss with her.

Someone had managed to discover an affair he'd had very early in his marriage to Candice, more than twenty years ago. Jim had repented his experimentation with homosexuality long ago and changed his life in the process. How anyone other than his partner at the time could have known was beyond him, but there was no question that it was out now. He harbored no personal feelings of distaste for gays, but if news of past homosexual conduct on his part became public, his career as an elected judge in Alabama was over, not to mention his marriage and everything else he'd worked all his life to accomplish.

It wasn't a difficult decision to make – rule in favor of the opposition on one case and let life go on, or stick with your guns and watch the house of cards fall. Jim knew his vote on the Whisenhunt writ before the first brief arrived at the Supreme Court, and he also knew that it might not be the last time he would be grabbed by the balls over his past.

* * *

Taylor arrived in Dallas early in the evening of the day he discovered Jack Garrett's betrayal. Arriving home, he proceeded straight to his makeshift office in the basement and called Bob, at his home in Birmingham.

"Have you heard about the writ we filed?" he asked.

"I've been out for a while," Bob said.

"The writ was granted, we have our expert."

"I'm glad I was of assistance."

"Like hell you were. Garrett went the other way; we only won because Stanley crossed over."Powell couldn't believe what he'd heard. "There must be some mistake?"

"I have the opinion in front of me now, Bob. Jack tried to fuck us."

"This doesn't make any sense; he assured me he understood what needed to be done."

"I need you here tomorrow," Taylor said. "The trial is in six weeks, and they're going to let Padgett get into all kinds of shit that will only give them a reason to turn on us. New information has come to light that we need to discuss."

"What new information?" Bob asked.

"I'll send Rick for you tomorrow morning and we'll go over it when you get here."

"Can't we do this over the phone, Taylor?"

"That won't be possible," he replied. "I'll see you tomorrow."

Taylor had hoped that it wouldn't be necessary to take the action that was now required, but Jack Garrett left him no choice, and though James Stanley had sided with them on this issue, Taylor couldn't trust him to go the distance. Stanley was still determined to be an adverse opinion and they had nothing else to use on him.

* * *

Bob Powell arrived in Dallas shortly before noon and was at the Plaza by eleven thirty. Taylor and Dan Spearman met him.

"Did I misunderstand you? I thought you said Jack Garrett wasn't our problem any more," Taylor said, emitting sarcasm.

"He assured me that he was with us," Bob replied.

"Well, I guess we know that isn't the case, now is it?"

Bob assumed no response was required.

"Come to find out, Jack has more significant problems than we first thought," Taylor continued.

"What are you talking about?"

"The tape that was released. It wasn't the whole story. There was a portion that was edited out for the media, and we have it."

"I don't follow you."

"I want you to see something." Taylor removed the disc from its case and placed it into his laptop. He played the video that Dan had acquired from his source, as Bob watched in disbelief.

When it was over, Bob was staring at the blank screen of Taylor's laptop. "What in the hell is going on here?"

"Jack is obviously not well, and I think his actions in the Whisenhunt case are proof that he's still not thinking clearly." Taylor studied Bob closely.

"What I want to know is how the hell the sex tape went public and this ended up in our hands." Bob stammered.

"The original tape that was released was sent to the media by an unknown individual," Taylor began. "We have no idea who she originally sent it to, but after it made its rounds, she began farming out this release. She'd contacted all the major national markets to see where the bidding would lead. Dan's source in Atlanta led us to her, and we were the highest bidder."

"How much did you pay for it?" Bob was still confused as to how this tape was in their possession.

"That's not the issue. We bought it to protect Jack from the fallout of its publication because we already knew, as you assured us, that he was an ally. You would certainly agree that we cannot afford to lose him, would you not?"

"I thought he was solidly with us and told you as much."

"Well, if that tape went public, and you know as well as I do that the national media would eat it up, then Jack would be done. But he has given us reason for concern."

"What exactly are you saying?" Bob saw where this was headed.

"I don't think he really understood the gravity of our situation in these cases, Bob, and it's your job to ensure that he does."

"You want me to go to him with this?"

"If he needs help for his problem, maybe you can assist. But we have a massive litigation crisis in the making. Your job is to make sure that our money is well spent. If you can't do it, I'm sure we can find someone who can." The tone of Taylor's voice assured Bob that it was not just an empty threat. Bob knew there were a number of former judges who would gladly take over his position. He was also mindful that he still needed an income source, and felt naked standing there with no contingency plan.

"This sounds like blackmail to me"

"I think that word is a bit harsh, Bob, but what would you call it if CNN got hold of it? Just a news story? The way I see it, you can help your friend and your career at the same time. Where's the down side of that?"

Taylor had a point. "What do you want me to do?"

"Get in touch with him and do what you do best, just don't fuck it up this time." Taylor gave a slight grin, suggesting he was kidding, although Bob wasn't sure if that was the case. "Call me after you meet and let me know how it went."

"I'll be in touch." Bob left the Plaza and was back at home in four hours. He had no idea how to approach Jack about this, but he was a professional, and he would find a way to help his friend and himself.

* * *

Jack felt invigorated. His life-changing decision had started paying dividends, and it showed first in his mood. Sharon noticed, too, that he had become happier, taking his staff to lunch regularly, and being significantly more talkative. He asked her out for dinner on two more occasions, one of which she was unable to make, but he seemed understanding. They both enjoyed their time spent together, and Jack had shown a renewed interest in handling his cases, spending some nights researching and reviewing briefs until long past his usual quitting time.

Their relationship had yet to become romantic, but Sharon began to envision that possibility, though she didn't know when, or if, it would ever happen. Jack thought about it too, and despite the fact that he had changed his mindset, he wasn't going to rush anything on Sharon. He was enjoying learning more about her and figured he would know when the time was right. She had become his best friend, the only person with whom he felt comfortable talking about life, and he reveled in the knowledge that there could be someone other than Stephanie who could make him feel that way.

* * *

Jack was in his office reviewing a brief submitted in a capital murder conviction when Bob Powell called.

"Jack, how are you, my friend?"

"Never better, Bob, and you?"

"I suppose I'll do. I wonder if I might have some of your time; there's something I need to discuss with you."

"Is this about the Whisenhunt case, Bob? I can only assume that's the basis of this call."

"To a degree. I just need to sit down with you for a bit."

"You have to understand that, like you, I base my rulings on the law and facts as I determine them to be. I respect that you may not have liked my position, but still the writ passed through, and who knows what will happen at the trial." Jack usually didn't provide an explanation to anyone about a ruling, but he figured he owed Bob at least that much.

"It's not as simple as that, my friend. Can I come down this weekend, if you have some time? I promise I won't take too long."

"Will Saturday afternoon work for you, say three-thirty? I'll pick up your favorite cognac."

"Three-thirty is fine with me. Don't worry about the cognac – I'll have to get back home anyway."

"Fair enough, I'll see you this weekend."

* * *

Bob arrived at Jack's house in Mt. Meigs at the appointed time, to find Jack sitting on his front porch in a wooden rocking chair, sipping on a glass of chardonnay. It was a warm day for February, even in Montgomery, as the temperature had reached seventy degrees, not unheard of, but mild nonetheless.

Garrett welcomed him and suggested that they enjoy the nice day and sit outside. As there were no neighbors for a mile or so, Bob didn't see the harm in discussing this with Jack in the open air.

After some small talk about the weather, Jack finally initiated the conversation, "About the Whisenhunt case…"

Bob interrupted him, "Jack, this isn't just about the case. Are you feeling all right?" Bob was subdued.

"I'm great, I told you that on the phone. What's going on?"

"I'm just concerned about you, Jack."

"I rule against your interests on a writ and you come down to tell me you're concerned about me. You're not making any sense at all now."

Bob thought this would be easier than it was turning out to be; he couldn't think of any other way to broach the subject other than to just dive in. "Jack, there are some things floating around about you, and I don't think you're being totally honest with me," he finally said, his heart beginning to race.

"Floating around? What in the hell are you talking about?"

"The tape that was released to the media…that wasn't the whole story and I think you know it." Bob was getting more nervous by the minute.

"I've told you before; I don't remember a thing about that night. And just so that we are on the same page here, what, exactly, is the 'whole story'?"

"The complete tape of that night…you are on video using cocaine, Jack. And you tell me you just don't remember something like that. I'm worried about you."

Bob's words almost knocked the breath out of him. "You're full of shit," Jack snapped.

"I've seen the video, Jack."

"You've what? How in the hell have you seen anything?"

Bob proceeded to tell him about the fact that whoever had the tape originally was trying to sell it to the media, and that Insure Pro had been tipped off and got it themselves to protect him from its publication. They were only trying to help him.

Jack sat silently, analyzing the situation. After several moments he said, "Now explain to me how in the hell a political action committee has obtained a copy of this so-called tape."

For the first time, Bob realized that Jack didn't know who his employer really was. "What did you think, Jack? I don't have anything to do with any political action committees. I mean we contribute to them, of course, but I don't work for them."

"If you're not a lobbyist for Insure PAC, then what exactly are you doing?"

"I assumed you knew. I'm the Judicial Liaison at Insure Pro."

Jack took several deep breaths, staring Bob down; his confusion was turning to anger now. "So I rule against your employer on this case, and all of a sudden here you are to blackmail me with a tape that you supposedly bought from some unnamed source? I think you know the so-called source, Bob."

"I swear to God, I have no idea who's behind this, but we certainly wouldn't have wanted the media to get it."

It was all coming together now. Jack had no idea exactly who was behind this, but he had a good idea what was happening. All he needed was the identity of the woman. Jack believed that Powell had no idea where this came from; he was simply the go-between. "Who sent you to see me?" Jack asked.

"What difference does it make?"

"You are going to tell me who sent you right fucking now, or I'm calling the police and having you arrested for blackmail." Bob had never seen him so angry. If he was bluffing, Bob certainly couldn't tell.

"Taylor Franklin, he's the Vice President and General Counsel at Insure Pro. I report to him."

"You look me in the eyes and tell me you really have no idea how any of this came to be." Jack stared at him.

"With God as my witness, Jack, I'm just the messenger here."

"Well then, messenger, I have a message for you. I don't have a drug problem, I never have and I never will. But I am going to get to the bottom of this, and you are going to help me." Jack explained what happened after the night in Atlanta, as Bob sat on his front porch, taking it all in.

Jack had no memory whatsoever of the events of that Friday night at the Ritz Carlton. He woke in his own room the following morning with a headache unlike any he had ever had before. He felt so bad that he was unable to attend the conference that day, and the sign in sheet would verify his absence. When he finally felt he was able to drive, he left Atlanta and headed straight home. By the time he got back, he still felt awful, so he called his personal physician and asked if he would see him, even though his office was closed on Saturday. Being a friend, his doctor agreed to see him on his off day. Jack explained his amnesia of the night before, his splitting headache and what other details he could provide. Dr. Echols ran some tests on him but they wouldn't be available until Monday. He told him to go home and rest, gave him some pain medicine for his headache and instructed him to call if his symptoms worsened.

By Sunday he was feeling better. Dr. Echols called him Monday afternoon to inform him of the test results. He had trace amounts of gamma-hydroxybutyrate, GHB, in his system. Jack had never heard of GHB before. The drug was known on the street under multiple names, but was most common in the dance and rave clubs. Most people recognized it by its name used in the media, the date rape drug. GHB is colorless, odorless and, for the most part, tasteless. It came in powder, pill or liquid form, but when used unknowingly, the liquid form was the easiest to

179

disguise. Its effects differed from one individual to another, and depended on the amount ingested, but intoxication, increased sex drive, drowsiness and amnesia were common. High doses could be, and in some cases were proven to be, fatal.

Dr. Echols informed him that he was likely experiencing anterograde amnesia, an inability to remember events that occurred while under the influence of the drug. It was similar to the drugs that were given before outpatient procedures such as colonoscopies, epidural blocks, and the like; the patient, although conscious, would have no memory of the procedure. The problem in using GHB for medical procedures was that it had severe and potentially deadly side effects, whereas other medications had proven reasonably safe.

When Jack got home, he realized that several hundred dollars was missing from his wallet, so after Dr. Echols told him about the test results, he assumed that he had been robbed by the woman he met – until the tape surfaced in the media. Once it was out, he revised his assessment, but there was no way he could figure out who was behind the matter.

Even so, he still assumed that the woman had simply tried to make some extra cash by disseminating the tape, so, as far as he was concerned, it was over. The JIC had cleared him, and life kept going.

"Then here you come with this," Jack said, "Whatever is going on is not the work of some random woman I met in the lounge at the Ritz Carlton. I could let it go if that had been the case, but here you are with allegations of my having a cocaine addiction. If it looks like shit and smells like shit, well, what do you think it is, Bob?"

Bob didn't know what to say. His nervousness blossomed into a severe case of anxiety, as he tried to process the sequence of events that Jack had outlined. There was no way his employer had been behind such a plot. Though he disliked Taylor from the beginning, he couldn't have been capable of such conduct. "I don't know what to say," was all he came up with.

"Then you will help me get to the bottom of this?"

"I'll talk with Taylor. There has to be an explanation."

"There is an explanation, Bob, and if you, or your employer, make this public, I'm holding you personally responsible. Quite frankly, I've had enough." Jack's new outlook apparently affected all aspects of his life, and he felt stronger than he had since he was twenty.

"Please understand, I have no idea why this happened. You are my friend, whether you believe that now or not, that's up to you, but I'll do my best to help you."

"I want to believe you, Bob, I really do, but actions speak louder than words." Jack set his glass down on the wooden floor. "If you don't mind, I would like to enjoy the rest of this beautiful day." He rose from his rocking chair and opened the door, leaving Bob alone.

As he drove off, Bob was still trying to convince himself that Taylor Franklin and Insure Pro had nothing to do with this mess, and he knew that they would reassure him of the same when he got back.

* * *

Jack spent the rest of the afternoon steaming over the fact that someone, or something, had gone to such lengths to ruin him. Having worked in public service for the last decade, making substantially less than he had previously made in private practice, he thought that he deserved better. The more he pondered the situation, the more questions came. Bob might be able to help him, but his career alone could be hanging in the balance. Jack's gut told him that Bob wasn't involved at the deepest level, that he was, in fact, a messenger. And if he was a messenger, the message was clearly being sent by Insure Pro.

There was only one thing left to do. He called Ray.

Raymond Carlisle had been a special agent with the FBI for twenty-five years. Ray graduated from law school with Jack, before spending two years obtaining his masters in business. He had always wanted to work for the FBI, but when he applied out of undergrad, he was informed that the Bureau was more interested in candidates who had bilingual capabilities, or law degrees, presumably to weed out those who simply thought it to be a glamorous profession. From what Ray had learned, their thinking was on point. If a potential agent had graduated from law school and still was willing to forego the higher salaries in the legal arena in order to go to the Bureau, he was serious.

Ray had been assigned to various field offices throughout the states, doing stints in Wyoming, Kansas and Michigan. When his seniority reached the point that he could request his own destination, he opted to return home. He was born and raised in Montgomery, attending Auburn University before his acceptance to law school at the University of Alabama. He loved the South and couldn't have been happier to return to his hometown for the remainder of his career.

Jack and Ray had been close in law school, more so as drinking buddies than anything else. They kept in touch periodically after graduation, usually when boredom set in, and one or the other was in need of reminiscing. When Ray got his reassignment to Montgomery, he called Jack and the two met for dinner and drinks. They had gone their separate ways in life, as they determined that evening, but vowed they would try to stay in touch more often. As it happened, they both fell back into their same routines.

Ray was surprised to hear from his old buddy. "Well, well, Mr. Chief Justice, it's been some time," Ray said.

"Indeed it has. How have things been in the world of organized crime and intrigue?" Jack laughed, knowing that such matters may have existed in some field offices, but certainly not in Montgomery, Alabama.

"Oh yes, the Hatfield and McCoy crime families are keeping very busy these days," Ray shot back. "How's the world been treating you?"

"Fairly well, I suppose." Jack engaged in some small talk to break the ice with his old friend for a while, as he didn't want to jump into his situation too quickly. Before long, he ran out of ways to avoid the reason for his call. "I have a little problem that you may be able to help me with. Have you got a minute?"

"For you, Mr. Chief Justice, I've got two."

* * *

Bob Powell called Taylor Franklin at his home. "I need to come to Dallas. When can you get Rick to pick me up?"

"What happened with Garrett?" Taylor replied.

"I said I need to come to Dallas – today. We need to talk."

"Is there a problem?"

"I'm not talking on the phone about this; when can Rick get here?"

Taylor put him on hold, not to call Rick, but just for the principle of it, then finally said, "He can pick you up first thing in the morning. Seven."

"Fine, I'll see you tomorrow."

Bob was at the Plaza before ten the following morning, explaining to Taylor the series of events that Jack Garrett had set forth two days ago. Before he was half way through his recitation, Taylor stopped him to get Dan Spearman to join them. Taylor and Dan listened as Bob told them everything that the chief justice had relayed to him about the night in Atlanta and, specifically, the days that followed. Taylor seemed amused at Jack's accusations that they had been involved in the matter. Dan sat stone-faced, acting his usual self.

"You need to tell me what the hell is going on here," Bob said to Taylor after he finished his briefing.

"I've already told you what happened. We got word of the existence of the video, we bought it so that it didn't hit the airwaves, and we are going to use it to our advantage – are you missing something?"

"So it is blackmail, then?"

"Come on, Bob, we didn't commission this thing; we just happened upon it. We are simply using information we gained legally, and if Garrett would rather we release it to the media, I'll be happy to do so. Just say the word."

"Then how did you get it?" Bob asked

"Dan had a source in Atlanta who turned us on to it. I've told you that more than once."

"Who is it?" Bob turned to Spearman.

"With all due respect, Your Honor, my source prefers to remain anonymous."

"Jack is sure that we are behind this, and I don't think he's going to let it go at supposition," Bob said, redirecting his remarks to Taylor.

"Well, we didn't do anything here, Bob. That much I know. I presume he didn't give you anything that suggests otherwise?"

"No, he didn't, but something is going to come out of this. He's not going to let this rest."

"If Jack calls you, just tell him what I've told you, because that's the truth, and keep me up to date. Don't worry, everything will be just fine."

Bob got just what he wanted. He knew that they were not responsible for what had happened. He had pressed Taylor as hard as he could for any semblance of an admission. He was adept at determining whether someone was lying, and he was as certain as he could be that Taylor was most definitely telling the truth. While Jack may have been the victim of unfortunate circumstances, his employer was not to blame for them.

* * *

Ray listened with interest to Jack's version of the events surrounding his night with the stranger in Atlanta and the consequences that followed. "Have you got any evidence at all that suggests that this company was involved?" Ray asked.

"They're using it in an attempt to persuade my decision in pending litigation, what else do you need?"

"But that litigation hasn't even ended yet; they might actually win, you know."

"That's not the point, Ray."

"I understand, but if they legally gained possession of the video and they haven't expressly asked that you do or don't do something in exchange for having it remain undisclosed, there is no crime. You should know that, Jack."

"All I know is something is happening here that doesn't pass the smell test."

"I want to help you, and I will. Just give me something to work with. Call me any time, Jack."

Jack understood his position. He wasn't going to let this go. He'd get something, anything, for Ray to go on.

* * *

As soon as Bob left the Plaza, Taylor asked Dan to join him for lunch. Though he played Bob's dissertation off at the time, he was concerned about what he'd said and he wanted to know if Dan had left out any details.

184

He questioned Dan about his source, an entity still unknown to Taylor by his own choice, asking whether Dan had gained any information he needed to know. Dan assured him that he was merely informed about the tape, brought it to Taylor's attention, and that was it.

"I trust you just as I always have, Dan," Taylor said. "Get in touch with your source and make sure we haven't been misled on anything."

"I'll make sure everything is taken care of," Dan replied.

They finished their meal, and the two went on their way.

When Dan arrived home, he had work to do. The next several days were going to be hectic.

* * *

Cara Patterson was still asleep when the phone rang.

"Cara, Ron Sullivan here. How are you?"

"Tired, what's up?"

"I may be interested in retaining your services again and was wondering if I might be able to set up a meeting. Will you be available in the next couple of days?"

"Um, yeah, I guess." She was slightly groggy, having only been asleep for three hours. "Maybe tomorrow?"

"Oh, I won't be in town until this weekend…how about I call you Saturday morning?"

"Can we make it in the afternoon? I'm not an early bird."

"Sure, baby, I'll call after three. We can meet that night."

"I have to work that night, sugar."

"Call Kip and take the day off. Tell him you're sick or something – I promise I'll make it worth your while."

"I'm not working at the club, baby – I'll just cancel my appointments."

"You're a sweetheart, talk to you soon."

Ron had two days to get to Atlanta to meet Cara and it was a twelve-hour drive if traffic cooperated.

185

TWENTY

Bob had just walked in from mowing the lawn when Jack called. "What have you found out?" Jack asked, after a brief greeting.

"It's just like I told you, Jack. The company got the lead from a source."

"Whose source?"

"Look, I don't know who it is. You've got to believe me here, buddy. Insure Pro is not behind this."

"If that's the case, will you do me a favor then?"

"I told you I would help you any way I can."

"Well, I've got a friend in the Montgomery bureau. I'm sure you wouldn't mind telling him anything you can that might be of assistance?"

"You've got the FBI involved – for Christ's sake, Jack, are you going insane?"

"Will you talk with him or not?"

"Are you accusing me of something here?"

"I'm not accusing you of anything; I'm holding you to your word."

"All I can do is tell him exactly what I've told you."

"Then you'll talk to him?"

"If that will make you feel better, sure."

Jack told Bob that Ray Carlisle would be contacting him in the near future, and thanked him for his willingness to help. An apology was thrown in for good measure, since Jack knew that Ray hadn't agreed to begin any investigation, let alone start interrogating people.

Bob didn't want to, but he had no choice, so he called Taylor to tell him that Jack had involved the FBI.

* * *

Ron Sullivan drove throughout the night, non-stop, to get to Atlanta. He used his driving time for reflection. The farm where he grew up was a distant memory now. He knew from an early age that country life wasn't for him. An abusive father and a mother who turned her head to the constant beatings didn't help matters. He took the first opportunity that presented itself to get the hell out. The army provided the outlet for the anger that his father had instilled in him. Even better, it was all legal. Special forces training combined with the later opening for a position on a strike force team meant a perfect fit for him. Most of the missions he participated in during his service were never officially sanctioned. He became a part of a team that did things the average citizen didn't want to think about. Things that, nevertheless, often needed to be done. *One man's atrocity was another's salvation.*

After his time in the service, success was bound to come his way. He was sure of it. It simply wasn't happening as fast as he imagined it would.

Taylor had given him this opportunity. He wasn't going to blow it. Ron Sullivan was a hero, he always had been…always would be.

He was totally spent when he arrived and checked into a room at the Motel 6 downtown. The meeting with Cara was not until the following evening, so he had time to get some rest. As he settled in, he ate a sandwich he had packed before he left then turned on the television until he fell asleep. It would prove to be a restless night for him.

When he awoke the following day, he proceeded with his usual routine of exercise and a healthy breakfast. When the time came, he made the call to Cara Patterson. There was no answer.

He called several times over the next few hours, but still nothing. He finally decided to call Kip. Kip was surprised to receive the call from his buddy, and started in right away with trying to set up a party for the two.

"I really don't have the time for it on this trip," Ron said. "I need to get in touch with Cara; do you know where she is?"

"Wow, you must have really enjoyed her last time!" Kip chuckled.

"Something like that. Do you know where she is?" he asked again.

"Yeah, she called me yesterday and told me that her mom had passed away. According to her, her mother was the only family she really had – sad story to be honest with you. Anyway, she had to go to Illinois for final arrangements and the funeral. She called me and said that if you were to call, she'd be back in town mid-week, and she sent her apologies, but she said she didn't have a number for you."

"Do you have any way to get in touch with her now?"

"She gave me the number at the hotel she's at." Kip gave him the phone number at the LaQuinta Inn in Champaign, and Ron quickly ended the call, thanking him. He wasn't able to reach Cara until later that evening, past the time of the scheduled appointment.

Ron extended his sympathies for her loss and inquired as to when she could get back to Atlanta, as he had a limited amount of time in town. The funeral was scheduled for Tuesday, and she would return as soon as the service was over. If he could wait around until then, she'd be back in Atlanta by nine or so that night. He was pissed off at her having ditched the meeting, but he knew she had no way to contact him, by his choice, and he would have to wait it out.

He called Taylor and told him that he was going to need a couple of extra days off for personal reasons.

Taylor granted the request.

* * *

Taylor's amusement at the Garrett situation faded upon hearing the news that he had an FBI agent investigating. His first thought was that Jack Garrett was losing it – he obviously had a closet drug problem and now it was leading to paranoia. Surely, if some agent had actually been notified, he would be able to see through this madness.

"Have you been contacted?" Taylor asked Bob.

"Not yet, but like I said, he's not letting it go, and I don't think he's making it up."

"Don't you think this is getting a bit ridiculous?"

"I don't know what to think any more, but you have to admit that there are a lot of questions that no one can seem to answer."

"Well, if someone does contact you, you know as much as I do, so cooperate with him, there's no need to get the feds on our ass."

Taylor and Bob had both had about as much of Jack Garrett as they could take for one day, and they agreed that Bob would simply do as requested by Jack, keeping his employer notified of the results, of course.

Taylor called Dan on his cell phone, passing along the information Powell had provided. "I don't know what Garrett is up to here, but he's got Bob sitting on the edge. Have you heard any new info?"

"Not as of yet. I'm out of town for a couple of days, but when I get back I'll check and see if anything is out there," Dan replied.

"I just don't know about Bob...he's really upset about the whole thing, and I think Jack's got his ear. If anyone even thinks that we are somehow involved, our reputation is going to suffer greatly."

Dan assured him that he had everything under control; the source in Atlanta had assured him that they were exculpated entirely from the incident that had almost brought Jack down.

* * *

Persistence finally paid off for Jack. He was being relentless on Ray to at least stoke the fire for him a bit to see if he could get someone at Insure Pro to budge with some information that could shed light on the case. After a week of constant phone calls from Jack, Ray figured that making a phone call or two couldn't hurt anything, and he hoped that appeasing Jack might get him off his back. Jack had suggested that Ray review a copy of the tape, which his lawyer still had from the incident. Maybe he could use something to identify that woman. She could have been in some of their databases, she could be found, and she would be able to tell him who did this.

Jack was grasping again, but he thought that Bob might flip on his employer if enough heat was put on him. Bob had to know more than he was acknowledging, and Ray knew ways to make people open up. His review of the tape proved useless, though he didn't say as much to Jack. The woman referred to herself as Jill.

Most women in her presumed profession used fake names. There was nothing in the tape that led to an identity, and a cursory review of criminal indexes revealed nothing. Ray had one last call to make.

Then hopefully he would be finished with things and Jack would move on. Ray called Bob Powell at his house, with Jack having provided his contact number. It was time for him to put on his show. "Mr. Powell, this is Ray Carlisle. I'm a special agent with the FBI; Jack Garrett said you would be expecting my call."

Though Bob figured that Jack was going to pursue things, he didn't actually believe that the FBI would get involved, and he was caught off guard when Ray announced himself. "Yes sir, Agent Carlisle, what can I do for you?" Ray detected the nervousness in Bob's voice.

"I would appreciate a couple of minutes of your time, if you don't mind?"

"Yes sir, I would be happy to meet with you tomorrow if you like. Any place in particular you have in mind?" His voice cracked.

"I'll be in Birmingham tomorrow on another matter, so tell me what's most convenient for you."

"You can come here if you like."

"Thank you for your cooperation. Mr. Powell, I'll call you around noon and meet you shortly thereafter."

* * *

Ray arrived at Bob's house after two in the afternoon, a tactic employed simply to make a suspect wait longer than expected so he could wear himself down dreading the encounter, over-thinking the issues.

Bob led him into the living room and offered him a drink, which he politely refused. They sat in opposite chairs as Ray began the inquiry. "Thank you again for allowing me to visit you, sir. I assure you it shouldn't take long." Ray appreciated that Bob Powell was nervous about the meeting and, to a degree, felt sorry for him that he was about to be accused of being a traitor to his friend, but he'd done this many times before and he held no allegiances to Bob or his company.

Ray told Bob about all the information that they had obtained during their investigation thus far into the Garrett file. He had brought a file with him that was filled with documents, only one of which actually pertained to Jack Garrett - his notes from his conversation with Jack. The rest of the file involved another case he was working on at the time.

Ray advised Powell that the Bureau had located the woman who was present with Jack Garrett in the hotel that evening and that she had provided a statement. The woman admitted to having been hired to lure the chief justice into a compromising position and to record his actions. She had been paid in cash for her work and, although she was unable to recall the name of the person who hired her, she gave a description of the man. She had been told little as to why these people wanted this to happen, other than that this was the chief justice of a court and the company he worked for wanted to ensure his loyalty. They were actively working on identifying the agent who hired her, and the woman was cooperating.

Bob's company was the only one to have possession of the tape and that was under the most suspicious of circumstances. Ray wanted the name of the person they allegedly bought it from, which Bob denied any knowledge of. Ray insisted that, with them being the only group seeking to benefit from the tape, it was clear to the Bureau that it had been of their design, and it was only a matter of time before they would prove it.

Everything Ray told Bob Powell was a lie. Another standard technique in interrogation was simply to make up the facts as you see fit. Whether they were true or not was of no consequence, because if it put enough fright in the suspect, he'd usually confess or, at a minimum, provide additional details or facts that would lead the investigation forward. Not only was everything Ray had told Bob false, it was also untrue that the FBI was going to do anything at all on this case. When he left Bob Powell's house he was finished with this and he'd tell Jack accordingly.

Bob was terrified when he heard what had happened in the investigation. Though Ray never intimated that he had specific facts or testimony implicating his employer, he was right about the circumstantial evidence . He assured Ray that he was in no

191

way involved in the situation and that his superiors had likewise denied any role. If someone in the company had been involved, it wasn't anyone he knew. He agreed that he would ask more questions and would assist Ray in any way he could with the ongoing investigation.

When Ray felt like he'd done all he could do for his old friend, he thanked Bob and lied to him one last time, telling him he would call him later when he needed more information. He had had enough of wasting his time on this, and he'd completed what he promised Jack he would do. Ray called Jack and told him the truth – there was nothing he got from Bob Powell that was of any help. He was sorry, but it was time for Jack to put this behind him.

As soon as Ray left, Bob called Taylor in a panic. The FBI had just left his house and they were deep into an investigation of the company, with evidence implicating them in an effort to blackmail the chief justice. They had the woman, and she was talking. They were hot on the trail. Taylor listened carefully to Bob's story before assuring him again that neither he, nor the company, was involved, and telling him he would cooperate to the fullest extent. Nothing he said made Bob feel any better, and as he hung up, Bob felt sick to his stomach, again.

Taylor had just talked to Dan several hours before, giving him some extra time off. He called him back within ten minutes of Bob Powell's call, and relayed the information that was now in the mix. Dan expressed some concern, but told Taylor that he, too, was sure the company had no reason to worry.

When their call was over, Dan was livid. Though he suppressed his true emotions to Taylor moments ago, he was now boiling over with them. *The fucking bitch is cooperating? Trying to make even more money. Fucking whore.*

TWENTY-ONE

Ron Sullivan called Cara every fifteen minutes, beginning at eight on the evening she was to return. Her cell phone was either off or she wasn't answering it, and he became angrier every time he got no response. She answered the phone on what felt like the fiftieth time he called.

"I'm so sorry if I've caused you any inconvenience, I hope you understand."

"You don't need to apologize," he interrupted. "I understand. I do need to meet with you tonight though."

"Of course you can, sweetie, when and where?"

"How about I pick you up, and we can discuss it over a drive?"

"Works for me. Can you give me an hour to settle in?"

Ron agreed to let her get her things unpacked and got directions to her apartment. It would be a forty-five minute drive, so he packed his things and checked out of the hotel before heading north.

Cara lived in an upscale apartment complex north of Atlanta in Marietta. It was home to many middle-class professionals who still could not afford the exorbitant house prices in the residential neighborhoods. The developer actually went to great lengths to give the complex a feel of a neighborhood, keeping many of the trees that existed on the property, and making a park and picnic area in the middle of the grounds. Autumn Gardens was a gated apartment living community, although the gates that secured the entrance had been out of service for more than a year and a half. Cara had advised Ron that no one would be present in the security guard's pavilion posted at the entrance to the complex, and he drove straight in and to her building. He called when he arrived at the gate to let her know he was there.

She was walking down the steps from her second floor unit when he pulled into the parking lot. He stopped in front of her building, got out of the car and opened her door, escorting her into his rented Ford Expedition. As he pulled out of the community, she asked about the new job, "So what is it that you need me to do for you now, baby?"

"There's a new case I need to discuss, but first I need to get some details about your last one if you don't mind, just some things that I forgot to ask about when everything was over."

"Sure, whatcha want?"

Ron drove toward the interstate, getting on I-85 south, heading into downtown Atlanta. As he merged into traffic he said, "Tell me how you went about it with the gentleman at the Ritz; I want the specific details." He wanted none of it, but he needed some time.

Cara began telling him about the night with Jack Garrett, going through the motions of the two, from when they first met in the lounge and on through the evening in her room. He continued driving into town, exiting the interstate in an industrial area several miles north of downtown Atlanta, listening occasionally to her story. She seemed more interested in hearing herself talk than paying attention to where they were going, until he finally pulled into a self-storage facility located four miles off the interstate. "What are we doing here?" she finally asked.

"The files pertaining to the new case are here, and I haven't had an opportunity to get to them yet." She accepted the explanation, as he pulled behind one of the units and parked the car. There were no other cars in sight, and the facility had no exterior lighting, making it almost pitch black, except for the moonlight. He turned on the interior lights in the Expedition and turned to face her, "Before I get into the new case, I need to ask some specific questions about your last one."

"Fire away," she replied.

"How exactly was it that you were able to get him into the coke?"

"I had some to party with and suggested that he try it, told him it'd make sex even better," she said.

"Are you saying you just asked him to do some coke and he agreed?"

"Basically, yeah."

"You didn't have any help in convincing him?"

"What are you getting at?" she asked.

"You know who he is now, obviously, but you probably don't know that he later found out what opened his inhibitions, and I think you know what I'm talking about. Now, do you have anything else to add about what happened?"

"So I used some cherry ecstasy, no harm no foul."

He assumed that she would come clean on using GHB to disarm Jack Garrett; the hard part was yet to come. "Who have you talked to about that night?"

"Other than you and the stations I contacted to sell the tape, no one."

"Tell me about Ray Carlisle."

"I've never heard of Ray Carlisle." Cara was nervous. She didn't know where Ron was going with this line of questioning, and Ron was growing impatient with her.

"Never heard of him?"

"I swear to God, Ron, I have never heard that name before." She was telling the truth, but Ron knew differently.

"So you have no idea why Ray would have told us that he has met with you and that you have been working with the FBI to cooperate in an investigation?"

Cara was speechless. She had never heard of Ray Carlisle before, never heard about an FBI investigation, never. *Why is the FBI involved? Why is Ron accusing me of something? What is he accusing me of? Where are we? Who is Ron anyway?* Her mind was racing and her heart was pounding and a bead of sweat began to fall from her brow as she evaluated the situation.

Ron took notice of her nervousness and the sweat was a dead giveaway.

"Can you take me home, please?"

"You are willing to walk out on a job paying more than the first one, Cara?" He quickly changed the subject in hopes that she didn't panic. He had to improvise and he was quite good at it. "You haven't talked with the FBI then?"

"Never."

"And if they were to contact you, what would you do?"

"I'd tell them to fuck off; it's my business if I record my sex life, not theirs."

Ron's demeanor changed; he had become subdued, almost calm now. "If you are going to work for me, I need to know that you are loyal. Are you loyal, Cara?"

"I am."

"Ray Carlisle doesn't exist anyway. I wanted to see what your reaction would be to an accusation being leveled against you – it may happen in this line of work, you know."

She wasn't sure she followed him, but although she was still nervous, he could tell that she had accepted his explanation and he wouldn't continue with the interrogation about Ray Carlisle anyway. She would continue to deny her involvement in the FBI's investigation because that's what she was instructed to do by Agent Carlisle. It would be pointless to hammer away at her, as he had what he needed. "I have a new job, if you're interested now?"

"I'm all ears," she responded, still a bit hesitant.

"It will pay two hundred grand, if you wish to consider it; otherwise, I'll take you home now."

The figure caught her attention immediately, and he knew it. "What do you want me to do?"

"My client needs dirt on the CEO of a major company that shall remain unnamed. He will be in town in three weeks for a two-week conference. He reportedly has an affection for the ladies, and has been known privately for having rather strange fetishes. It's all been rumor to this point, but if you can successfully get what we need, your pay will be wired to an account of your choosing."

Sliding back into her curiosity of their trip, Cara asked, "So what does that have to do with us coming to this storage place?"

"My client has kept the files on this man very private. They are here for your review and instructions if you wish to proceed, and I assumed it would be best if we got down here before it got too late."

"Let's see what you've got then, I need to get home soon."

Ron Sullivan had rented the storage unit the day of his arrival. Officially, cash had been paid by Mr.Sullivan for a one month, one term rental. Storage unit G-37 belonged to a ghost for the next thirty days – Ron Sullivan from Seattle, Washington. He opened the car door, as did she, and they exited the vehicle. He went over to the padlock, pulled his key ring out and flipped through the several keys on it before finding the right one. He popped the lock open and removed it from the metal latch, sliding the latch open while holding onto the padlock, then slid his foot under the handle at the bottom of the door, pulling it up with his leg. As the door rolled up on its track, it gave way to total darkness inside. From the outside, nothing was identifiable in the blackened pit. Ron reached his hand inside the opened frame as Cara watched.

"Son of a bitch, the manager told me he'd have the lighting repaired by this afternoon. There should be a couple of storage boxes in the corner," he said to her as she was standing at his side, in front of the open unit. "I'll get my flashlight out of the trunk. If you don't mind, see if you can locate the boxes while I get us a light."

Cara moved slowly into the darkened storage unit, shuffling her feet so as not to trip over anything and holding her hands in front of her. The only sounds were of the traffic on the interstate, several miles away from the entrance to the unit. "I've got it," she finally heard from outside. Ron had apparently found the flashlight and they could get this over with.

"How about a little help then, I can't see shit in here, Ron." Cara noticed the glow of light on the pavement outside moving from the parked SUV toward the unit. As Ron rounded the corner, the flashlight was still focused on the ground at his feet. The brightness of the bulb contrasted against the blackness of the evening in such a manner that she couldn't focus on anything other than the light itself. "Shine it in here, I haven't found anything."

The beam was slowly raised from the ground, initially toward her feet, and proceeded up her body to her face. It momentarily blinded her as it hit her eyes. "God damn, Ron, get that fucking thing out of my face." Her left hand was cupped over her eyes as she stretched her right arm out to block the beam. "Quit being an asshole."

* * *

197

Over four hundred lawsuits were pending against Insure Pro in Baldwin County by early spring. Padgett & Keeler alone had filed at least one hundred fifty. That was the way things worked in south Alabama. Most of the small town lawyers who had managed to land a case such as this simply couldn't afford to prosecute it, but they wanted to keep a hand in the pot. Buck was widely known in the area, and his referral base was massive, consisting of practically every lawyer south of Montgomery who came upon a plaintiff's case that would prove costly.

He also picked up a number of referrals from out-of-state attorneys as well. In light of the fact that most of the damaged properties were vacation homes, owned by people primarily throughout the southeast, lawyers from several different states found Insure Pro cases coming in the doors. Buck was a member of several networking associations, the American Trial Lawyers Association being the largest and most popular, and a standard search of their database pointed many outside lawyers to Buck as the first choice. The referral agreements meant that Buck had to give a third of any fee generated to the referring lawyer, who undertook no actual work on the case, but it was standard in the industry, and without the referral Buck would have made nothing from the case.

Though he had many pending cases, most of them were still in the early stages, with discovery pending. The Whisenhunt case was still the benchmark case and would set the tone for future negotiations and trial strategy. He had wanted to file a class action, joining all the plaintiffs in a single case, but each homeowner's claim had factual differences that precluded the class action from being approved. Each case would be tried on its own, unless an agreement was later reached on some or all of the remaining claimants. Buck knew a victory in Whisenhunt would open the doors to substantial settlements in most of his other cases.

Buck scheduled a review of the Whisenhunt case with the associates, and Chief was called to attend as well. "Where do we stand on the pattern witnesses?" he asked Chief.

"I've been able to track down maybe ten or so that we've been able to talk to and obtain statements from. Most of the others who have begun rebuilding don't want to get involved."

198

"We do have the homeowner next door lined up, do we not?"

"We have Mr. Littleton, yes sir, and I believe we have a commitment from two others in the same neighborhood, but I'll have to check and see if we've reduced those to writing yet."

"Excellent work, Chief. Stay on the others and get affidavits as soon as possible. If I need to talk with any of them personally, let them know I'll be happy to do so."

Buck reviewed the remainder of their pre-trial preparations with his trial team, going over the expert opinions, proposed exhibits for use at trial, witness lists and the like. With less than two months until trial, it was time for the final push. He also called Steve Whisenhunt to schedule a meeting with him before trial to explain to his client what to expect in the process. He was starting to get excited about the trial, right on time.

* * *

Ray Carlisle called Jack several days after his meeting with Bob Powell to give him the news that he wasn't looking forward to receiving. "Jack, I've had a meeting with Bob, and as expected, he assures me that they were not involved in it."

"Surely there's something else you can do, Ray, there's got to be a way to get to the bottom line here," Jack replied.

"Like I said before, there is no evidence out there that connects them to the tape, outside of their having possession of it, and they have provided a reasonable explanation as to how that occurred."

"But they have intimated that they will use it against me. That doesn't give probable cause for further action?" Jack still wasn't letting it go.

"I didn't say it was the only explanation. I said it was a reasonable one, and they haven't demanded anything from you in exchange for keeping it private."

The light bulb went off for Jack Garrett, "That's not true, Ray. Bob said, and I quote, 'you certainly wouldn't want the media to get ahold of that tape'."

Ray showed some renewed interest, "Do you have him on tape, anything I can go on here?"

"No, he just said it when he came to me about the new information they supposedly had."

199

"Do you think you can get him to say it again? Because I assure you that if I call on him, he's not going to be as forthcoming as he might be with you." Ray said.

"I can try. How do you want me to go about it?"

"Just use your standard Dictaphone, call him up and see if you can get the admission. If what you are saying is true, and you can get him to own up to it, I might be able to convince someone to open a formal file."

Jack had found hope; all he had to do was confront Bob again. Bob was a man of his word for as long as Jack had known him, and there was no way that he would sit idly by and watch a fellow justice be humiliated, possibly lose his career, over such matters.

* * *

Jack called his friend later that evening from his house. Bob had been at home sick for the past several days, and Jack chatted with him to warm up the tone of the conversation, asking about Susan and the grandkids. When he finally had run out of small talk, he turned on the recorder. "Can I ask you something about this whole tape issue?"

"Why are you bringing this up again, Jack? I thought I made myself clear when we talked before."

"I guess I wasn't clear on a couple of things, and you said you'd help in any way I needed. Or were you just placating me?"

Bob sounded exasperated, "What is it, Jack?"

"Why did you come to me with the information about the drug allegations?"

"I told you before, I was concerned about you. If you were having a problem, I wanted to get you help," Bob replied.

"But you came right after I ruled against your employer on the writ of mandamus. The timing is quite a bit curious, isn't it?"

"We didn't get the tape until then, and I came to you as soon as we got it."

"And didn't you say that I certainly wouldn't want the media to get ahold of it? As I remember things, that's exactly what you said."

"I most certainly did not. What in the hell is wrong with you, Jack? I said 'we' wouldn't want that out, not 'you.'"

"You were using it as a threat and you know it! Don't try to backpedal now." Jack was getting louder, verging on losing control.

"I never threatened you in the least, sir, and I don't appreciate your accusations. Quite frankly, I'm not comfortable continuing this conversation."

"You said you would help me, you fucking liar!"

Bob Powell had had enough; he hung up on the chief justice without saying another word. He had not been spoken to in such a manner in his entire professional career, and he wasn't about to sit back and tolerate it now.

He immediately called Taylor and told him about the conversation.

"He's losing his mind, Bob. It must be his addiction," Taylor offered. "Where do you think he was headed?"

"First of all, I doubt seriously that he had a drug addiction. I believe this whole thing is just getting the better of him. But his tone was accusatory, as though he badly wanted me to agree with him." Bob answered. "I figure I'll let him calm down and call him back when he can be rational."

"I don't know if that's a good idea," Taylor said. "It seems like there's more to it."

"I can talk to him. I've known Jack for a long time and he just needs to unwind. I'll give him a day or so and try to put an end to this once and for all."

"Well, from now on, I am washing my hands of him," Taylor started. "I want you to report to Spearman with any new information you get. I've got a shitload of cases to work on, and we are getting ready for the Whisenhunt trial as well. Dan can handle anything that comes up, and I'll let him know you will be touching base with him."

Bob was somewhat relieved that he didn't have to keep going through Taylor on this issue, but he wasn't sure if Dan was the proper person to handle the matter either. "Are you sure that's best?"

"Dan is completely on top of this, he knows everything I do, and I'm tired of micromanaging you. Dan will update me on anything I need to know. Do you have anything else?"

Bob was insulted, and rightfully so. It was typical Taylor Franklin, and with that last jab, Bob resigned himself to report to Dan Spearman. "No, Taylor, I don't have anything else, but thank you for your time." Bob offered his best at sarcasm as he put the phone down.

He would wait a day or so before calling Jack.

* * *

The sound reverberated in his head for what seemed like an hour.

Cara Patterson dropped to the floor after Ron fired a single round from his Beretta M9 into her forehead. The .45 caliber slug ripped through her within microseconds of Ron's flashlight identifying the target. It had been louder than he would have thought, but he wrote it off to the metal walls of the storage unit that surrounded them on three sides. The sound exited the opened door, facing east, toward the interstate, and there were no residences or offices within several miles. No one could have identified the muffled shot by the time it had an opportunity to reach an ear.

Ron shined his light around the empty room, searching for the casing that had been deposited after the pistol discharged. He carefully picked up the casing and canvassed the floor to ensure that no other evidence had been left. When he was satisfied that he had cleaned the scene of any incriminating evidence, he returned to the Expedition and put on his latex surgical gloves.

He removed the new master lock from its packaging and placed the old lock on the passenger seat. He returned to the storage unit and carefully lowered the rolling door, installing the newly purchased lock on the latch. A final review of the area was completed, and within ten minutes he was back on I-85. Fifteen minutes after that he made the transition to I-20, heading westbound, straight toward Dallas.

Somewhere between Meridian and Jackson, Mississippi, the lock that had originally been on unit G37, the packaging for the new lock, various items from Cara's purse and the casing from the M9 were strewn about the interstate, approximately thirty miles apart from each other. Her purse found its way into a garbage dumpster outside a Burger King in Shreveport. By midday, Dan Spearman was back at home, having driven twelve hours straight, stopping only for gas.

* * *

Over the next few weeks, Cara Patterson was missed, but never missing. Kip tried to call her several times; when she continued to refuse to answer, he assumed that she had gone on her own, leaving him out of the mix to take all the fees her clients paid for herself. Clearly, she had amassed a client base that could support her. Since she had paid her rent three months in advance, the apartment manager had no reason to call. She had no real friends, other than her party friends, and they assumed she had left town, probably avoiding legal problems at home. Her clients thought the same, and none of them would go to the authorities to report that their prostitute wasn't returning their calls.

The duty manager at U Store It discovered the body when Ron Sullivan failed to renew his month-to-month lease. Following the facility's procedures, he cut the lock off unit G37 and was preparing to take possession of the contents to cover fees and penalties. The woman's body was all there was in the unit, no identification, no purse – nothing.

The local police were called and performed their investigation, while her body was removed to the county morgue, where no one came forward to identify it. The news of the unnamed woman's death at a storage facility aired for ten seconds on the local news – once. It never made its way out of Atlanta.

* * *

Spearman checked in with Taylor after a night's rest. His time off was appreciated and he wanted to thank Taylor again for allowing him to recharge.

Taylor asked him to come in for an update on Jack Garrett, as well as to get his monthly update on the Security Division's reports. Dan reviewed the appropriate documents that his staff made available each month first, so that he could provide his report. Most of the forms were for the last month's terminations and any reports of vandalism, destruction of property on the premises, and most often, allegations of employee theft. When Dan finished his update, Taylor jumped straight to Jack Garrett.

"I have informed Powell that he is to report straight to you with regard to the Garrett matter. I assume you have no problem with it?" Taylor began.

"No sir. May I ask what you want me to do?"

"Garrett has called Bob again, trying to pry more out of him. You are certain that we will have no problems from your source in Atlanta?"

"You asked me to handle this, sir, and I assure you that it has been taken care of," Dan replied. Is there anything you need me to do with respect to Powell?"

"He will simply update you; I don't want to be bothered with him anymore. You can advise me if anything new surfaces. Just handle him."

"Yes sir."

Dan knew the meeting was over when Taylor turned back to his computer, returning to his other work. He left Taylor's office and walked next door to his own to review the Garrett file again, making sure he had not missed anything. If he were in control of Bob Powell from now on, he would take control. That's what Taylor always wanted out of him.

* * *

Against Taylor's instructions, Bob called Jack several days after the chief justice's rambling call accusing him of being a traitor to the friendship. He knew that Jack had been under a tremendous amount of stress and he wanted to make sure he had calmed down; after all, Jack was still a necessary ally to his employer on the Court and Bob believed he not only could reassure Jack about the issue, but still keep him in their good graces.

"I hope you don't mind me calling, but I've thought a lot about our last conversation and I didn't like the way things were left," Bob said after Jack answered.

"I suppose I owe you an apology." Jack began," I had no right to speak to you the way I did." His honesty was apparent.

"I understand that you're going through an awful lot these days, Jack, and your apology is accepted."

"It's still no excuse. What is it you want, Bob?"

"I want to make sure you're all right, that you and I are all right."

"If you are asking whether I am giving up on finding out the true nature of this situation, then the answer is no. I intend to find out why this has happened and I truly don't care how long it takes. I'm not letting it run my world, but I have changed the way I look at things, the way I am going to live my life, and I'm doing it with no regrets whatsoever."

"I'm not following you. What do you mean you've changed? Personally, professionally, philosophically –?" Bob asked.

"In every way I can," Jack said. "I don't want to wake up one day wishing I had done something differently and know in my heart that I could have done it right the first time around." Jack repeated the Walter Broussard method that he had adopted as his own.

"Well, if there's anything I can do for you, I would hope that you would let me know," Bob said, still unsure as to what Jack meant.

"Since you ask, there is one thing you can do for me."

"Yes?"

"Give me the disc."

"What do you mean?" Bob asked.

"You said that Insure Pro is not behind this – had no idea how it came to be. You took it off the market to protect me from the ramifications of its going public, right?"

"Absolutely, like I said before."

"Then if you have no reason to hold it over my head, you should have no problem giving it to me so that we can both be assured that it remains private."

Jack's reasoning was unassailable. "I don't have it, Jack; I've also told you that."

"But your employer does, and if I am to believe that your intentions are as you state, you should be able to obtain it. Am I wrong?"

"Jack, I'm sorry this has happened, I really am, but..."

"There should be no buts," he interrupted. "As the saying goes, my friend, actions shall speak louder."

"I suppose you have a point. I will see what I can do," Bob finally said.

Jack thanked him for calling and apologized again for his actions during their last conversation. When the call ended he realized that he had forgotten to set his recorder. He hadn't expected Bob to call and got caught up in the moment of putting Bob on the spot about the tape. It was improvisation on his part, and he had come up with the perfect plan, with the exception of having real evidence to prove it had actually occurred.

* * *

Powell took a couple of days to consider the request that had been made by the chief justice. He knew that the company would use the evidence against Jack if they needed to, of that there was no question, just as they used anything they could to get an upper hand. There was no crime in that; it was politics, and it happened all the time. If they were involved in the planning or execution of it, that was a different matter – but they weren't. A case for blackmail had not been made – yet. He just didn't know if it would come down to it later.

Dan was in his office when Powell called in about Garrett. "I spoke with Jack yesterday and wanted to give Taylor an update."

"I'm listening," was all Dan said in response.

"Garrett seems to have calmed down, and I think he is still with us," Bob started, "but he did make a request."

"And what would that be, Bob?"

"He wants us to give him the disc."

"What did you say?"

"I didn't say much of anything, actually. I just told him I would get in touch with the company. But if we aren't going to make it public, is there any point in not handing it over? I mean, wouldn't we gain much more headway with him if we saved him from the publication?" Bob asked.

"And if we did decide to use it to our benefit, Bob?"

"For Christ's sake, hasn't this gone far enough? Look, just talk to Taylor for me, since he apparently has no interest in hearing from me directly."

"I will pass this on. In the meantime, I would suggest that you refrain from talking with Garrett any more. I'll be in touch."

After Dan Spearman had blown him off, as was becoming the case lately, Bob felt compelled to call Jack. It was a brief conversation, but he wanted Jack to know again that they were on his side, and he was working with the corporate office to try to get the tape released to him. Though he didn't say it to Jack, Bob had come to the conclusion that Jack was absolutely correct in his analysis, and, though Bob was in the business of lobbying judges for his employer, he only approved of it being done the traditional and legal way. This had gotten old, and it was wearing on him almost as much as on his friend.

* * *

It was time to upset Taylor Franklin again, something Dan didn't take any joy in, but which always resulted in Taylor's gaining more insight into the value that Dan provided to the company. He called Taylor and asked that he come to his office for an impromptu meeting.

"I told you that you were to handle Bob for now. What's the problem?" Taylor asked.

"I believe we may be heading for a problem."

"What kind of problem?"

"Bob has suggested that we turn over the disc to Garrett."

"This is a joke, right?"

"Far from it. He called me earlier and said that since we had no intention of using it, he assumed we could get more from Garrett by turning it over."

"We would be giving up any leverage we have on him if it was released. What do you think Garrett is going to do when these cases come up?" Taylor prodded.

"He's already ruled against us and, to be honest, I don't think Powell is shooting straight with us any more."

"What do you base that on?"

"Call it a hunch – but as you know, my hunches are usually correct." Dan answered.

"Are you concerned about Bob?"

"I believe we may be losing him, sir; he obviously isn't performing as he has in the past. Take the writ and the JIC matter – first he goes in and gets Garrett off the hook, adamantly assures us of his allegiance, and all of a sudden we have to rely

207

on a crossover vote to avoid a disaster. According to my information, Powell had nothing in any way to do with James Stanley switching sides, and it seems like he's becoming more interested in working for Jack than us. Shit, Taylor, he knows we need that material and he's still asking us to roll over."

"For the time being, monitor him closely. Don't let things get out of hand," Taylor said.

"As you wish." Taylor left Dan's office to get back into the case reviews that he had been working on for Hurricane Peter.

* * *

Garrett had given plenty of thought to his last conversation with Bob Powell, and he was encouraged that his friend might be standing on higher ground than he originally believed. There would be no better time than now to make the push, so he called Raymond Carlisle. He informed Ray that Powell had been receptive to the idea of turning the disc over to him, and had acknowledged that using it would, at a minimum, border on unethical, if not criminal, behavior. Jack thought Ray would be best suited to approach Powell from this point forward.

"Do you have any of these statements on tape?" Ray asked.

"I don't, but he's opened up to talking to me now and I think he's having a tough time with the whole situation."

"Let's look at the pros and cons, Jack. If we assume that they're not stupid enough to come out and demand a ruling from you in exchange for the information they have, which I don't think they would do, the only possible alternative would be to leak it to the outside. What results then?"

"I would assume that my career would be over. There would be no question that a formal investigation of me would begin, and from an election standpoint, I would never survive," Jack said.

"And if they simply hold it without demanding anything of you?" Ray asked.

"Then they've got me by the balls, if I go against them."

"Do you have any idea how you are going to feel when the case comes up, regardless of who may prevail?"

"I don't know any of the facts right now. I can tell you that they insured my home at the coast and paid my claim, so clearly there are factual differences in each case. But I can tell you that I will rule in accordance with the law and the facts as I determine them to be at the time. I just don't appreciate anyone trying to manhandle me."

"I guess I'll give Bob a call then," Ray decided.

"I may not have said it before, but if I have, then I'll say it again. I can't tell you how much what you're doing means to me."

* * *

Agent Carlisle called Bob at eight that evening, asking if he had a moment to talk about Jack Garrett.

"Yes sir, I suppose so."

"Jack told me you two have spoken again, and I want you to understand that I appreciate how hard this must be on you as well."

"I've been through easier times, yes."

"Bob, you would agree with me, would you not, that using this information against Jack would be against every notion of justice that the public should expect?"

"I've never said that anything was going to be used, sir."

"Then you would also agree with me that, if that be the case, it should be released to him or his attorneys?"

"I told Jack that I understood his reasoning on that point."

"From everything Jack has told me about you, it appears to me that you are an honest and genuine man. You have dedicated most of your life to the judiciary, and I hold a tremendous amount of respect for you for that, sir. When we look at this matter in its entirety, I think you know as well as I do that the right and just thing to do is to turn it over." Ray paused, waiting on a reply.

"I don't have possession of it though; I also told Jack that several times," Bob stepped in.

"Can you get it?" Ray asked.

"Do you mean will they hand it over to me?"

"I mean will they hand it over to you voluntarily, or do you think you could obtain it in any way?"

"I'm working under the assumption that they wouldn't be inclined to just give it to me," Bob answered.

"Then you would consider locating it and bringing it to me?" Ray was getting firmer in his tone.

"You're asking me to steal it from my employer? Do you realize what would happen to my career if that occurred?" Ray could tell he wasn't angry now; he was evaluating the request.

"I'm asking that you do what you know is just. If you're the man you seem to be, are you really doing what you love or are you just collecting a check? Can I ask you a personal question?"

"I suppose."

"Do you believe in God?"

"Most definitely. Why?"

"I firmly believe that when people do the righteous thing in difficult situations, God has a way of rewarding them, that though one door may close, he opens another. So many times I have seen people come out cleaner, in all aspects of their lives, when they follow Him." Ray was rolling now. "Do you believe in the Bible, Bob?"

"I read it regularly, yes."

"Then how could you not agree with what I'm saying?"

Bob fell silent for a while, and Ray was content to allow him to process the conversation. In his soul, Bob knew that Ray was right. His intuition had been leading him to the same conclusion, but fear had been standing in the way – fear of losing his job, fear of failure, fear of retribution. He was overcome with a sense of shame and embarrassment; he had become what he had despised for so many years as a judge.

After more than a minute of silence, Ray asked if he was still there.

"Give me time to figure out how to go about it, and give me your word that you will not say anything to Jack until I say so."

"You have my word, Mr. Powell. May God bless you." Ray put the phone down, impressed again at his abilities of persuasion. He would honor Bob's request and hoped he would be able to pull it off.

Bob contemplated how he could retrieve the disc from Insure Pro. It was not going to be an easy task, and he knew his career would soon come to an end. This would take some serious planning, and a lot of lying, but righteousness couldn't always be accomplished through complete honesty.

TWENTY-TWO

The Broussard method was lifting Jack to new heights. His workload had grown, at his request, and he was enjoying every minute of his role as a justice, save the capital murder cases that always caused him to pause over the finality of what his decision would mean to a human being. After his last conversation with Ray, he knew the best course would be to let the matter with Insure Pro go. He understood that it would work its way out the way God wanted. He had done everything he could do, and had placed far more on himself than he deserved in doing so. He trusted that Ray would see it to its natural end, for better or for worse, and he ultimately determined that he would accept the outcome of it with open arms. Even the loss of Buster was accepted as part of the plan, and considering that the dog had been a faithful companion for so many years and that his hip dysphasia had crippled him, his passing was almost welcomed. There was one thing left for him to do to accomplish his goals, so he called her.

Sharon had been to dinner with Jack on a number of occasions over the last several months, usually discussing cases, but there were times when they drifted into outside topics. She seemed to enjoy his company, and he most certainly did hers. She was at home when he called on a Thursday night.

"Would you be interested in getting away for a day or so?" he asked.

"I suppose, where to?" A hint of excitement resonated in her voice.

"I need to get down to the coast to check on the house, and wouldn't mind some company. I was planning on heading down tomorrow after work, and should get you back here mid-afternoon on Sunday."

"Is this a date?" she asked coyly.

After a brief pause, Jack replied, "As a matter of fact, it is." He had wanted to admit to that idea for so long, and now it finally managed to escape his lips.

"You're on, then." As they discussed the details of the trip as far as clothing, meals, etc., neither of them was able to hide their anticipation. They agreed that Jack would follow her home after lunch, and they would take a couple of hours off Friday afternoon so that they could get to the beach at a reasonable hour.

They talked during the whole three-hour drive, meandering from work-based topics to cooking, gardening, exercising (a topic about which he lacked much knowledge) to discussing how Keith had been doing. They arrived in Orange Beach shortly before five in the afternoon, to find the spring colors already beginning to show. The sun had another hour or so left before it crossed the horizon of the gulf, and its reflection made the relatively calm waters of the gulf sparkle with brilliance.

When they had unpacked his Tahoe, they settled in on the upstairs balcony for a glass of chardonnay, looking out over the gulf and enjoying the cool breeze that would gradually warm over the coming months. They stayed outside until eight-thirty and watched the sunset, before retiring to the living area. Jack suggested that she relax while he went about dinner preparations, and she reluctantly agreed. As she rested on the sofa, flipping through the channels, he began making their dinner for the evening – grilled veal chops with roasted asparagus and wild rice. When he was satisfied that he had done all he could do to perfect the arrangement, he called her to the table he had previously set up on the rear porch.

He had arranged the small table with two chairs and placed a white linen tablecloth over the wooden table top. It was a brisk evening, perfect for dining outdoors. When summer would fully arrive, eating on the deck would be unbearable.

They enjoyed their meal and talked about the house. She was interested in hearing about the changes that had been made, compared to the previous structure that Peter had demolished. They discussed potential additions that Jack was interested in making as well, and he knocked around the idea of putting in a

212

swimming pool. She suggested the possibility of a hot tub, with an endless pool.

"What in the hell is that?" he asked.

"You've never heard of them? It's a small pool that forces water toward the swimmer, so you essentially stay in one place while swimming; it's an excellent workout," she told him.

He told her he would take it under advisement, as they both laughed. They had managed to talk about a variety of subjects throughout the night, and they both found themselves more comfortable than ever in each other's company.

As midnight approached, Jack finally decided to confess. "There's something I've been debating on bringing up with you," he said softly.

"You can say anything, Jack, you know that."

He slid down into his chair, stretching his arms over his head and bringing his clasped hands down behind the back of his head as he leaned his head back, staring at the night sky. He took a deep breath and exhaled, "It's not that easy."

She could see he was struggling to find the words he wanted. "What is it?"

He realized that this was going to be much harder than he first thought; certainly more difficult than the conversations he had recently had about his career. He continued to peer at the stars, searching his vocabulary. He wanted to be poignant and poised, but the words eluded him. Eventually he gave up, "I like you Sharon. I've liked you for a long time, but in recent months I have come to the conclusion that I'm falling for you." He dropped his hands into his lap, looking at her face for some clue as to what was about to come. His anticipation was giving way to fear again – of rejection, and he took his gaze off her face, staring at the wooden deck.

"I've been wondering if you were ever going to say anything," she said in a soothingly calm voice. "I have enjoyed myself too, you know. Keith was so impressed with you at Christmas, and you have brought me back to a place I didn't think I could find again. I like you too, Jack."

Sharon moved her chair next to his and perched herself on the edge, reaching toward him; she took his hands in hers. Jack was still staring at the floor, trying to convince himself that he had heard her correctly. His hands were sweating as she took them.

She held both his hands in her left as she moved her right hand to his chin, lifting his face to hers. "I know the past while has been difficult, but it will get better. And I will do everything I can to see that it does." She leaned into him and gently kissed his lips. It seemed as though she had lingered for five minutes, as Jack moved a hand to her face, holding her smooth skin timidly.

She pulled away and sat back in her chair, smiling at him, and was able to coax a grin to his face. "So now what?" he asked.

"Now we enjoy the rest of our weekend," she replied. "Let's just ride things out, and see how it goes. I've never known planning a relationship to be the ideal way to start. I'm just happy to know how you feel, and hope you can believe me when I say that I feel the same way."

They talked a bit longer before deciding that they needed some rest, and she made her way upstairs to the guest room while he slept in the master suite.

When he woke the following morning, she was sitting on the back porch sipping a cup of coffee. As he walked out, she embraced him and gave him a soft kiss to greet the day. "Good morning," she said cheerfully.

His second kiss from her meant more than the first, as it confirmed that last night's revelations were not alcohol induced. After breakfast they spent the rest of the day walking on the beach, with lunch at a beachside café, followed by lounging about at his house. They continued to ask questions of each other, about their past, their stories, their lives. They ate dinner at a cozy restaurant on the beach, sitting outside to listen to the surf wash on the shore.

When they returned to the house, Sharon asked if he would think less of her if she joined him for the evening in his room. She was not ready to be completely intimate with him, but she did want the companionship. He understood and agreed that sex could wait, and accepted her invitation to share the bed.

It was the best night of sleep he'd had in years, and when he woke in the morning at five-thirty, she was still asleep next to him. He quietly got out of bed to make them breakfast before they had to begin packing for the return trip home.

The drive home was even more enjoyable than the one down, especially since Jack had made his move.

No regrets. Never *again.*

* * *

Buck Padgett was in the final stages of trial preparation. With a month to go, no time would be wasted from this point forward. His team was busy preparing witnesses, serving subpoenas, copying exhibits and organizing the files for trial. Buck spent most of his evenings reviewing the pertinent documents and preparing outlines for his direct examinations. He also reviewed the depositions that had been taken of each witness who would be called to testify, making sure he knew exactly what they had previously said under oath. Other than a last meeting with his trial experts to discuss their testimony and give them a mock cross-examination, he would spend each night repeating the process, until it was ingrained in his memory as though he had been the witness himself.

The week prior to the trial he would move all of his files and documents to Bay Minette, where he planned to spend the last week of preparations repeating the process. He arranged to reside at a local hotel in Bay Minette for the duration of the trial. Though he still kept a home in town, there were too many distractions there; he needed a place that was simple and quiet to keep his skills sharp.

* * *

Final trial prep at Gibson Vance was no different. Les and Luther had six associates assigned to the Whisenhunt case, and each was putting in fourteen hours a day, all billable hours to the client. The two trial attorneys also reviewed depositions and exhibits, and met daily to discuss potential theories that they guessed Buck might be using. Months ago they had solidified their position, but now they had to try to get inside Buck's head – the direction of his cross-examination of their witnesses, what questions would he be asking – all questions that would aid them in witness preparation.

Gibson Vance prepared to spend their trial time in South Alabama, too, although their projected expenses far exceeded those of Padgett & Keeler. They arranged to rent a house in Bay Minette to accommodate five lawyers and a support staff of four.

Judge Willingham had already informed the parties that their case was number one on his docket, and he had set aside two weeks for the trial. If it spilled over, he would cancel the next docket, but this case was going to be heard.

* * *

Ray Carlisle received the call from Agent Kelly Gentry, a Birmingham field office agent with the Bureau. After being briefed on the details, he called Jack.

"Bob Powell was found dead in his house yesterday morning. I'm sorry, Jack." Ray knew it was going to hit him hard.

"Was it a heart attack?" Jack assumed that the stress had gotten the best of him.

"He hanged himself in the basement, Jack."

Jack was astonished. "He hanged himself – there's no way he would have done such a thing – I've known him for…"

"There was a note," Ray interjected. "He left it upstairs in his office."

"What did it say?"

"I don't have that information yet; they're going to forward it to me from the Birmingham office."

"Jesus Christ, how is Susan doing?"

"She's not doing too well. She had been out of town visiting friends, and when she got home yesterday she was the one who found him."

"I need to call her," Jack said.

"I'd recommend that you didn't, Jack. You were mentioned in the suicide note, and I think it's best that you keep your distance."

"What do you mean I was mentioned?"

"Listen, I don't have all the information yet. Just hold tight and I'll call you when I get a better handle on things."

"What are they going to do with the body?"

"Susan is making arrangements today; I assume the funeral will be within the next day or so."

"Surely they're going to perform an autopsy?" Jack asked.

"She has refused it, Jack. He's gone and an autopsy won't bring him back."

"You know as well as I do that this could be a crime scene, for Christ's sake!"

"Jack, he was found hanging in his basement with a suicide note. His wife has specifically rejected the notion of an autopsy, and not only can I not, I will not attempt to persuade her otherwise. You're the one who got me in the middle of this whole mess, and now the man I have been pressuring on your behalf has committed suicide. I feel responsible for his death, Jack, and I'm not going to inflict any more suffering upon his widow than I already have. It's over, Jack. You have to let it go now."

"Maybe someone in the Birmingham office can..."

"I said let it go." Ray shouted, "If I so much as hear that you have contacted another agent about this, I will file charges against you, do you understand me?"

Jack knew he was right. Jack had been the one to heave all that pressure on Bob, and now it was time to let it go. He knew that Bob couldn't have killed himself, but trying to force Ray deeper into it wasn't going to get him anywhere. "Will you please call me when you get the note?" he finally asked.

"You'll be the first to hear, and, Jack, I know you considered him a friend, but I recommend that you don't attend the funeral."

"I understand."

Bob Powell was cremated and laid to rest three days after his death, with Jack not in attendance. At Susan's request, no autopsy was performed.

Two days after Bob's service, Jack received the call from Ray Carlisle. "The Birmingham office sent me a copy of the note that Bob left and I told you I would call when it came in." Ray was matter-of-fact in his tone.

"Thank you, Ray, go ahead."

"It reads as follows: 'Jack, Let me first take the opportunity to apologize to you for all the pain that you have been put through over the last year and a half. You have been not only an outstanding judge, but a true friend, and you deserved to be treated fairly and with respect. I am ashamed at having been involved in the events that have caused you such public and private humiliation, and for that I find it hard to forgive myself.

My only hope is that you will find it in your heart to be able to forgive me.'"

"He apparently left the note upstairs and went to the basement for his final act of penance. It wasn't signed."

An inner pain swelled in him unlike any he had experienced. He couldn't believe that Bob had been deeply involved in the scheme; he still couldn't, but Bob's manner of death could only be interpreted as evidence of his guilt. Jack concluded maybe it was finally time to let it go.

Taylor received notice of Bob's suicide from Les Vance, and it shocked him as well. Taylor was unable to make it to Birmingham for the service, but sent his condolences to Susan, along with a note that she was to call him if she needed anything at all.

After Les' call he walked over to Dan's office to break the news to him, "I've just been informed that Bob Powell committed suicide several days ago."

"So I've heard."

"What do you mean you've heard? I just got off the phone with Les."

"It's time you and I have a talk, Taylor."

* * *

Despite the promise he made to himself, Jack wasn't able to let it go. Bob's death was haunting him, and he found himself unable to sleep. The guilt he was placing on himself was eating away, and he was slipping into depression. There were so many unanswered questions and, with Bob's cremation and the end of Ray's participation, they would never be answered.

There was now only one person he could talk to, and he asked Sharon to come over one evening. If anyone could bring him back to sanity, it was Sharon.

She arrived at his Montgomery home to find him lying on the sofa. The room was quiet and he was staring at the ceiling. "All right, we need to get you up and moving," Sharon said playfully as she walked in the open front door.

"Please, I just need someone to talk to now. I don't need exercise."

"What's going on?" she asked, realizing he was seriously hurting.

Jack explained to her the circumstances surrounding Bob Powell's death, along with each detail of the conversations he had been having with Bob and Ray Carlisle that eventually led to it. He expounded on his feelings of guilt, as well as the paranoia that had begun to set in as a result of the situation. Sharon sat on the sofa next to him and listened. "I don't feel safe in my own home anymore, and I can't begin to tell you why, but something doesn't feel right to me, Sharon. I recently made a decision that I would live my life to the fullest, with no regrets, and every decision I've made since that day has been spot on. Something just isn't right."

Sharon sensed his loneliness and pain over the situation. She sat silently beside him for several minutes, thinking to herself, as he stared into nothing. "I think you need some company for a while," she announced. "Nobody should go through a thing like this alone. So, get your ass up and throw on some clothes."

She had caught his attention. "Where are we going?"

"You're coming with me to my house; I'm going to grab some things and come stay with you for a while. I don't think you'd be terribly comfortable in my little place, and together we can get you through this, right here where you belong."

"Are you sure that's a good idea?"

"Am I sure? I'm positive. Now get up and let's go."

They drove into the city so that she could pack some things, and within an hour they returned to his house. Jack Garrett had a roommate, and a pretty one at that.

* * *

Taylor was standing at the entrance to Dan's office, trying to figure out how in the world Dan could have gotten the news about Bob Powell before he did. Taylor Franklin was always the first to get the news, whether good or bad.

"Shut the door, please, and have a seat," Dan said, propping his feet on the corner of his desk. "There's a storm brewing – one that has the potential to cost us dearly, and it's time we plan for it."

Taylor was totally lost. "What in the hell are you talking about?"

"The Whisenhunt case, sir. As you are well aware, the trial is about to begin, and I feel certain that we have lost Jack Garrett. Worse than that, I don't think the information we've obtained is going to be of much value to us at this point." Dan was straight-faced and staring at Taylor.

"You haven't answered my question, Dan."

"I will if you will bear with me, sir."

"Humor me then," Taylor shot back.

"You hired me to do a job, did you not?"

"Get to the point." Taylor had no time for games.

"I have always performed above and beyond what has been asked of me, and you will agree that you trust me to do what's best for the company?"

"I've always believed that, Dan."

"As far as I'm concerned, sir, you *are* the company. You hired me, you have put me where I am, and, as you continue to climb the ladder, I feel a great deal of pride in being a part of your success. Towards that end, you have entrusted me with a great deal of responsibility. I do the things that others either don't want to think of or don't want to think could be done. Do you follow me?"

"You have been an asset to us, Dan, and I believe that I've taken good care of you in the process," Taylor replied.

"Well, there has been a glitch in the program, sir – one that has required rather unpleasant actions on our behalf."

Taylor's pulse quickened as he sat straight up in his chair. "Tell me what is going on."

"The Atlanta episode didn't turn out as expected, sir." Spearman proceeded to tell Taylor the story of how he hired the woman in Atlanta to set up the chief justice, figuring that Jack's background made him a prime target for such a mission. When Taylor expressed immediate concern that he would put the company at so much risk, Dan assured him that they were completely insulated. He explained that Ron Sullivan, a man who didn't exist, had undertaken the task and that Insure Pro's name wasn't stamped on any aspect of it.

"She got what we needed, and that was the end of the matter. We could have sat on the information until it was needed," he continued, "but she got greedy and sold the information to the media in Alabama. It was all done in an effort to find me, because she couldn't find Ron Sullivan – and it worked. When Ron contacted her to investigate, she told me about the drugs. This whore held it out to extort more money from us. I know I wasn't completely forthcoming about it, but she was going to sell it to someone and we had to act."

"Why didn't you tell me at the time?" he asked.

"I wanted you to be protected – nothing more – and you were. But then Bob comes along and tells us that the FBI was involved, and more than that, they'd found the girl and she was cooperating. I had to go talk with her, so I went to Atlanta; well, Ron went to Atlanta and talked with her."

"Who is she?"

"Who she is, is of no relevance to you. You have no need to know. But it was clear from our conversation that she was cooperating. There was only one way to be sure she didn't cave."

Taylor had a look of horror on his face. "You killed her?" He was trembling now, barely able to breathe.

"She was a money-hungry whore who was going to bring us down, Taylor. She had to be silenced. Hell, she probably already had plans to make more money on the back end."

"What in the hell were you thinking?"

"I was thinking about the company, about you, about me – about survival. And if I hadn't just told you about it, you would have never known a goddamned thing. No one has called, no one has been questioned, the whole thing wasn't even worthy of a fucking news story."

"Then why tell me now?" Taylor's brain still couldn't comprehend the sequence of events.

"Because it has led us to where we are now."

"I'm not following you in the least." Taylor replied.

Dan went on to explain how Jack had continued to press the issue, involving the FBI and the contacts between Jack, Ray and Powell. "You instructed me to keep my finger on the pulse, did you not?"

"Go on," Taylor said.

"I was concerned about Bob's loyalty, as I have been for some time. There was no way I could keep up with him and the others without interjecting myself into the equation, which would have been impossible, so I had his phone tapped. That way I could at least monitor what was happening on his end."

"Wiretapping is a federal offense. Jesus fucking Christ, Dan!"

"I just told you I shot a fucking whore to death. Do you think I'm afraid of the consequences of listening in on a conversation or two?" He paused, shaking his head, "Anyway, Bob was getting serious pressure to cooperate with Jack and the FBI agent. When he came to us about it, that's when the lying started. Garrett told him that he had changed his philosophy, he wasn't going to listen to anyone anymore – he had become his own man, according to him. Then the hammer fell – the agent convinced Bob that his best way out was to steal the disc from us and turn it over. He was in the planning stages of the theft when it happened."

"Why in the world would he hang himself if he had decided to cooperate with them?"

"He didn't. He had help." Dan was unapologetic and straightforward.

"NO. NO, NO, tell me you did not." Taylor was nauseous, the bile from his stomach had reached his mouth and he was on the verge of vomiting. "Please tell me you did not."

"I have the tapes if you would like to confirm that what I am telling you is true, sir."

"I never told you to kill anyone and you know it."

"You employ me to do those things that others find unpleasant, sir, and you asked me to take care of the situation, which I did. If Bob had stolen the disc, Garrett was a total loss. He would have taken possession of our only collateral and have been sufficiently pissed off at us that it wouldn't have mattered what the outcome of the case had been. Once the collateral was lost, we were sure to be next in line for investigation."

"But you murdered the former chief justice of the Supreme Court?"

"And tell me who has come knocking on the door asking questions? No one – his death was ruled a suicide."

"I suppose now you want to tell me just how that happened?"

"Like I said, it's time for you to get up to speed," Dan started. "Bob wanted the disc; he asked me explicitly to do so, which I relayed to you. Again, you instructed me to handle the situation."

"I never told you..."

"Please, sir," Dan stopped him. "I have acted as instructed for my entire career, with an understanding that I am to do what needs to be done to accomplish our goals. With respect to Powell now, I called him to inform him that we were going to give Jack the disc, but that we wanted him to draft a letter of apology to Jack, just for goodwill, so that he would be appreciative of our generosity down the road. I met him at his house, bringing the disc along so that he knew we were sincere. When he had written just enough of the scripted letter I had provided, I broke his neck and took him downstairs where the suicide ultimately played itself out."

Taylor felt as though the rug had been pulled out from under his feet, with no floor to fall on. His head was spinning and he wasn't sure if he was about to pass out or simply keel over. "I never..."

"Sir, we now have our storm to deal with and I would hope that you can put your attention to the matter at hand," Dan said sternly.

"What storm? I'm lost." Taylor still couldn't find his bearings. Having been informed that an executive of his company had committed two murders, one of which was a fellow executive – was too much, too quick.

"How about we take a break," Dan said, realizing that Taylor was incapable of comprehension at that moment.

Taylor went to the restroom and splashed cold water on his face, trying to regain some semblance of composure. He walked into his office and poured a cup of coffee, before returning to Dan's office. Dan was leaning back in his chair, exuding confidence, awaiting his return. "Are you ready to proceed, sir?" Dan asked.

"I'm fine," Taylor lied.

"I don't know for a fact where Garrett stands at this point, other than I would surmise that he is dealing with a great deal of guilt over the death of Bob. Because it was ruled a suicide, and it was his pressure on Bob that ultimately led to it, he may have turned the corner, at least as far as we are concerned. If we prevail at trial, I don't think there will be any issue that could stand up on appeal. Bob had previously assured me, and on this I believe him, that Judge Willingham will give the plaintiff every inch of leeway they ask for. A loss, on the other hand…" Dan stopped suddenly, evaluating Taylor to see if he appreciated where he was heading.

"You think he would uphold a verdict against us?" Taylor asked.

"Based upon his conversation with Bob several weeks ago, I am sure of it."

"What is it you are suggesting?"

"I suggest we wait and see what happens at trial. If we get a negative result, it seems to me that our only hope on appeal would be for the Governor to appoint a new chief justice who would be more receptive to our cause."

"You want to have him assassinated too? This can't be happening."

"I have taken care of the company, sir. I have gone to great lengths to protect you as well. But if Jack Garrett manages to ruin this case, don't think for a moment that Leo wouldn't replace you in a heartbeat. I listen to the talk amongst the board members, you know, and your name keeps coming up as the next replacement when Leo gets too sick. If we can get through this, you will be the official head of the largest insurance company in the country."

"I need some time to process everything, Dan. Let me get some rest and we can talk more tomorrow."

"Very well, sir."

Taylor left Dan's office and went directly to his car. When he arrived home, he asked Dee to take the kids out for dinner, as he needed to review some files for the upcoming trial and wanted to have some peace and quiet. When she had been gone for ten minutes, Taylor went into the bathroom and vomited.

Then, for the first time since the birth of his first child, he cried.

When he was finally able to pull himself together, he thought about how everything had gone so wrong. Failing to properly oversee Dan Spearman would mean a certain end to his career if knowledge of his actions were ever uncovered, regardless of what happened with the pending litigation. Taylor's whole life had been modeled for success, he had worked harder than everyone else to attain the level of prosperity he had, and in an instant it could all be gone. His family would be shamed – no more private school, no more vacations, no more life, even if Dee stayed with him, which she probably would not. He always had the highest of aspirations, and now, with Leo Kirschberg on the verge of retirement, he had the greatest opportunity of his professional career, and Dan had put it all in jeopardy.

With his mind overwhelmed and his body overworked, he took a sleeping pill, and was out before Dee returned home. When she came home she knew he was exhausted, so she slept in the guest room that night.

* * *

The following morning, Taylor was in the office at six-thirty, waiting for Dan Spearman. For the last two hours, he had gone over every possible scenario and compared it with the potential outcome. He had made a decision as to how they would proceed.

Dan arrived an hour after Taylor and noticed that his boss was already in the office. He knocked on the door as he walked through. "Good morning, sir," he said as he took a seat at Taylor's desk. "Where do we stand?"

Taylor was a different man from the mess that had ended up in Dan's office the day before; he appeared confident and poised. "You have jeopardized everything I have worked so hard for, Daniel."

"With all due respect, sir…"

"You will listen to me now." Taylor cut him off abruptly. "You have placed us both in a difficult position, but there is nothing you or I can do about what has happened in the past. I have made a decision as to where we go from here."

"Yes sir." Dan eased forward in his chair.

"We will await the outcome of the Whisenhunt trial. If we are fortunate enough to avoid a beating in that case, I don't see how an appeal could hurt us. Willingham will give them everything they ask for, and there should be no grounds to support a reversal of any verdict. If we get hit, I believe that we will have lost Garrett as an ally, and Governor Holliday should be given the opportunity to appoint a replacement. I know Mike Holliday well, and he wouldn't be the governor if it weren't for InPAC. I recognize there is some risk involved in keeping Garrett on the Court, but another murder should not be our first option, and with a victory for us, any re-trial would take place more than a year from now, giving us time to re-evaluate our position then."

"I think you're making the right decision, sir."

"You've drug me into this mess, Dan, and if we must have Garrett off the Court, you will clean it up."

"I understand, sir."

"If, by the grace of God, we are able to come out on the other side without a scratch, I assure you that your position here will be sealed in stone, with an increase in compensation, of course." Taylor was in too deep and he knew it. His first inclination had been to call the authorities and notify them of Dan's conduct, but Ron Sullivan had covered Dan's tracks to perfection, and there was no evidence preserved against him in either of the murders, other than what testimony Taylor himself would be able to provide. And if he had chosen to take that route, he would have implicated himself. He had no doubt that if he didn't give himself away in the process, Spearman surely would after having been informed that his boss had ratted him out. Even worse was the prospect that, if he became an informant, Dan would bring him to the same fate as Bob Powell and that woman in Atlanta, which was definitely not an option he wanted to entertain.

With the Whisenhunt trial about to begin, Taylor Franklin, Vice President and General Counsel, as well as counsel of record, of Insure Pro, the largest insurer in the country, and defendant in a pending lawsuit in Baldwin County, Alabama, was already guilty of conspiracy to commit murder.

TWENTY-THREE

Jury selection in the Whisenhunt case would take longer than anyone had expected. To begin with, the original panel of thirty-six potential jurors had to be extended to forty-eight in order to weed out the folks who had their insurance coverage with Insure Pro. Once they arrived on a panel that was acceptable, the questioning began.

Buck used his time with the panel to show Les Vance just how many people he knew in the group. He asked the usual questions that most lawyers in these cases asked – which jurors had undergone bad or good experiences with insurance claims, which ones had filed lawsuits themselves or had cases filed against them, which ones believed that lawsuits shouldn't be filed at all, and so on. He deviated from there to talk with each juror on a personal level.

"Mrs. Jacobs, is Johnny still living in the area? Mr. Farmer, when did Jan finish her radiation treatment?" The questions weren't designed to determine whether the juror should be struck from the panel or not; they were asked to show Les that Buck was a local, and these people were his friends and neighbors, as well as to let the jury know that he was one of them.

Les took twice as much time with his questioning. He was meticulous and precise in his address to the panel, asking each juror his or her religious affiliation, political ties and leanings, memberships in community groups, and also ensuring that every person who had a predisposition against his client was identified.

After two days of questioning, the jury that would decide the Whisenhunt case was selected. Pursuant to the Court's rules, each was a resident of Baldwin County, over nineteen years old and had not been convicted of a felony – other than that, it was the lawyer's gut feelings that determined who stayed and who didn't. The jury was comprised of twelve individuals, plus two alternates – there were eight women and four men, with both alternates being men. Their occupations were from across the spectrum – the women consisted of a teacher, factory worker, secretary, homemaker, medical technician, sanitation manager, cashier and nurse. Amongst the men, there was an iron worker, plumber, mechanic and a high school football coach. The alternates, who would sit through the entire case, only to participate in deliberations if another juror was excused, were a construction superintendent and a local butcher.

Buck Padgett knew, within one degree of kinship, more than half of the jurors who were ultimately seated to hear the case. As for Les, Luther, and their associates, they were familiar with none of them.

After Judge Willingham gave his preliminary instructions to the jury, advising them of the general nature of the case and admonishing them not to talk with the lawyers involved, it was time for opening statements.

* * *

Buck was first to go.

Although he was well known for his theatrics during argument, Buck played down his opening statement. He told the jury about the Whisenhunts' dream home, the one that they had saved a lifetime to buy, the one that Hurricane Peter took from them, the one that the defendant insured and was wrongly refusing to pay to rebuild. He told them that when the evidence was in, they would find that Insure Pro had absolutely no reason to deny paying their claim, and, in fact, that the company had engaged in a calculated effort to deny many others through a bogus scam. He figured the evidence would speak for itself, and left the jury to accept what he had told them at face value.

Les presented the opening statement for Insure Pro. He talked of the thousands of homes that they insured throughout the state and the statistical nightmare that was involved in adjusting such an outrageous number of claims following a devastating natural disaster. His client had paid millions and millions of dollars in claims already, relating to the storm. He told the jurors that they would hear testimony from his expert, who had determined that the damage sustained by Stephen Whisenhunt's home was a result of flooding or structural and construction inadequacies that his policy simply did not cover. Though the Whisenhunts disagreed with their findings, Insure Pro had relied upon sound expert advice in coming to their determination, certainly not a concerted effort to refuse paying one homeowner's claim.

Both lawyers felt that they had the jury's full attention during their opening remarks, and neither had a feel for the panel's initial impression.

Following a short break, it was time for Buck to begin presenting his case.

Mr. Whisenhunt was the first to take the stand, as Buck wanted the jury's first impression to be of the devastation that the defendant's conduct had caused. Buck led him through the purchase and renovation of the home that he and his family had struggled to buy over the years. Steve spoke about the feeling of hope when he received the initial letter from his insurer informing him that they were working on his claim – then the betrayal that followed when he was told that they would pay nothing. At one point, Judge Willingham ordered a recess so that he could compose himself to resume testifying.

Les knew that he had to be cautious with his cross-examination, initially expressing his apologies that Peter had destroyed the family's home. His only question to Mr. Whisenhunt was whether he agreed that the company should only be required to do what they had contracted to do – to which Stephen replied, "Yes sir."

Buck then called his engineer to the stand to provide the plaintiff's expert testimony. Following a brief recitation of his qualifications, Buck steered him through his investigation and review of the circumstances surrounding the damage to his client's residence. Buck sensed that the jury was becoming lost in the scientific details of his expert's analysis, so he proceeded to the conclusion that the expert had reached from his studies – the Whisenhunt home's damage was caused by Hurricane Peter's massive wind – certainly not flooding or structural problems.

On cross-examination he repeated that there was no question that wind – nothing else – had caused the structural failure. Les hammered away trying to get him to budge, before the expert finally said, "Sir, with all due respect, no matter how many ways you try to rephrase your question, the answer remains the same – the wind velocity was the primary cause of this particular structure's demise." Buck's witness was well prepared; he was instructed to keep it simple, without reference to the details that Buck wanted to save for later testimony.

When his expert left the witness stand, Buck announced that the plaintiff rested. Les turned to Luther Abercrombie in amazement. "You've got to be kidding me," he whispered. "Surely he can't be done."

"Are there any issues we need to take up at this time?" the judge asked.

"May we have a brief recess Your Honor?" Les asked.

"Very well, we'll take an hour and a half for lunch. Ladies and gentlemen of the jury, we are in recess until one-thirty, please return to the jury room by that time, and remember not to discuss this case with each other, or anyone else, until further order of this Court."

* * *

Once Courtroom 1 cleared, Les asked Luther, "What is he thinking? Padgett calls two witnesses in a case of this magnitude?"

"I have no idea. He had twenty people on his witness list," Luther replied.

"Do we have anyone ready to go?" Les asked, knowing that Willingham would be pissed if they were going to be responsible for a delay in the proceedings.

"If he wants to keep this simple, I say we play the same game. Call Roger to the stand and then rest," Luther responded. "This jury has been told about all the people they could hear from, and if there are only three witnesses that testify, they're bound to assume that this isn't that big of a deal after all. They've been primed for a big show, and when they don't get it, they'll be too disappointed to render a big verdict."

Luther's analysis made perfect sense to Les. "Fair enough, we'll ask to break until tomorrow and get Roger here early."

When the lunch recess was over, the lawyers returned to the courtroom with the jury sequestered in their quarters. "Any motions for the Court at this time?" Willingham asked.

"The defense would like to make a motion for a directed verdict at this time on the plaintiff's claim of bad faith failure to pay, Your Honor," Les began. "As the Court is aware, if the plaintiff cannot prove that they are entitled to a verdict on the claim for payment of the house, there can be no bad faith."

"What says the plaintiff?" Willingham asked Buck.

"I can only assume that the defense intends to present at least some witness to dispute the evidence we have presented in this case, Your Honor, and I would ask the Court to reserve a ruling on their motion until such time. Unless, of course, they have no witnesses, in which case I wish to make the same motion on behalf of my client, considering that there is no evidence whatsoever before this jury that would support their defense."

"Do you have any witnesses to call, Mr. Vance?" the Judge asked.

"We do, Your Honor."

"In that event, I will reserve my ruling until the defense rests their case. Are you prepared to call your first witness, Mr. Vance?"

"Your Honor, we expected Mr. Padgett to spend more time with his case in chief. Our expert can be available first thing tomorrow morning, so we would ask for some leeway in order to get him in town." Les said.

"I don't like to keep our jurors any longer than necessary, and you should be aware from the pre-trial order that all parties are required to have their witnesses available on the day of trial. Did you bother to read the order, Mr. Vance?"

"Yes, Your Honor, but we would hope that the Court would not require us to have our expert witness on standby, considering the cost involved," Les answered.

"I understand your scheduling difficulties, Mr. Vance, but I want your witness ready to go at nine in the morning, is that understood?" Willingham's chastisement was for his own fun more than out of a serious concern – he enjoyed watching city lawyers squirm.

"We'll be ready, Your Honor."

Les called Taylor to inform him that Roger needed to be in Baldwin County that evening. Franklin assured him that Roger would be there by seven, and called Stoltz to tell him it was time.

* * *

Roger was briefed, for the third time, on the evening before his testimony was to begin; it was the second time by Les Vance. Les reminded him to keep his responses as brief as possible and not to volunteer information that was not directly asked. Les went over every issue that he foresaw Buck getting into and was reasonably confident that Roger would be able to hold his own.

Roger Stoltz took the stand at nine in the morning.

Les guided him through his investigation of the Whisenhunt property, including the site visit, review of weather data from the National Weather Service, and a short dissertation of his qualifications as a structural engineer. Following a description of the damage that had occurred at the home, Roger testified that, in his expert opinion, it was caused by the hurricane's surge of water, twenty feet according to information provided by the weather service. To the extent that the water didn't finish the job, inadequate construction and design was to blame for the remainder.

"What do you mean when you say that there was inadequate construction, sir?" Les asked.

"Had the structure itself, meaning the walls and joists, been adequately connected to the foundation, the surge would have simply washed through the house. This structure was built on a concrete foundation, and nothing but the slab remained after the storm. Based upon my review, had the connections been sound, there would have been a strong probability that the structure itself would have remained intact."

Les continued, "So you are saying that the surge was the primary cause of the damage, then?"

"Most definitely. I don't believe that this house survived the flooding. The structural problems certainly didn't help though."

Les had given the jury a reason that supported the denial of the Whisenhunts' claim. Whether they accepted it or not wasn't the issue; as long as Willingham let them weigh the experts' opinions against each other, the bad faith claim would not be submitted for their consideration, and the worst case scenario was a judgment against Insure Pro for four hundred thousand dollars, the value of the house itself. Though most people would think that to be a substantial sum, it would be a victory for Insure Pro, setting the stage for the other pending cases.

Roger Stoltz was then handed over to Buck Padgett for cross-examination.

Buck jumped in asking how much money he had made on this case so far, to which Roger replied that he hadn't figured the fees yet – that would be done upon the completion of his testimony. "Give me a ballpark number," Buck requested.

"I would guess around fifteen to twenty thousand."

"How much money has your company received in fees over the last five years, Mr. Stoltz?"

"I'm not sure on that, sir." Roger said.

"Then I'll help you. According to the documents we subpoenaed from your company, you have been paid a total of approximately four and a half million dollars in fees over that time period," Buck stated.

"If that's what the numbers show, I'll accept it."

"And you would agree with me that you have a staff of more than twenty-one, with seven engineers, including yourself, and an office building out in Texas?"

"That is correct, sir."

"What is your overhead per year, Mr. Stoltz?" Roger had a blank look on his face as he glanced over at Les.

"Objection, Your Honor, this has no relevance to this case," Les interrupted.

"Overruled. We have gone over this before, Mr. Vance." Gibson Vance had filed a motion before trial asking that Buck not be allowed to get into the matters of the funding of Roger's company, which the judge quickly denied. "You may proceed, Mr. Padgett."

"Do you wish for me to help you with the numbers again, sir?" Buck asked the witness. Roger nodded affirmatively. "According to the records, your company's annual expenses totaled over a million and a half."

"If that's what they show, sir." Roger looked confused and he didn't know the numbers anyway.

"All of your revenues in those years came from Insure Pro, did they not?"

"I believe that is correct, sir."

"So if we do a little simple math, your company had four and a half million in income over the last five years, and seven and a half million in expenses, leaving you three million in the hole. Tell these ladies and gentlemen how much money your company has in the bank as of your bank statement, please sir." Buck handed him the company's statement from First Federal Bank & Trust.

"Slightly over three hundred thousand dollars," he answered.

"I guess we're all interested to know where all this money came from then." Buck was looking at several jurors as he questioned Roger.

"Jerry Shanks provided the shortfall in funding."

"Tell the jury how you know Mr. Shanks, please sir."

Roger informed the jury that Jerry Shanks had been introduced to him by Taylor Franklin, general counsel at Insure Pro. Jerry was looking for an investment opportunity and his company provided start up cash for Forensic Engineering. He also helped out when cash flow problems arose.

"This Mr. Franklin, is it the same Taylor Franklin that was listed as co-counsel in this case for the defendant, but didn't bother to show up here for this trial?"

Les stood up. "Objection, we told the Court that Mr. Franklin had a conflict, and that is totally improper."

"Sustained. Mr. Padgett, please move on."

Buck proceeded to ask Stoltz about Fairway Investment Group, Shanks' company that had sent several million dollars to him, then proceeded up the ladder of corporations that ultimately led to Insure Pro. Though Roger was unaware of the nature of the corporate organizations that had been created to funnel money to him, he was well aware that Insure Pro had been supplying his shortfall over the years.

"Let me summarize this if I may, Mr. Stoltz, and you tell me if I have missed anything at all in my assumptions – you have testified for no other company, other than the defendant in this case, for the last five to seven years, and thus have received no income from any other source, you have an operating shortage of over three million dollars that has consistently been replenished by a maze of corporations that were created simply to funnel money into your company; and each and every dollar of that money has come from the very company on whose behalf you are testifying for right now. Have I misstated anything, sir?"

Roger was leaning forward on the witness stand, with his elbow on the desk. He dropped his head into his hand, rubbing both eyes with his thumb and index finger, and shook his head slightly from side to side.

"You need to say 'no' for the record, Mr. Stoltz," Judge Willingham ordered him.

"No sir."

"Thank you very much," Buck continued. "Now let me ask you some questions about this house that you say was damaged by the surge." Buck was picking up steam now, ready to crucify the so-called expert.

"How much water would be required to enter this structure in order to cause a structural failure?" he asked.

"This was a two-level house, so ten feet of water would carry sufficient force to cause a failure." Roger was finally on a subject that he knew something about.

"Would you agree with me then, that if there was… say, five feet of water in this structure that it would have held together?"

"Most certainly. There are a number of properties that had that amount of water and they survived the surge," Roger answered.

"Well, please tell us why you say this house didn't make it when the others did, Mr. Stoltz?"

"I've already provided you with the data from the National Weather Service, reflecting that the surge in their area was twenty feet; that's almost to the roof, Mr. Padgett."

"Did you review the building codes for this area before coming to your determinations in this case, sir?"

"Absolutely. The 1980 codes required that structures be built no less than five feet above sea level, which would still translate into fifteen feet of water in this structure, more than enough to cause a total failure." Roger was gaining confidence, sitting more upright now.

Buck turned to face the jurors again. His next question was directed to Roger, though he simply stared down each member of the panel as he asked it. "So I take it then that you didn't review the revised building code that was enacted in 1988, which

235

required new construction to be built a minimum of fifteen feet above sea level?"

Roger's demeanor changed again. He was nervous now. "What year was this house built?" he asked Buck.

"1990."

"Uh, I –I..." Stoltz was lost for words.

"You didn't catch that did you, Mr. Stoltz? There was, at the most, five feet of water in this residence, which you testified earlier would not have caused a failure."

"There was still an inadequate construction of the residence," Roger jumped in.

"Is that so? Is that the last thing you are relying on, Mr. Stoltz?"

"I've already testified to that, I believe."

"Fair enough. Let me show you a picture of another residence in Orange Beach. This is a house located at 1664 Pecan Drive, right next door to the Whisenhunt property. Did you investigate this property?"

"I was not asked to, sir."

"Looking at the photographs, you can see that this structure survived the surge and the wind as well, correct?" Buck approached the witness stand, showing the photos to Roger and holding them up for the jury to see.

"Correct," Roger answered.

"Would there have been any structural defects in this house that you could identify as you look at these pictures?"

Roger studied the photos carefully before answering, "This is how a house should be built. You can tell that the connections to the foundation were strong and held as designed."

"So you would agree that this house had no structural defects at all, sir?"

"None."

"Very well, then," Buck said, "With that I have no further questions."

"Mr. Vance, you may call your next witness," Willingham announced.

"The defense rests," he said to the amazement of the judge.

"You have no other witnesses?" Willingham asked again.

"No, Your Honor, we are satisfied that the case can go to the jury at this point," Les responded.

"Anything in rebuttal, Mr. Padgett" the judge asked Buck.

"As a matter of fact, we do, Your Honor. At this time I would like to call Glen Moore to the stand," Buck asserted.

Les jumped to his feet. "Objection, Your Honor, the plaintiff did not list any 'Glen Moore' in their witness list, and we object to being blindsided at this juncture." Les had never heard of the man and was taken off guard.

"Mr. Vance, with all your years of experience you should know that rebuttal witnesses are not required to be listed on pre-trial filings. Overruled."

It was embarrassing enough that he jumped the gun with his objection; Willingham only made it worse with his admonishment in front of the jury, but there was nothing he could do about that now. "Thank you, Your Honor, I apologize," he said meekly.

* * *

Glen Moore was called to the stand after a lunch recess, arriving in a buttoned down plaid shirt, blue jeans and tan work boots. He looked about fifty, with a neatly trimmed gray beard and mustache, his face a bit reddened, obviously from spending a lot of time outdoors.

Buck asked him to identify himself, then asked, "Would you mind telling these ladies and gentlemen your occupation?"

"I am the owner of Moore Construction Company."

"As the owner of Moore Construction, do you also participate in the actual building of the homes you are contracted on?"

"I personally oversee the building of every home we have working at any given time. I am on site on a daily basis."

"Mr. Moore, were you contracted by Mr. Stephen Whisenhunt to construct his family's residence at 1660 Pecan Drive?"

"Yes sir, I was."

"Do you recall what year that house was built?"

"It was started and completed in 1990, sir."

"Did you have any other projects in Orange Beach that were under way in that time frame?"

"We actually had a total of five different houses we built in the area that year."

"Where were the other residences you built that year, please sir?"

"There were three of them that were all located on the western end of the area; as I recall they were three adjoining lots. The other was located next to the 1660 Pecan address."

"You built the house at 1664 Pecan Drive?"

"Yes sir, I did."

"Was the residence at 1664 constructed with the same degree of workmanship, planning and materials as the one located next door, at 1660 Pecan?"

"They were identically built, the only exception being the interior design. The floor plans were the same, building materials identical, same crew even. We spent different days working on each house." Glen answered.

"So, from an engineering and structural design standpoint, these two houses were…?"

"Identical in every way," Glen interrupted.

"Thank you very much, sir, your witness," Buck said as he glanced over at the defense table.

"May we have a short break, Your Honor?" Les asked Willingham.

"We'll take a fifteen minute recess," The judge ordered.

* * *

During the recess, Les asked Luther whether he thought cross-examination could render anything useful to them. Buck had already obliterated Roger's opinion regarding the surge, and now Glen Moore had nixed the design and construction theory.

"What in the hell are you going to ask him, Les? Is he sure he built that house? For Christ's sake, Roger just got abused. You need to let it go, and while you're at it, you might want to call Taylor and see if you can get some settlement authority. I don't like the feel of things." Luther had litigated enough cases to know when he was in trouble, and right now Insure Pro was deeply in trouble.

When they returned from the recess, Willingham asked the parties if they were ready to proceed. Les rose from his seat.

"Your Honor, if I may, would the Court allow us to break for the day, as we would like an opportunity to speak with our client at length regarding some issues that have arisen?"

"Mr. Padgett, do you have any objection?"

"No sir, I suppose this jury has heard enough for one day. If the Court is inclined to recess, I have no problem with it."

Judge Willingham excused the jury, asking the lawyers to remain until the jurors had left the courtroom. Once all the jurors were gone, he looked at Les Vance and said, "Mr. Vance, I assume that you understand the nature of the testimony that has been received today?"

"I do, sir," Les responded.

"I would suggest that you contact your client about getting this matter resolved. I don't want to see you get hurt here."

"That was the reason I asked for the recess, Your Honor. I hope to have something to present to Mr. Padgett in the morning."

"I hope you can come to an agreement, but you might want to inform your client that the Court has been less than impressed with their expert's testimony." Judge Willingham was no different than any other trial court judge – he didn't mind sitting through a trial, but his job was to encourage parties to resolve cases without the necessity of a jury's verdict. For one thing, settlement allowed the case to get off his docket, but more importantly, it meant that there would be no appeal, thus no opportunity for a reversal.

"Thank you, Your Honor," Les said as he and Luther packed their briefcases and left the courthouse.

* * *

When they returned to their hotel, the two Gibson Vance partners made their conference call to Taylor Franklin, hoping that they would be leaving Baldwin County by lunchtime the following day.

Les informed Taylor about the day's events and how Roger Stoltz' testimony had been essentially eliminated by Buck Padgett and his surprise witness. He also relayed the veiled warning provided by Judge Willingham.

"What are you asking me to do, Les?"

239

"We need settlement authority, Taylor; I have a bad feeling about how this case is going," Les replied.

"Is he going to let the bad faith claim go to the jury?" Taylor asked.

"He hasn't said yet, but the indications are that it's quite possible, maybe even likely."

Taylor thought to himself for a moment before continuing, "How much is the policy?"

"In the neighborhood of four hundred grand," Les answered.

Taylor wasn't too naïve to know that sometimes you had to cut your losses in a case, and he figured that even though the Whisenhunts were a test case, if it could go away they could try again later, and the later the better. "Tell Padgett our top offer is five hundred thousand, but I want a confidentiality agreement so that no one can publish the settlement," he finally said.

"I don't think that's going to get it done," Les shot back.

"Then finish trying the goddamn case, Les. That's your authority and if he doesn't accept it, I am willing to take our chances with the Supreme Court, which you may want to remind them, is still on our side."

Les felt sure that the offer would be rejected, but he knew from Taylor's tone of voice that it was useless arguing any longer. "We'll present it tomorrow."

"If I don't hear from you by noon, I'll assume there's no deal then." Taylor hung up.

* * *

When the lawyers reached the Courthouse the following morning, Les asked Buck Padgett to join him outside for a talk. "I've been given some authority to settle the case, Buck, and I don't want to play any games, so I'll just tell you what I have," Les said.

"I'm listening," Buck replied.

"Five hundred and a confidentiality agreement."

Buck didn't flinch. "I'll certainly present it to my client, but you know that after fees, that doesn't leave him with enough to rebuild, Les. And the way I see it, I've got you bent over the table as it is and I think you know it."

"The offer is five hundred with confidentiality, Buck."

"Give me a minute,' Buck said, as he walked back into the courthouse. He went back to the courtroom and found Steve Whisenhunt sitting at the plaintiff's table. "Steve, can I talk to you for a second?" Steve got up and joined his lawyer as they walked out of the courtroom and down the hall to an empty office.

"The defendant has offered to pay five hundred thousand, with an agreement to keep it confidential and I have an obligation to present it to you."

"What do you think?" his client asked.

"When our fees and expenses are taken out, it leaves you with about three hundred – not enough to rebuild, but a start nonetheless. I think we are in a good position in the trial, but ultimately it's your case and your decision to make." Buck wanted to push forward, but the reality was that Steve Whisenhunt could put an end to the trial if he accepted the offer.

"I trust your judgment, Buck, so whatever you want to do, I'm good with."

"Like I said, I like where we stand. If you are in agreement, I say we press on."

"Then do it."

Buck walked outside and informed Taylor that the offer was rejected.

The lawyers proceeded back into the courtroom and waited for Willingham to come out of his chambers.

The judge made his way to the bench, cloaked in his usual black robe, and took his seat. "Have we got a settlement?"

"I'm afraid not, Your Honor," Buck said plainly.

"What was your offer, Mr. Vance?" Though such matters were not routinely inquired into by a trial judge, Willingham had all the latitude he needed and was genuinely interested in helping the parties reach a compromise.

"Five hundred thousand, sir," Les answered.

"I would have assumed you'd have been able to convey to your client your situation somewhat better, counsel."

"Your Honor, I informed my client of everything you stated yesterday, and that is their position."

"As you like it. Do you have any other witnesses to call, Mr. Padgett?"

"I have one more, sir."

Judge Willingham turned to his law clerk, "Get the jury back in, Tom."

Once the jurors had returned to their seats, Willingham leaned back in his chair, then said, "Mr. Padgett, please call your next witness."

Buck stood from his chair and faced Les, demanding his attention. With a look of utter glee he said, "Plaintiff calls William Littleton to the stand."

Les' initial reaction was to jump up with an objection, but his memory from the day before caught him. He didn't need another dressing down from Willingham.

The witness casually walked into the courtroom, dressed in a blue suit with a red and white striped tie and immaculately shined black leather dress shoes. He took his seat next to the judge and was sworn in.

"Tell the ladies and gentlemen your name, please sir," Buck said.

"William Littleton, but I go by Bill."

"Where do you live, Mr. Littleton?"

"My home residence is in Macon, Georgia, but I spend a good deal of my time in Atlanta, so I have a residence there as well."

"What is your occupation, sir?"

"I am an associate justice on the Georgia Supreme Court."

Les was lost. He knew that Buck would be given wide latitude in calling rebuttal witnesses, but nothing was making even the least bit of sense.

"Judge Littleton, do you own property in Orange Beach, Alabama?"

"Yes sir, I have a house located at 1664 Pecan Drive."

Les went limp. *This can't be happening. What in the hell did they do?*

"Did you own the residence at 1664 Pecan Drive during Hurricane Peter, and if so, was it insured?"

"Yes sir, I did, and our coverage was with Insure Pro."

"After the hurricane, did you file a claim under your homeowner's policy with Insure Pro?"

"I did."

"Please tell us what the outcome of that claim was, sir."

"They paid it in full," the judge replied.

"Was there ever any investigation that you were made aware of?"

"I just submitted my proof-of-loss forms as they asked me to, and within a month or so I got a check."

"Let me ask you this, sir, are you an elected judge?"

"Yes sir, but in Georgia, judges are elected in a non-partisan election."

"But you still have to raise money to run a campaign, do you not?"

"Most definitely. Without the funds, there is no way to compete."

"Can you please tell us how much money you received from Insure Pro during your last campaign?" Buck asked.

"They contributed about a hundred thousand dollars, to the best of my recollection."

"Do they have cases that come before you on the Supreme Court?"

"Sure, as do many other parties, but I certainly don't rule in favor of any one individual or group simply because they contribute to my campaign."

"I wasn't suggesting that you did in any way. Thank you for your time, Your Honor." Buck turned to Les with an 'eat shit' grin, "Your witness."

Les knew full well that cross-examination was a lost cause with Judge Littleton; there were absolutely no questions that he could think of that would help his client. "I have no questions of this witness."

Judge Willingham looked towards Buck. "Does the plaintiff have any more witnesses?"

"No sir, we rest."

"Mr. Vance, anything from the defense in rebuttal?"

"No, Your Honor."

Willingham instructed the jury that they would recess for the day and resume in the morning with closing arguments; they were to be back in the jury room by nine. "Counsel, I assume we have some matters to take up?" he asked the lawyers.

"Yes, Your Honor," Buck said.

"Very well, as soon as the jury is gone, the Court will entertain any motions that the parties may have."

Once all jurors had exited the courthouse, Willingham asked if the defense had any motions that they wished to present. Generally, the plaintiff went first in every matter in a trial; however, when it came time for these matters, it was usually the defense that had first priority.

Les stood and made a motion that the Court dismiss the Whisenhunts' claim for bad faith. "Your Honor, we have presented evidence that conflicts with the plaintiff's expert on the cause of damage to this house, and it is a matter for the jury to determine at this time. As such, there can be no bad faith, because my client had an arguable reason to deny this claim at the time the decision was made."

"Mr. Padgett, do you have response?" Willingham asked.

"I do, Your Honor, and in addition, we would ask the court to grant our motion finding that the Whisenhunts are due to be granted a verdict on the breach of contract claim." Buck knew that the only way for the jury to consider the bad faith claim was if Judge Willingham ruled, on his own, that Insure Pro owed them for the damage to the residence. If he did not, the Whisenhunts would be limited to the payment of the policy proceeds for the house, at the most.

Buck recited the testimony that he relied on in making his motion, omitting the financial connections between Insure Pro and Roger Stoltz' firm, as that was a matter for closing argument. The primary reason that the Court should rule in his client's favor at this point, he argued, was that the defendant's expert admitted under cross-examination that the flooding couldn't have been the cause of the damage; and furthermore, Glen Moore's testimony that he built both the Whisenhunt and Littleton homes to the same standards, when viewed along with Roger's admission that Bill Littleton's house was soundly constructed, clearly proved that the Whisenhunts had been a victim of a scam by the defendant. They had paid Judge Littleton's claim, first of all because it was a valid claim, and, secondly, due to his position as a Supreme Court Justice in Georgia who considered cases involving them.

Les tried his best to assert that Buck's theories were best left for a jury to determine, but he had already resigned himself to the notion that it was a lost cause.

When Les concluded his argument, Judge Willingham sat up in his chair, pushing his glasses to the top of his head. "Counsel, this Court normally would take a matter such as this under advisement, but I believe that I have a firm grasp on testimony in this case. Mr. Vance, this Court finds that the testimony given by Mr. Stoltz is unworthy of belief. He admitted to failing to properly review the existing building codes before coming to his determinations; then, when confronted with an identically built structure, had to admit that he wrongly asserted a building defect. In light of these findings, it is the determination of this Court that the plaintiff's motion for a judgment on the breach of contact claim is due to be granted. We will have closing arguments tomorrow morning regarding the bad faith failure to pay claim. We are in recess until ten tomorrow morning. Have a pleasant evening, counsel." Willingham rose from the bench and disappeared into his chambers.

* * *

Les dreaded the call he was going to make tonight, and he hoped that Taylor would be willing to make a real effort to make this nightmare go away.

He called Taylor at home after he and Luther had eaten dinner; he didn't want to ruin his meal by having the discussion too early. Taylor didn't take the news that Buck had won on the contract claim very well. "So this is the legal work that we're paying three hundred dollars an hour for? Is your firm inept or are you just plain stupid?"

Les had had enough of the humiliation and disparagement. "You listen to me, you dumb motherfucker. You were the one who planned out this scheme and kept us in the dark from day one. If you had any ounce of intelligence, you would've at least given us something to work with, so don't give me any more shit about me not knowing what the fuck I'm doing, because all of this falls on your shoulders." It felt good to finally get it off his chest and, by now, Les had decided that he didn't care if Taylor pulled their business from his firm anyway. "If you want to make a new offer, tell me. Otherwise I have a closing argument to prepare."

"Look, I'm sorry Les. I've had a lot going on and I shouldn't take it out on you." Les thought he sounded sincere. "We'll go up to one million – how you choose to negotiate is up to you, but after that, we're going to have to take our chances. The Supremes are with us, wouldn't you agree?"

Les appreciated the apology, but it couldn't excuse Taylor's conduct over the last year or so either. "As far as I know, the Court's still five-to-four, but I certainly can't predict what they would do. Is the million all you want to put on the table?"

Taylor waited a few seconds before finally responding, "That's a final offer."

"I'll call you after the verdict."

* * *

Les approached Buck Padgett on the morning of closing arguments and informed him of the new offer of a million dollars to settle the case. He wasn't going to bother low-balling him.

"I appreciate the offer, Les, but I'm afraid we're going to have to pass." Les already knew that Buck wasn't going to be interested in the offer, but he had an obligation to present it at any rate.

Closing arguments went exactly as Les had imagined they would. Buck laid out the case of a grand scheme to deny valid claims by the big bad insurance company. He went through each and every piece of evidence and testimony with precision, painting Insure Pro as a greedy corporation that cared nothing about the dreams of the Whisenhunt family. Insure Pro had spent millions of dollars in their quest – a plan formulated not just against his client in this case, but thousands of others, and they, the jury, should tell them that the citizens of Alabama demand better treatment. The only way that Insure Pro would listen was to hit them where it hurt most – the pocketbook.

Les tried his utmost to be an advocate for his client; that was, after all, what he was being paid to do. Part of him almost welcomed a large verdict against his client, but being associated with the losing side of such a case was bad for business. He argued that there was no scheme or deceit, but that Roger Stoltz had simply done a poor job investigating the case for his client, that had he discovered the correct building codes, the Whisenhunts claim would likely have been paid. The jury, he urged, should not punish his client for the shortcomings of their expert. It was a stretch, but it was all he had, and it seemed as though the jurors were paying close attention to his closing.

When the lawyers had concluded their arguments, Judge Willingham instructed the jurors on the law that they were to apply in the case, then sent them back to the jury room to begin their deliberations. It was all over now but the waiting.

* * *

The door to the jury room had been shut for three hours when there was a knock from the inside. They had been instructed to knock on the door if they had a question or when they had reached a verdict. Willingham's law clerk cracked the door open and eased his head inside. No one could hear the conversation that took place. He shut the door and walked into Willingham's chambers, saying nothing to the participants.

Judge Willingham emerged from his chambers. "Counsel, it appears we have a verdict." He instructed Tom to tell the jurors to return to their seats in the jury box for the reading of the verdict. One by one they filed back into Courtroom 1, taking their seats. "Ladies and gentlemen of the jury, I have been advised that you have reached a verdict in this case. Who have you chosen as your foreperson?"

"Me, Your Honor." Sandra Farrow, a fourth-grade school teacher from Bay Minette, announced that she had been chosen to lead the deliberations.

"Mrs. Farrow, has the jury reached a unanimous verdict?"

"We have, Your Honor."

"Would you please read the verdict aloud so that the court reporter can hear you?"

Mrs. Farrow rose from her seat in the jury box. "We, the jury, in the matter of Whisenhunt v. Insure Pro, on Count Five of the Complaint for bad faith failure to pay, find in favor of the plaintiff, Stephen Whisenhunt, and against the defendant, and assess damages in the amount of eight million dollars. Signed, Sandra Farrow, foreperson."

Stephen Whisenhunt began to sob.

Buck put his arm around him and congratulated him on his victory. "They will appeal, Steve, so we still have work to do, but enjoy this moment for the time being."

Les stood and extended his hand to Buck Padgett, and the two shook hands, complementing each other on a case well tried. Within a half hour, all parties had left the courthouse, making their way home.

TWENTY-FOUR

Les waited until he got back to Birmingham to make the call.

"We got a verdict late this afternoon, eight million," was all he said to Taylor.

"Are you going to file a motion for a new trial?" Taylor asked.

"If you want us to, we will, but I can tell you that Willingham will deny it, so it's only going to prolong the inevitable."

"I believe you're right, Les. Go ahead and start preparing the appeal."

"We'll get started on it right away."

Gibson Vance had forty-two days to file the appeal on behalf of their client.

* * *

Within a couple of days of being there, Sharon began to feel as if she were at home. Though Jack's home lacked the feminine touch that could make it more livable, it was still a warm and inviting place. She had rearranged some furniture to make the main level more pragmatic, and the kitchen needed some work. Jack was an excellent chef, but had lousy organizational skills, with silverware located too far from the plates, and the pots and pans weren't easily accessible from the cook top.

She had managed to gradually settle him down, though it did take some time. Jack continued to entertain thoughts of calling Ray Carlisle back to urge further investigation into Bob Powell's death, but Sharon's realism ultimately convinced him that it would likely destroy any friendship that he and Ray may still have had. While she persuaded him to stop harassing Ray, his concerns over the suicide did not wane; he just decided they were best kept to himself.

Even though they had shared a bed at the beach several weeks ago, Sharon was sleeping in the guest room upstairs. They had agreed that they still needed to take their time with each other, and both were all right with the sleeping arrangements. They drove to work separately, with one of them leaving fifteen to twenty minutes earlier than the other each day. Although they weren't ashamed of the blossoming relationship, neither wanted to deal with the questions that would inevitably arise around the office if eyebrows began to rise.

In like fashion, they left the Supreme Court building at different times. Eventually they would be comfortable enough with the situation to stop worrying about what their co-workers thought, at least they hoped they would; but in the end, it was an office, with many types of people co-existing on a professional level, and employees of the Supreme Court were no more immune to the dangers that rumors and innuendo could create than any other work place.

The intimacy they did share was privately expressed, mostly during walks around Jack's four acres in Mt. Meigs. It became a simple, yet very real, pleasure – sitting by the pond behind the house just holding hands and talking about life. They were both amazed at how much more they had learned about each other while cohabitating. They also discovered some of the small things about each other that irritated one or the other – he never deemed it necessary to clean the dishes until the morning after dinner, and she could only imagine that the sink was crawling with bugs overnight; and Jack would swear that he could hear her chewing ice from the other side of the house. Both of them recognized that the other's idiosyncrasies were minimal in the big picture and that learning about them, and coming to accept them as a small part of the greater whole, was a part of the process that they were experiencing. After a week or so, even those things began to seem less bothersome when compared to the alternative of a return to loneliness.

Jack Garrett and Sharon Waters were becoming a couple, at least as far as they were concerned.

* * *

Gibson Vance dedicated three of their associates to research and draft the appeal of the verdict in Whisenhunt v. Insure Pro. Amongst the group, a total of thirty years' experience writing appellate briefs existed. Any type of supporting case from any jurisdiction in the country would be uncovered and cited in the argument that would eventually be submitted. With just over a month to prepare and have the final draft ready for filing, the appeals team worked fourteen hours a day, six days a week. Les couldn't afford to wait until the last day to have the official copy in the clerk's office in Montgomery. Consequently, reviews of the working draft were held every third day.

A secondary goal in the briefing process was to make the other party have to work their asses off responding to a multitude of issues that wouldn't necessarily provide a basis for a reversal of the lower court's findings – a tactic used in hopes that they got so caught up answering every allegation of error that research on the valid claims was neglected. The Gibson Vance appeals team was skilled in burying their meritorious arguments amid the bunk, and they were aware that the staff attorneys who would eventually review their brief wouldn't overlook any rational argument.

It was a long and tedious process, but they were paid handsomely for their efforts.

* * *

Upon being notified that the redneck jury in Baldwin County had ruled that his company had to pay over eight million dollars to some dumb bastard from east bumble fuck Alabama, Taylor decided that he needed to get away for a week. He had done the math in his head over and over again – five hundred cases pending, with Padgett & Keeler being lead counsel in half of them – assuming smaller verdicts of five million per case, they were staring at more than a billion dollars in judgments just on the cases that Buck had, not to mention the others, many of which were bound to have negative results. Everything was riding on the appeal and the wisdom of the Alabama Supreme Court.

He told Dee that the kids could stand a break from school for several days – then he called his travel agent to book a trip to the

Grand Caymans. Dee was reluctant to take the kids out, but Taylor insisted that he needed a vacation, and he wanted his family to be with him. She enjoyed traveling immensely and didn't put up much of a fight.

They were gone for five days.

His hope was to get his mind off the pressures that Hurricane Peter had created in his life, and though he played the part of the happy father vacationing with his family, the situation in south Alabama never left his mind.

The Franklins returned to Dallas on a Sunday – three weeks before the deadline for Insure Pro to file the appeal. The following morning Taylor called Dan Spearman into his office.

"I've given every ounce of thought I have to the Garrett matter, Dan, and I have come to the conclusion that, in light of what we are facing in that hell hole, we would be most likely to prevail in the end if Mike Holliday was given the opportunity to appoint a new chief justice." Taylor spun his chair around, not wanting to face Dan, and stared into the wooded area behind the Plaza. "Make sure nothing can come back to us."

"I understand, sir, I'll take care of it." Dan simply turned and walked out of his boss's office. Taylor sat at his desk, staring into the distance, for almost twenty minutes – trying to come to terms with the fact that he had just authorized his Director of Security to murder the sitting chief justice of the Supreme Court of Alabama.

* * *

Dan left the Plaza and drove home, where he would begin planning the mission Taylor had ordered him to complete. When he arrived at his two-bedroom home, on the eastern side of Dallas, he proceeded straight to the basement, where he had set up his home office in a small room originally designed as a storage room. He maintained most of his files in the attic, keeping only working files in his office. When meetings were scheduled at the Plaza he would bring the required files from home and ensure that they came back with him – he didn't want his work available for just anyone to see at the Plaza.

He retrieved the Garrett file and began to review it. Since the Atlanta incident, Garrett had dropped under the radar, keeping to himself as far as Dan could determine. There was no indication that he had been traveling, other than occasionally making weekend trips to Orange Beach, which, according to his sources happened an average of twice a month.

The most important issue to decide upon was where the mission would be carried out. Montgomery was the capital, and the third largest city in the state – their police force was skilled, and with the legislature in session, there were plenty of officers on duty. Federal authorities also maintained offices in the capital – another negative. Several interstates ran in and out of the city, however, which would provide for an easier exit, but he would have to drive there himself, so shooting up to Atlanta, just two hours away, and catching a flight was not an option.

Orange Beach was a vacation town whose police force was more accustomed to handling drunk drivers, bar fights, underage pranksters and the occasional domestic disturbance call. Last year there had been only two homicides in the area – one, involving a young male, that was still unsolved but presumed to be drug related, and a convenience store clerk who was killed in a robbery, also still unsolved. It was forty-five minutes or so to I-10, which ran from Jacksonville, Florida, to San Diego. With numerous opportunities to head north along the way, once he made it to that point, he could be headed to virtually anywhere.

Another factor in favor of Orange Beach was the fact that spring break had ended, and they were in a lull before the summer vacationers overran the community. When he had thoroughly examined the possibilities, the safest choice was to confront him in south Alabama.

He made the call to his source to check on the chief justice's schedule – he was in Montgomery this weekend. Dan would have to check in the first of the following week.

* * *

Jack watched the news religiously, as he had always done. Over the last several weeks he waited for the story to air telling the voters about his cocaine addiction, but apparently it hadn't made its way to the newsrooms yet.

Word spread quickly through the legal community about Buck's eight-million-dollar verdict against Insure Pro, and Jack knew it was a matter of time before they let him know they were

253

counting on him. Statewide newspapers ran a story on the verdict, always sensationalizing the size of it without printing any details informing the public about why the jury awarded what they did. Most readers were simply told, in a cursory fashion, that a Tuscaloosa couple was awarded eight million dollars when their insurance company denied a claim on a four-hundred-thousand-dollar beach house – another jackpot in an Alabama courtroom.

Although he was working hard at keeping the Broussard method in action, he couldn't fight back the nervousness and worry that inevitably crept back in after the verdict in the Whisenhunt case was issued. It was time to escape to paradise for a couple of days and get away from the pressures of normal life. He would leave for Orange Beach after lunch on Friday.

* * *

Spearman called Cindy Driscoll, Jack Garrett's secretary, on Tuesday morning. "Cindy, this is Howard Feldman with ProPac. How are you this morning?"

"I'm fine, Mr. Feldman, what can I do for you?" she answered politely. She was accustomed to receiving phone calls from a variety of lobbyists at all times of the year – most wanted to schedule an appointment with the judge to talk politics, or whatever it was that they did. She lost track of all the names and groups that wanted to give Judge Garrett money, and Mr. Feldman's name didn't ring a bell.

"I have some potential donors to ProPac who were going to be in the capital this weekend, and I was wondering if His Honor will be in town?" Howard was pleasant and courteous.

"I'm sorry, sir, but Judge Garrett is going to the beach this weekend. I can check his calendar for next week if you like?" she asked.

"Please don't go to the trouble – our donors will only be in this weekend. Thank you so much for your time, and we'll see if we can't set something up down the road."

"You're welcome, have a nice day."

* * *

Ron Sullivan left Dallas on Wednesday afternoon, headed for Orange Beach. He needed to get there early to prepare.

On Thursday morning, Ron checked into a hotel five miles down Highway 98 from Jack Garrett's paradise. It was time to go to work.

After several hours of sleep, Ron was rejuvenated and ready to get his day started. He had a small meal and a quick workout, then showered and spent the rest of his day waiting for nightfall. Shortly after nine in the evening, Ron drove down the front beach road to Jack's house. He parked at a beachside restaurant's parking lot about three hundred yards from Jack's gated entrance. He strolled down the roadway, along with a handful of other tourists enjoying the late spring air. When he arrived at Garrett's place, he walked north, away from the beach, along the perimeter of the iron fence that surrounded the property, until he was sure that no one was close.

He scaled the fence, landing in the sandy yard on the western side of the house, opposite the garage, proceeding to the rear of the house. He examined the residence from every side, assessing his options. The riskiest part of the mission was underway. Ron had to find a way in – and he hoped that Garrett either hadn't had time, or bothered, to activate an alarm system. The reality was that Jack had never paid the monitoring company to establish service at the house. The original home was equipped with an alarm system, as was the reconstructed one, but Jack didn't have much in the way of valuables in the house, and Orange Beach was such a low crime area that he never gave it a second thought.

Ron walked around the house, studying the windows and doors, evaluating the possibilities – he needed quick, easy access. When he'd circled the house several times, he finally decided that the door leading from the study off the master bedroom was the best option – it was a standard, single-bolt locking mechanism door. There wasn't a keyhole from the outside, so the door had clearly been designed as a means of exit from the bedroom, rather than an entrance. He slid a prepaid phone card he had purchased on the drive into the door jam, slowly bringing it down towards the secondary lock. When it was breached, he pulled a small screwdriver from his pocket, wedging it into the primary lock, and gently pushed the lock open. The door eased open, with no audible warning. Ron waited outside the residence for five minutes, figuring that if a silent alarm had been activated, he would have heard the approaching sirens within a minute or so.

Once he was satisfied that no alarm was present, he entered the residence. He toured the main level quickly, mentally noting the layout. Once he was sure that he had familiarized himself with the floor plan, he returned to his entrance and placed a piece of masking tape over the throw from the door to the frame. He then pulled the door shut and took two additional pieces of tape, stretching one from the top of the door to the frame and the other on the left side of the door, also attaching it to the frame. When he returned in two days, if the tape was gone he would know that there was a problem, and he would improvise. In forty-eight hours, Ron would be on his way back to Dallas, and Governor Holliday would begin the process of appointing a new chief justice.

* * *

Jack and Sharon arrived late Friday afternoon.

After unpacking, they went to Phil's Oyster Bar for dinner. Phil's was far from gourmet, but they had some of the best fried oysters on the gulf coast. The beachside diner had dark wooden floors and the walls were covered with baseball caps that had been signed by the donors; Greg Maddux, Randy Johnson, Charles Barkley and a handful of other celebrities were represented on the wall, along with hundreds of beachgoers who enjoyed coming back every year to show their friends their spot on the walls of fame.

They enjoyed the fried seafood platter, a staple at Phil's and the most popular item on the menu. It was a warm evening, so they decided to walk down the beach for a while, enjoying the weather and sea breeze – an added benefit was that it was helping them digest the unhealthy meal they had just finished. Following a forty-minute stroll up and down the beach, they were tired and made their way back to the house.

They agreed that sleep would be a welcome relief after a day of traveling, so they turned in.

* * *

Saturday was a brilliant spring day, with bright sunshine and warm temperatures, common for Orange Beach, but appreciated nonetheless. After a breakfast of bacon, eggs and toast, prepared by Chef Jack, they decided that the day was too good to waste indoors, so they opted to spend the afternoon on the beach. In only a couple of weeks it would be packed with summer vacationers, the majority from farther north, but this weekend the crowd was largely local. They sat under rented umbrellas and relaxed. Spending an afternoon on the gulf coast was the perfect prescription for what ailed most anyone – stretching out on the pristine white sands, listening to the gentle crash of waves against the shore and feeling the warm soft breeze off the Gulf of Mexico on the skin – it made worries disappear. They made sure they didn't waste a minute of the experience, waiting until shortly before sunset to pack up and head back to the house.

Jack decided that he would prepare gourmet pizza for dinner, and he received no objection. Italian food wasn't his specialty, but he'd recently picked up a cookbook with a recipe similar to one he had tried in Birmingham. Grilled chicken pesto pizza proved easier to make than he expected, though he thought he might have kept it in the oven slightly too long. His intuition was wrong on this occasion, and it came out perfectly. After dinner, they retired to the back porch to enjoy some merlot, along with the star-filled night sky.

The mosquitoes decided to come out early this year, and by nine-thirty they'd had enough of slapping them off, so they headed indoors for the evening.

* * *

Ron Sullivan left his hotel at ten o'clock, stopping by one of the convenience marts along the way to gas up – once the mission was over, he wanted to get a couple hundred miles out of Alabama before he had to stop again.

He drove in front of Garrett's property, first taking note that, unlike Thursday night, the lights were on – Garrett had made his way to the coast. He slowed as he passed the house, preparing to turn north as soon as he reached Carroll Street. There were three small homes that sat across the street from Garrett's property to the west, all of them one-level, concrete block wall structures built in the early 70s, and each of which was empty that night. Ron pulled his rented Jeep Cherokee into the driveway of the second house he came upon, stopping it in the covered carport that abutted the residence. He pulled the keys from the ignition and placed them under the driver's seat, then got out and walked around to the trunk. He lifted the rear hatch and pulled up the cover that hid the spare tire. Reaching into the wheel well, he retrieved the 9mm pistol he had acquired from a pawn shop just outside Slidell, Louisiana. The gun was registered – if the store's owner bothered to file the required paperwork – to the gentleman from Seattle who was on his way to New Orleans to visit his daughter and son-in-law. He had been concerned about their safety and wanted to bring them something for protection.

He slid the pistol into his waistband, checked his watch, then shut the rear hatch and began walking across the street, to the fence that surrounded Jack Garrett's property. He climbed the fence at the same location he had two nights earlier, landing in the yard. The house was fifty yards from the fence, with the rear located to his left. There was no traffic on either the front beach road or the side street, and thus no headlights to avoid. He jogged to the rear of the house, alternating his attention between the street and the residence. When he reached the rear end of the house he was protected from the front beach road, as well as Carroll Street – now he could focus on his plan.

He had to walk across the back porch or detour deeper into the yard if he wished to get to his pre-determined entrance. Ron decided he didn't want to arouse any suspicions by making any noise crossing the wooden deck, so he proceeded deeper into the property, into the darkness. Most of his attention was focused on the surrounding streets as he made his way to the house – there was plenty of time to deal with the occupant when he got in.

He worked his way through the back yard, eventually making his way to a palm tree located twenty feet from the marked door that would provide his entrance to the master bedroom. Ron slowly walked toward the door, peering in the windows to see if Jack was moving around. When he reached the door, he checked to see if the strips of tape he'd placed there earlier were still firmly in place. Nothing had been disturbed – his initial visit to

Garrett's house had gone unnoticed. He studied the master bedroom carefully – Jack was not in the room and, from what he could tell, there was no activity in the bathroom that was directly across from the door, either.

Ron Sullivan was looking forward to meeting Jack Garrett for the first time – he knew so much about the man and now he was going to have his first face-to-face encounter. He peeled back the three strips of tape from the door to the frame, and gently pulled the door toward himself.

It opened without a sound.

He stepped in the door and slowly pulled it shut behind him. It was time to introduce himself to the chief justice.

* * *

The first meeting of Insure Pro's Hurricane Peter Litigation Review Committee took place in the main conference room at the Plaza. Leo Kirschberg requested that Taylor organize a group of the company's executives to convene in order to update the board on the status of the numerous lawsuits that were pending, as well as to provide a reasonable estimate of their future exposure for shareholders.

Taylor was asked to lead the meeting. The committee members were all involved in the claims process and included Taylor, Leo, Hugh Capelli, two of his southern regional district managers, three divisional managers for the gulf coast and Kyle Varden, the vice president for claims in the western division. Kyle had not been involved in the hurricane claims, but Leo trusted his judgment and wanted a disinterested voice present for the discussion.

Taylor began by outlining the number of outstanding lawsuits that had been filed against the company. As of May first, a total of seven hundred fifty lawsuits had been filed, and according to the estimates, they could expect up to a thousand more, give or take a few.

"The Whisenhunt verdict was what, again?" Leo asked.

It was a sore subject for Taylor to discuss. But then again, none of the committee members knew any of the details of Taylor's plan, Roger Stoltz, or any of the other facts that the Baldwin County jury heard that had inflamed them so much.

"Just over eight million, sir, but our appeal is pending and we are confident that their Supreme Court will vindicate us," Taylor replied.

"Assuming they do not, we are left with more than seven hundred pending cases, Mr. Franklin; how do you propose that we properly reserve these claims?"

"We know the policy limits of each claim, Leo, and I honestly don't expect that the punitive damage claims will stand on appeal. We had a bad jury, and everyone knows Alabama's reputation for such awards. The majority of the Court ran on a platform to stop these miscarriages of justice, and I am confident we will prevail," Taylor answered.

"I'm just concerned that we have no way to accurately predict our exposure in those cases," Leo said.

"That's my point, Leo. Their system doesn't allow us to predict our exposure, and the Court knows that. You hired me to do a job and I assure you that, not only am I doing it now, I have been doing it for the last several years." Taylor was respectful, but slightly perturbed at Leo's persistence.

"I trust that you have that matter in hand, Taylor." Leo had hired him to handle all the company's legal matters, including judicial relations, and so far he had performed exceptionally. There was clearly no reason to start doubting him now.

"I think we need to focus our attention on the outstanding denials," Taylor said, referring to the other two thousand or so claims in the zone that had been denied. "Although we are confident that we have a valid basis for denying those claims, I don't think it would hurt to approach them with an offer to pay a nominal amount, out of goodwill, in exchange for a release. It would help us tremendously in the PR department with the pending cases, and we could get press releases out informing the public." Taylor wanted damage control and he wanted it badly. He knew that the company's exposure was huge, but if he could get through the appeal, and get Leo out of the picture in the meantime, everything would be fine.

"I like it," Leo said. "Hugh, get to work on drafting a proposal to the denied claimants – no admission of liability, of course – and let's see what kind of response we get."

Most of the members of the committee understood that they were not there to question Leo or Taylor's judgment; it was more of a formality for the board. They took notes and nodded in approval when necessary.

The meeting was adjourned, with nothing of substance having been accomplished. Hugh would prepare the draft letter to the denied claimants, but Taylor was ready to put a hold on the mailing – if the Supreme Court ultimately ruled as expected, there would be no reason to offer anything.

TWENTY-FIVE

Ron walked over to the door that led from the master suite into the living room, and glanced through. Jack was not visible from his viewpoint.

Jack had gone into the half bath, located off the living room and toward the front door, to take a leak. When he emerged from the bathroom, Ron was standing just outside the bedroom door.

Jack didn't realize that anyone else was present when he exited the bathroom and began walking toward the sofa. He caught a glimpse of another person in his peripheral vision and turned, assuming that Sharon had walked out of the bedroom.

He saw a large man, dressed in black slacks, a dark long-sleeved shirt and dark shoes, standing at the entrance to his bedroom. The man had a closely cropped haircut, partially covered by a black baseball cap. Jack's pulse picked up rapidly as he looked the man in the eye. He didn't know what to say, but he finally managed, "Who are you?"

Ron knew that Garrett was taken off guard. "Who I am is not important, Mr. Garrett. Why I am here, that is what's important."

Jack swallowed hard, trying to figure out what was happening, "Then why are you here?" Jack asked.

"There is something I need for you to do for me."

Jack began to step back, toward the front door. "This is private property, sir, and I suggest that you leave." Jack stumbled on his second step.

When Garrett requested him to leave, Ron reached into his waistband, and brandished the 9mm he had acquired for this mission. "I don't think you understood me," he said, pointing the gun directly at Jack. "There's something you are going to do for me, Mr. Garrett."

When his eyes focused on the firearm aimed at him, Jack realized that he was in a bad situation – a very bad situation. If the man was here to rob him, he could have whatever he wanted. Jack just wanted him to take what he was after, and get out without being shot. "You can have anything you want, there's no need for anyone to get hurt. My wallet is in the bedroom. Take it – take everything, just take it." Jack was visibly distraught, and Ron knew that he would do as requested.

"I don't want your money, Mr. Garrett," the man said, still pointing the gun in Jack's direction. "I need your signature and a brief note; then I will leave."

My signature?

A note?

What in the hell?

Jack's brain was spinning, still trying to assess the situation, when it finally sunk in. *He doesn't want money, he wants me. Bob Powell – a suicide note – not signed. Oh shit.*

The man motioned Jack toward the master suite. "In the bedroom, Mr. Garrett – now." The intruder followed him into the bedroom. Jack was standing at the desk along the rear wall, facing the doorway, and the stranger was standing partially in the door frame, target still in sight.

Just as Jack was coming to the conclusion that the man pointing the gun at him had no intention of leaving him unharmed, they both heard her.

"Jack, mind if I turn the air down?" Sharon said as she stepped off the stairs, coming back to the main level. Jack thought he was going to faint.

Someone else is here. That was certainly unexpected. Ron had no indication that the chief justice was traveling with company. He turned and caught her attention just as she reached the landing, and pointed the 9mm directly at her.

Sharon let out a short scream at the sight of the gun.

"Shut up," the huge man said. She saw Jack behind the man, standing near the wall of the bedroom. "Please join us, ma'am," the man said, waving her into the room with Jack.

"Who are you?" Sharon asked him nervously, as he moved aside to let her through the door to join Jack in the master suite.

263

"I will ask the questions here, miss, and the question is who are you?" He was very forceful in his tone. Sharon looked at Jack and saw nothing but fear in his eyes.

"Sharon Waters."

Sharon Waters. The name was familiar and Ron knew he had seen it before. *Sharon Waters.* He studied her closely, alternating his attention back and forth between the two. *The staff attorney.* It finally dawned on him who she was – his file on Garrett, after all, had the names and positions of everyone he was affiliated with at the Court.

"You're the staff attorney," the man said, a slight grin appearing on his face. *The old bastard was banging his staff attorney at his beach house, sneaking her down here for extracurricular activities, what a fucking riot.*

"What's this about, Jack?" Sharon turned to him, whispering, as the intruder stood ten feet away, moving the pistol back and forth between the two.

"I don't know, just do as he asks." Jack wanted to calm her, but recognized that he had to do something. The man in front of him knew who Sharon was, which meant he knew much more about Jack than he would be willing to discuss. Whoever he was, he had done his homework, and that didn't bode well for explaining his presence in the house.

Ron had been prepared to improvise in the event his entrance to the house had been compromised – he had not anticipated an additional body. He had mapped out Jack's suicide in his mind, and now this whore staff attorney threw a wrinkle in the plan. He stood there, studying the two in front of him for a moment before his analytical skills came through. The woman had to go as well; there was no question about that, but he still needed the initial aspect of the mission to be accomplished. It was quite simple, actually.

Murder/suicide. Jack's drug problems would surface soon enough.

Sleeping with his staff attorney. Sneaking off to the coast.

Get the note. Get this done.

Ron was proud of himself, and Jack had unknowingly made his mission much simpler. When the authorities found them at his house and finally determined who she was, it would be clear to them what had happened – that Jack had killed his lover, then turned around and hanged himself, out of shame and guilt and as a tribute to his friend, Bob Powell, who had done the same for him.

"You," Ron said to Sharon, pointing the 9mm at her. "Lie on the bed, face the bathroom."

"What is this…?" she started to say when he stopped her. "Shut up and do as you're told," Ron snapped, raising his voice.

Sharon complied with his orders, lying on the opposite side of the bed from where the two men were standing, and faced away from them. Tears started to well in her eyes, and she began to sob quietly.

"Sit, Mr. Garrett," the man instructed him, "at the desk."

Jack, too, did as he was told, still trying to think his way out of the situation, without alarming or angering the man.

"Get a blank piece of paper." Jack removed a blank piece from the desk drawer and placed it on the desk. "Now," the man continued, "I want you to write down exactly what I say. Do you understand me?"

Jack nodded affirmatively. He was sitting at the desk, facing the wall. The man stood behind him, looking over his shoulder to ensure he was complying.

Sharon wept more audibly now, and the intruder looked over at her.

"Enough of that – be quiet and this will all be over soon." She toned it down slightly.

He could ignore her for now. The plan was coming to a close Standing over Jack's shoulder, the man put the 9mm to the right side of his head, placing his left hand on Jack's shoulder. "Now, write the following words: 'I'm sorry.'"

Jack was confused, "Write what?"

"I'm sorry," the man said again.

Jack's mind was spinning, but he had to find a way to stall the man long enough to think of something. If he was responsible for Bob's death, then Jack was surely a dead man now. It was just a matter of how much longer he had before the trigger was pulled. Jack didn't write anything. He simply turned his head to face the gun that was touching his skull. "You're going to kill me anyway, I'm not writing a goddamned thing."

Had it just been Jack at the house, Ron would probably have gone ahead and finished the job then. But he had options. He stared the chief justice in the eyes coldly. "Are you sure about that?"

"Go ahead and do it." Jack could only hope that Sharon might have a chance to get out during the commotion that would come. He knew he was no match for the intruder physically. He was a lost cause.

Ron stepped away from the target, still pointing the gun at him. He walked to the other side of the room, to Sharon. She was still facing away from Jack, but now looking directly at the man's legs. Ron reached down and ripped her shirt, exposing her bra. She began to sob louder. "Mr. Garrett, you may wish to reconsider," he said.

"She has nothing to do with this," Jack began, "leave her out of it."

"You will not bark orders at me, Mr. Garrett." Ron moved the gun away from Jack, pointing it directly at Sharon now. Jack was terrified. Sharon's death would be his fault, completely. It would haunt his soul for eternity.

Ron slapped the side of her face violently, leaving his handprint. He stared back at Jack as her sobbing grew louder. She was unable to speak, facing sheer horror for the first time in her life.

"Open your mouth, you fucking whore!" The intruder's face was turning red and the veins in his neck were bulging. Sharon was paralyzed with fear. "I said, open your fucking mouth." Ron looked straight at Jack as Sharon slowly opened her lips.

Ron placed the barrel of the 9mm into her mouth, almost gagging her. "Mr. Garrett, I will give you five seconds to change your mind, before I make a mess of your pretty little friend's head. Give me what I want, and she can leave the house, unharmed."

Jack struggled with his thoughts for a split second. Anything to delay Sharon's execution would be acceptable. As the man began counting down to Sharon's death, Jack interrupted him, "OK. I'll give you what you want, but she has to be let go now."

Ron removed the gun from Sharon's mouth, pointing it again at Jack. "You're right, sir, this is not about her. She'll be allowed to leave when I have what I need. Then you and I can talk. It is not a matter for negotiation." He pointed the 9mm back at Sharon for an instant.

"Fine," Jack finally said. "I'll give you what you want." He had no choice. His mind was blank.

Ron left Sharon, a sobbing mess, on the bed and walked back to Jack at the desk. He returned the gun to his side, leaning over Jack's shoulder and rested his left hand on the top of the chair.

Jack began writing as instructed, with the man looking over him.

Garrett took his time, writing each letter slowly, to make sure that he didn't misunderstand his directions.

Ron thought for a moment that the gun had misfired – the cracking sound resonated in his head as he began to stagger toward the floor. The gun that had been in his hand dropped to the floor, as he fought desperately to get air into his lungs. He didn't know what was happening, but suddenly he couldn't breathe, and the pain in his left side was unbearable. He felt something, or someone – he couldn't quite discern which – grabbing hold of his right arm. He was violently thrown to the floor, and caught a brief glimpse of a bald headed man, possibly mid-twenties, before he saw the flash of a leg coming toward his head. Ron still couldn't breathe. Gasping for air, he realized that the leg had missed its target, until he felt it on the side of his head. The assailant had tightened his legs around Ron's upper torso, pulling his right arm straight. His arm was being bent at the elbow – the wrong way. The pain grew more intense as Ron screamed, trying to slip the hold that had been put on him. It was no use, the attacker had him gripped too tight, and Ron's arm was bending far past the point that it was designed to go.

He heard his attacker yell, "The gun, Jack, get the fucking gun." The woman was screaming hysterically, and the man on top of Ron screamed back at her to call the police. Ron was about to pass out from lack of oxygen when it broke. The sound alone made him sick, but the pain was worse than any he had ever felt before. He saw the remnants of his right arm; the lower part of his arm was now dangling at an absurd angle, much closer to his head than it should have been, and the attacker still had him in his grasp. Ron used the last bit of consciousness he had to look over at the man who was breaking him in two. He saw a red-faced man, straining with every ounce he could muster – the veins in his head and neck were pulsing, he was not backing off at all.

Ron Sullivan slipped into unconsciousness, his body limp.

* * *

Keith Waters had been upstairs in the guest room, reading a book, when the intruder had made his way inside. He didn't hear the initial commotion, as he had the television on, and there wasn't any screaming. When his mother poked her head in the door to tell him she was heading to bed, he turned the TV off, and kept reading. Sharon's brief scream got his attention, and as he got to the bottom of the stairs, he saw the strange man in the bedroom, holding them at gunpoint.

He crept slowly to the side of the bedroom door, listening to the commands the stranger was making to Jack and his mom. When he realized that he had an opening, he took advantage of it. He peered through the space between the door and the frame, and saw that the man had turned his back, pointing the weapon at Jack. He saw his mother sobbing on the bed, facing away from them, and slowly made his way into the room. The attacker's left arm was elevated high enough for a devastating roundhouse kick to the ribs. Keith put everything he had into the kick, hoping it would be enough to disable the man, or at least open another avenue of attack.

As the man fell to the ground, he knew the kick had done its job. He could tell that he was having difficulty breathing, but he wasn't going to take any chances. He threw him to the floor and straddled him, grabbing the exposed arm and falling backwards to the floor himself. It was a traditional jujitsu maneuver, most commonly referred to as an "arm bar." Once it was fully administered, the victim had no way out – the aggressor could put as much pressure on the elbow joint as he wanted, and it didn't take much for an arm to break. Keith had performed the move thousands of times, and taught it regularly in his classes – but he had never broken anyone's arm before, and was surprised at how little effort it actually took.

When the man passed out, Keith released the pressure. The injuries he had inflicted upon him were not life threatening, but the man certainly wouldn't be a threat to them when he woke, if he even did before the police arrived. Sharon called 911 immediately and reported the crime that was in process. Jack had given Keith the 9mm that the attacker had brought into the house, and Keith stayed with the disabled man in the bedroom. He instructed Jack and his mom to wait in the front of the house for the police – Keith would make sure nothing happened if the attacker came to.

The man on the floor slipped in and out of consciousness, occasionally muttering something incomprehensible. His breathing was so labored that Keith began to think he might actually be in respiratory distress, but he wasn't going to provide medical attention. The man had come into the house with a gun, why he didn't know, but he wasn't going to give him the benefit of the doubt.

The police arrived at Jack's house five minutes after the call came through. Officer Patrick Capps was the first to arrive. Jack informed him that an intruder had been subdued by his companion's son and that they were in the master bedroom. He escorted the officer into the house, as Capps called for another cruiser for assistance.

Officer Capps found Keith holding the man at gunpoint. The man was awake, but groggy, with an obvious deformity to his right arm. Capps called dispatch requesting additional backup and an ambulance.

"An ambulance?" Jack protested. "That man came into my house with a gun, and you are going to send him to the hospital?" He was outraged.

"Mr. Garrett, he will be guarded at all times, but we have to follow protocol, and the man is clearly badly injured."

Jack knew there was nothing he could do about it, but he was still reeling from the night's events.

Officer Capps' colleagues arrived and began taking statements from the victims. The intruder was taken to Baldwin County Hospital, under the watchful eyes of two Orange Beach PD Officers. Jack and Sharon told the officers what had happened, to the best of their recollections – the entire nightmare had lasted less than ten minutes or so, but it had felt like hours.

Keith was questioned afterwards. He had originally traveled from Nashville to Montgomery to spend the weekend with his mother, whom he saw once a month or so. She was coming to Orange Beach with Mr. Garrett, so they invited him to join them for the weekend. He told them how he'd heard the commotion downstairs and went to the aid of his mother and her friend. He made no apologies for what he'd done to the intruder, and none were asked of him.

The officers asked the three to stay in Orange Beach until Monday morning, if at all possible, to assist in the investigation. Keith needed to get back to Nashville to his martial arts studio, but understood that his assistance would be required here. He called a friend and asked him to cover his studio for a couple of days.

Jack told the lead investigating officer about his concerns regarding the intruder – he knew entirely too much personal information, he knew who Sharon was – he was there for a very specific reason, and Jack wanted reassurance that he would not be set free on bail.

"Due to the use of a weapon, we are charging him with burglary, attempted armed robbery, assault with a deadly weapon and attempted murder, Mr. Garrett. Bail will be set by a county judge on Tuesday."

Jack took some comfort in knowing that the man would not be able to post bail and walk away, but the circumstances of that night were too bizarre to chalk up to coincidence. He hated to do it, but maybe now Ray would listen to him.

TWENTY-SIX

According to the Washington driver's license the police found in the Jeep Cherokee across the street from Jack's house, the man in their custody was Ron Sullivan, from Seattle. The Cherokee had been rented in Dallas, and other than that, they had very little to go on. The resident on call notified them that Mr. Sullivan had sustained five broken ribs, a partially collapsed left lung, and a compound fracture of the right arm. He was in surgery to repair the arm, and would probably be ready for discharge the following afternoon.

"When will he be able to talk?" the officers asked.

"He'll still be sedated from the surgery tonight, but he should be fine in the morning."

The two officers spent the night at Baldwin County Hospital, sitting next to Ron Sullivan in his room. Ron had been brought out of surgery shortly after midnight, and was not responsive overnight.

The following morning, he woke to find himself in the hospital, the cobwebs still in his head – handcuffed and shackled to the hospital bed.

One of the police officers standing over him looked down, "Mr. Sullivan, we have some questions for you."

* * *

Ray Carlisle was getting ready for bed when Jack called him at home.

"Ray, I know I'm the last person you want to hear from, but can you give me five minutes, please," Jack asked.

"What is it now, Jack?"

Garrett proceeded to tell Ray about the intruder in his house earlier that evening, how he knew who Sharon was, and wanted him to write a note.

Jack was clearly distraught. Ray could tell in his voice that this was not the same as before, when he wanted to pressure Bob Powell about the disc. Jack was terrified now. "What did he ask you to write?" Ray asked.

"All I got to was 'I'm sorry,' then everything went crazy," Jack started. "The note started out just like Bob's, Ray, and I have a feeling that the same ending was planned for me."

"Where is the man now?" Ray inquired.

"Orange Beach PD took him to the hospital, but they said bail wouldn't be set until Tuesday. Look, I know you don't want to be involved in this anymore, but I think this is much bigger than the disc."

"Let me get a couple hours of sleep, and I'll head down first thing in the morning. Are you okay for now?" Ray asked.

"I'm fine, and, Ray, thanks for your help, I sincerely appreciate it."

Ray called the Orange Beach Police Department as soon as he got off the phone with Jack, and asked for the ranking lieutenant on duty. When Lt. Small answered, Ray informed him that a prisoner they had apprehended earlier that evening, who was at the hospital, was a suspect in a federal case, and that he would be down by midday to interrogate him. The officer expressed his understanding, and thanked the agent for his call.

Ray slept for five hours before making the three-hour drive to the beach. He arrived at the station shortly before nine a.m.

* * *

Ron looked at the officers standing over his bed, and said nothing.

"Mr. Sullivan, what were you doing at that house last night?" one asked.

"I was out of cash, just needed some money, that's all. Have you arrested that animal that did this to me?" Ron answered.

"You went to burglarize the residence, then?"

"Like I said, I was out of cash." Ron knew a small theft charge would mean he's out of jail in days, free to go home.

"What are you doing here all the way from Seattle, Mr. Sullivan?"

"Just traveling through, I wanted to see the country."

"When did you get here?"

"I'm still a bit tired, sir, can we do this later?" Ron said, not wanting to get too far into a story he wasn't going to remember.

"Are you asking for a lawyer?" they inquired.

"No, just some time to let this anesthesia wear off," Ron replied. He didn't need to get a lawyer involved. If things worked out the way he needed, the charges filed against him would result in a bond, and he'd disappear, never to be found.

The officers called the station to inform them that the prisoner would be released after noon, and they were told that someone from the FBI was waiting for their return. They stepped back into Ron's room. "Looks like you've pissed someone off. The FBI wants to talk with you," one officer informed him.

The FBI? What in the hell are they doing here?

Shortly after one-thirty on the afternoon following Ron's breaking and entering of Jack Garrett's home, he arrived at the Orange Beach Police Department, escorted by two officers, with his arm in a cast.

* * *

Ray had been waiting for several hours when the lieutenant on day shift told him that the prisoner was being processed. When the officers had completed all the required paperwork, fingerprinted him, and gotten him the standard issue orange jumpsuit, Ron was placed in the interrogation room, where he sat for thirty minutes, waiting for the FBI.

Ray entered the room to find the prisoner sitting still, straight-faced and confident. Jack's girlfriend's son had done a number on this guy, and Ray knew he still had to be in a good deal of pain. "So your name is Ron Sullivan?" he asked.

"You have my identification."

"You seemed to know quite a bit about Mr. Garrett, Mr. Sullivan, and I'm interested in knowing how you came to acquire that knowledge."

273

"I don't know what you're talking about, sir."

"You told them last night, when Ms. Waters identified herself, that she was his staff attorney. Now how exactly would you know something like that?"

Ron didn't reply.

"You need to tell me the truth, or things are going to get much harder on you, Mr. Sullivan. Why did you come to Orange Beach?"

"I told them it was a robbery, sir, and I am prepared to be charged for my crime."

"Oh no, sir, you are being charged with attempted murder, Mr. Sullivan."

Ron stared back at the agent, showing no signs of concern. "Mr. Carlisle, I threatened no one with violence, sir."

"Putting a loaded 9mm pistol to someone's head is not a threat, Mr. Sullivan? Come on, you can do better than that," Ray shot back. "You say you are from Washington?"

"Just look at the license, agent."

Ray pulled a chair up to the metal table, sitting opposite Ron, and forced his attention. "Why don't you tell me about Bob Powell, Mr. Sullivan."

Ray got what he wanted out of the question. He focused on Ron's neck, where his pulse was visible. As soon as Bob's name was mentioned, Ron's pulse quickened. Then he blinked more rapidly than he had been doing since their conversation began – both physical cues that he was in distress.

"Who is Bob Powell?" Ron finally asked, though it didn't matter to Ray. Ray expected a denial from him.

"What is your name?" Ray asked again.

"I believe we've been over that, sir."

Ray got up and left the room, and went to talk with the lieutenant. "Run a check on this license; compare it with the social and date of birth, if you don't mind." Ray took a seat next to the window that peered into the room where Ron was sitting and waited for the license check to come back. Ron remained calm in his seat, occasionally adjusting the position of his right arm when it began to throb. About thirty minutes after the request was made, an officer came back and presented Ray with several printouts from their computer. He studied them for a few minutes before getting up and walking back into the room.

"I'm sorry to hear about your loss," he said to Ron. Sullivan had no idea what he meant by that comment.

"Pardon me?" Ron replied.

"I said I'm sorry for your loss. It appears that you died last year, Mr. Sullivan, and I am very sorry to have to be the one to inform you of your death." Ray had a shit-eating grin on his face. "It's time you tell me who you are now."

"Your information is wrong, sir, and I have nothing else to say to you." The prisoner turned his head away from Agent Carlisle.

"You may change your mind, we'll see about that." Ray left the room again. He asked the officers to put the prisoner in his cell until he was ready to talk with him again, and they obliged him. Ray then asked for a complete copy of the file they had on Ron Sullivan, including all the personal belongings, paperwork, prints and anything found in the rental vehicle. Once they had everything ready, it was handed over. Ray thanked them for their assistance and informed them that he would return as soon as he got what he needed.

He left Orange Beach and headed east – it was only about a thirty-minute drive to Pensacola, Florida.

* * *

Ray arrived at the Pensacola field office with his file on Ron Sullivan, and walked in. He greeted the receptionist and showed her his credentials, then asked if he could speak with one of the field agents on duty. Being a Sunday, there were only two agents present in the office. Agent Carol Gordon came out and introduced herself.

"I need to run some comparisons through our databases on an ID," Ray said. "I don't really need any assistance, but could you direct me to a connection?"

Agent Gordon nodded in approval, then led Ray through the electronically locked door that led from the lobby into the main office complex. She showed him around the floor for a moment before finally reaching a terminal that he could use. "Here you go, Agent Carlisle, can I get you anything?"

"No thank you," he answered, "I'll just get to work." She left him to his duties and Ray logged into the system using his password. He didn't know how long it would take, but he was confident that eventually he would be able to determine just who Ron Sullivan was – and when he did, the real fun would begin.

Ray had compared his data against more than two hundred databases, run NCIC checks and reviewed photos of hundreds of suspects, yet nothing had come up matching this man. Knowing that his identity had been stolen, the only thing they had to go on was the fingerprints they had obtained.

Four hours into his research, just as dusk was setting in, Ray found what he was looking for. It was one of the last data comparisons he was going to do before calling it a day and returning in the morning for another round. The FBI, in conjunction with the CIA, had maintained open lines of communication with the armed services, and Ray took a shot that the prisoner might have been a soldier at some time. The comparisons were being performed by the system when a match appeared on the screen. Apparently, Mr. Sullivan had been in the Special Forces for some time, having been discharged approximately fifteen years ago. Daniel George Spearman's last known address was in Dallas, Texas. Now it was time to find out what he did.

Ray began the second part of his research immediately, and picked up the phone to call the Dallas field office to see if they had any information on Spearman. Likewise, he would scour the databases that they had in order to determine who Daniel Spearman really was. As he was beginning his search, he thought to call Jack. Maybe he could give him something to work with, and anything was worth a shot.

"We've identified the man from last night," he said, when Jack answered. "His name is Daniel Spearman. Does that name ring a bell with you?"

Jack was encouraged to hear the news, but the name was foreign. "I've never heard it before."

"We have a last known address in Dallas; does that help you in any way?" Ray asked.

"Not that I can think of. Shit, Dallas is a huge city, Ray."

"Well, if anything comes to mind, you have my number, just give me a shout." Ray went back to his search on the computers at the Pensacola field office.

* * *

Jack started to knock around ideas with Sharon and Keith on ways to help Ray Carlisle in his quest. They had plenty of wild ideas, none of which would have been beneficial to give to Ray, as they didn't want to cause him to go off on a tangent due to their imaginations. Ray was the professional when it came to these matters, and they would intervene only with good cause.

Over the course of the evening they continued to discuss things, when Sharon finally made a comment that resonated with Jack. "Didn't Bob Powell do some work in Dallas, Jack?" she asked.

Jack hadn't given it any thought, but Bob had told him that he had been in Dallas on several occasions, though he maintained his office at home. It wasn't until shortly before Bob's death that Jack found out that he worked for Insure Pro. If that's what he was doing in Dallas, surely Ray would want to know.

Jack called him at nine that night and told him about the potential connection. "They've got a case coming up, and Bob was hounding me about it over the last year. I just thought you might be interested," Jack said.

"Thanks for the tip; I'll see what I can find."

Spearman was clearly using an alias, and who he was working for would eventually be determined, but Ray had a hard time believing that the largest insurer in the country was involved in this. Out of sheer curiosity, he decided to make a call.

"Thank you for calling Insure Pro, we're always there for you, this is Faith, how may I direct your call?"

"Daniel Spearman, please ma'am." Ray said.

"One moment, please," Faith said, putting Ray on hold. Ray was waiting for her to come back on the line and inform him they had no one by that name, when she said, "Thank you for holding, I will connect your call, have a wonderful day and thank you for calling Insure Pro."

There's no way. Ray waited while the phone rang five to seven times and then he heard a familiar voice, "You've reached the voice mail of Dan Spearman, Director of Security with Insure Pro. I am currently out of the office, so please leave a detailed message and I will get back with you as soon as possible. Thank you for calling and have a nice day." Ray hung up before he heard the tone, indicating to begin your message.

The Director of Security at Insure Pro is at the chief justice's house with a 9mm pistol, making him write a note of apology to some unknown person, carrying the identification of a deceased Washingtonian, driving a rented car, and carrying nothing whatsoever that would lead to an insurance company. None of it made any sense, but he wanted to call Jack.

When Jack heard the news he began to sweat. He had to sit down for a minute. "He works for the company?" he asked, still in disbelief.

"It appears that he is a director of their security department, whatever that means," Ray said.

"He was going to kill me, Ray. I have no doubt in my mind about that, and he would have killed Sharon and Keith if he had to."

"I believe you're right, Jack, and I'm sorry you've had to go through this. I'm going straight to the station to have a talk with Dan Spearman; we're going to get to the bottom of things before too long."

Jack began to settle down. "Thanks again, for everything."

* * *

Agent Carlisle walked into the Orange Beach Police Department at ten-thirty Sunday night, just before shift change, and asked that the prisoner be brought back to the interrogation room. The duty officer had been present when Ray was there earlier, and he immediately left his post to get him. Ray waited outside the room until Spearman was seated and cuffed to the chair.

He walked in with a smile on his face. "I told you I had nothing else to say to you earlier, sir. Did you forget?" Dan said smugly.

"No, I recall our conversation, but I think you might want to reconsider, Dan."

He couldn't hide anything this time, though he tried – "What are you talking about?"

"I'm talking about you telling me what's been going on at Insure Pro. As the director of security, I would assume that you have some insight into the company." Dan was completely silent now. "You've got an awful lot of explaining to do, Mr. Spearman."

Dan remained quiet, and Ray presumed he was weighing his options. Usually when suspects were presented with the evidence against them, they would cave. Though Ray didn't have anything solid yet, it was only a matter of time before all the pieces were put together – a fact that Dan was fully aware of by this point. After several minutes of silence, Dan spoke, "I want a deal."

"I'm not sure what you mean, Spearman," Ray replied.

"I can give you something much more valuable than myself, but I want a deal first."

"That will be up to the U.S. Attorney, but before I go to him, I need to know what it is you are offering to provide."

"Cut me a deal, and I can give you the vice president of the company."

Ray was startled, but kept his calm upon hearing that whatever was going on went to the highest levels of the company. "I'll talk with the U.S. Attorney in the morning and we'll get back with you." Ray left the interrogation room.

He needed to get some rest before calling the U.S. Attorney tomorrow morning – this case was getting more and more interesting.

Dan was returned to his cell for the rest of the evening. He realized that he had just offered Taylor on a platter to the federal government – the man who was responsible for everything he had become, the man he had worked so hard to protect and insulate from the authorities – but the situation had evolved and now it was survival of the fittest. And Dan was in much better shape that Taylor Franklin.

* * *

Ray called Jim Longwell, one of the prosecutors in the Southern District of Alabama, and filled him in on what had transpired over the weekend in Orange Beach. Jim's office was in Mobile, just across the bay from where Spearman was being held. Jim was a career prosecutor, and had been with the U.S. Attorney's office for over a decade. Ray was unable to provide many details to him, other than that Spearman had been found in the chief justice's home, armed and with false identification – and now he was offering up an executive of the company he worked for in exchange for a deal.

It was widely known in criminal practice that if a prosecutor had a shot at bringing down a big fish – and a highly-paid corporate executive was definitely a big fish – then the prosecutor would routinely agree to immunity deals or significantly lighter sentences for the informant. The big fish brought media attention, and that meant more money in the private sector when the prosecutor decided to get out of public service, which they always did inevitably. Jim agreed to talk with Spearman and hear him out, so he traveled the short distance across the bay to meet with Ray and the inmate.

Dan was brought back into the interrogation room and waited about ten minutes for the two lawyers to come in. Ray introduced Jim and let him take over from there.

"Agent Carlisle tells me that you can provide us with an executive, is that so?"

"You cut me loose, and I can give you what you want," Dan replied.

"I can't agree to anything until you tell me what it is that this person has done, Mr. Spearman. I need to know what happened, first," Jim said.

"His name is Taylor Franklin and he is the Vice President and General Counsel of the company. He ordered me to kill the chief justice so that the governor would have to appoint a replacement." Dan was straightforward in his assertions.

"Why would he want him dead, sir?"

"Garrett had already ruled against us in a proceeding that stands to cost the company millions, if not billions, and it was clear he would continue to do so. I have it on tape, Mr. Longwell."

"You have a recording of this?"

"I do. But I want to walk – do we have a deal?"

"We will escort you back to Dallas, and, once we have the information we need, I will agree not to prosecute you for this crime."

"I want it in writing, Mr. Longwell."

"Once I hear the tape, you will have it in writing, sir."

Ray and Jim Longwell made the arrangements for Spearman's transfer to Dallas to obtain the tapes. He would be driven by a deputy sheriff from Baldwin County, and Jim and Ray would meet them there.

* * *

Two days later Jim and Ray met at the small two-bedroom home that belonged to Dan Spearman, along with the deputy sheriff and Dan. They went into the house and were led to the basement, to his home office. Dan retrieved his files and removed a two inch tape from one of the folders. He pulled out his Dictaphone and placed the tape inside, then pushed "*play.*"

Taylor Franklin's voice, according to Spearman, was the other one on the tape. He was heard saying that Governor Holliday should be given the opportunity to appoint a new chief justice, along with a statement that Dan was to make sure nothing fell back on them. Jim had what he needed; he drafted and signed an agreement to give Daniel Spearman immunity from prosecution for the crime that occurred the previous Saturday evening. Dan had to remain cooperative and not leave the state, pending the prosecution of Taylor Franklin, and he signed an agreement to do so. He was off the hook now, with no reason to leave anyway. He would have to find a new job, that much was clear, but he could return to personal training or get back into private security. There were plenty of options for a man of his caliber.

Ray Carlisle and Jim Longwell left the house and drove to the FBI's Dallas field office, where the arrest of Taylor Franklin would be planned.

* * *

Taylor hadn't heard from Dan in almost a week, but he knew that the task he was performing had no exact timetable, and he trusted that Dan wouldn't act until he was sure the time was right. On Wednesday morning, ten days after Keith Waters had broken Dan Spearman's ribs and arm, Taylor arrived at the Plaza for another day of work. Nothing was out of the ordinary until about ten-thirty, when the phone rang. He answered in his usual fashion: "Taylor Franklin" was all he'd ever said to greet callers. The other party didn't say anything, but simply hung up immediately. It was strange because incoming calls were routed through the switchboard, so someone had to specifically request his extension. Hang-ups were rare, and he hadn't had one in a long time.

He figured he shouldn't worry himself too much about it, and began reviewing his calendar for the rest of the week and checking e-mails. Ten minutes later he heard the sirens.

Taylor's office opened to the rear of the property, so he had to step outside to see what the commotion was about. Emergency vehicles routinely came to the compound, as Insure Pro employed thousands of people, and illnesses and accidents were bound to occur. He heard the sirens drawing nearer, and stood at the railing staring out over the foyer into the driveway. Two Dallas police cruisers pulled into the Plaza, accompanied by a black sedan with flashing red and blue lights on the dash. The officers exited their vehicle, waiting for the occupants of the sedan who got out shortly thereafter. Brian Kelly, one of the U.S. Attorneys in Dallas agreed to participate in the arrest. They were dressed in suits and carried nothing in their hands. They went through the lobby and entered the elevator, proceeding to Taylor's office. When Ray, Jim, Brian and the two officers exited the elevator, they saw a man standing outside the office they were heading toward.

"Mr. Franklin?" Jim Longwell asked, as they approached.

"Yes, how may I help you?" Taylor responded.

"Taylor Franklin," Jim continued, "you are under arrest for conspiracy to commit the murder of Jackson Garrett." Jim proceeded to read Taylor his Miranda rights as he handcuffed him and they began to lead him back to the elevators. As they left the Plaza, a number of on-lookers gathered to see the spectacle of the executive being led away in handcuffs. The rumors would begin immediately.

Declining to be interviewed, Taylor informed the agent and prosecutor that he wanted to speak to his attorney. He was booked in the county jail, where he was held overnight without bond. He was allowed to call Dee to tell her he wouldn't be home – he told her that there had been a mistake, but that he was arrested and she needed to call Bill Hawkins and ask him to come to the jail as soon as possible. Bill was a prominent criminal lawyer in Dallas, and Taylor and he played golf together at times. Bill was allowed to see him that evening in the county jail.

"What's going on, Taylor?" he asked, in the client meeting room.

"I don't know, Bill, but you've got to get me out of here. We can pay any bail they want to set."

"I understand, but they can hold you for seventy-two hours before setting one. I'll try to talk with the prosecutor and see what we can do.

Bill left Taylor and went about trying to find out who he could talk to about the pending charges. After being blown off by several deputies, he finally saw one he knew fairly well who was willing to help.

Hawkins was able to schedule a meeting the next morning during which he would be informed of the nature of the charges that were pending against Taylor Franklin. Although he was not allowed to hear the recording, he was assured that they had possession of it and he would be provided an opportunity to hear it shortly. Based upon what he was told, Taylor had gotten himself in deep shit, maybe too deep for Bill to be able to get him out.

Taylor's bond was set at two million dollars. After spending two nights in jail, he was released, under the conditions that he surrender his passport and agree not to leave the state without express permission from the U.S. Attorney. Bill greeted him upon his release, and took him straight to his office to discuss the case – they would spend the next four hours going over the options and details. The last three days had been the worst Taylor had ever experienced, and, in light of Bill's advice and opinions, the days to follow weren't going to get any better.

* * *

Three weeks after Taylor Franklin was led away from the Plaza in handcuffs, Brian Kelly, chief prosecutor for the Central District of Texas, along with local authorities and Ray Carlisle, who had asked to be allowed to witness the event, descended on the home of Dan Spearman. It was early on a Monday morning when Dan opened the door and was informed that he was under arrest for the second time.

"My deal is in writing, you can't do this," he told the police who were effectuating the arrest. "I'll show you the fucking letter."

Ray corrected Spearman, "We have the agreement, Dan; it provides immunity for the actions that took place in Baldwin County, Alabama, several weeks ago. It does not provide immunity from all prior criminal acts."

"What in the hell are you talking about, agent, we had a fucking deal!" Dan shouted.

"You're under arrest for the murder of Robert Powell at this time, and you are a prime suspect in a Georgia murder that is currently under investigation." Ray read Dan the Miranda rights he was entitled to receive, before being informed that Dan wasn't interested in talking this time. He wanted a lawyer.

* * *

The weeks following the near miss at the beach proved to be some of the best that Jack Garrett had experienced in a long time. Ray was keeping him up to date on the status of the situation in Dallas. Before long, Taylor would be extradited to Alabama to face his charges, unless an agreement was made, and it appeared that Dan was going to be traveling to Georgia. The vindication was the sweetest part of all – Jack knew all along that what had happened in Atlanta was, for the most part, beyond his ability to control, but he still had reservations as to whether Sharon fully believed his version and wondered whether that might have anything to do with the continued delay in the sex department.

Taylor Franklin was able to fill in the details of his program designed to maintain control over the Alabama Court – as well as the other states with elected judges – to the prosecutor, and Jack was later informed via Agent Carlisle. Another bonus was the fact that the material Insure Pro obtained from Cara Patterson was never shared with the media, giving Jack comfort that he would avoid more charges before judicial investigative groups. Being back at the Court without fear of those issues made judging enjoyable again, and he wasn't looking over his shoulder wondering who knew what about what.

Sharon stayed with him for another two weeks after they returned from the beach, mostly to get him acclimated to normal life again, but she had to return to her house eventually, she said. They continued to see each other privately and the relationship was still good, but he wanted more from her – they had been through so much together, and not sharing the most intimate part of herself was wearing on his psyche. He began to doubt himself again, usually wondering if she was simply not physically attracted to him, or maybe the age difference was an indication that she viewed him more as a father figure. Whatever it was, she had not made a move, though he hadn't either, and they hadn't talked about it in quite some time.

* * *

The appeal in the Whisenhunt case was filed in the clerk's office of the Alabama Supreme Court on the fortieth day, two days before the deadline. The random assignment was made to Beth Callahan, the attractive Democrat. The response from Buck Padgett would be received within two weeks.

Everyone on the Court knew it was coming, with the verdict making all the statewide newspapers; it was a foregone conclusion that the Whisenhunt case would come up. The Democrats figured that the jury must have been presented with some seriously bad conduct on behalf of the company for such a verdict to be handed down – over the last few years there had been nothing approaching such a large amount, as jurors had bought into the hoopla being thrown at them from the tort reformers.

Republicans assumed the same must have been true, but they were concerned about their financial backing if they ruled

285

against a member of their supporters' groups. They mentioned it privately, but public discussions were strictly off limits.

The Whisenhunts reply to Insure Pro's appeal came in earlier than anticipated, and both sides' arguments began their circulation around the nine members of the Court. A couple of judges assigned the matter to one of their staff attorneys, but the majority were too intrigued to pass the matter off and they began their review personally. Normally, Jack would have let Sharon handle this one, but he had far too much invested.

* * *

Jack finally decided that his deviation from the Broussard method was hindering him too much. He had made a commitment to live each day to the fullest. Now, unless he talked with Sharon, he would have broken his promise. By early summer they had a standing date for dinner every Friday night, sometimes eating out, but most often staying at Jack's. This evening Jack suggested that they eat in, as he didn't want his discussion with her to be unknowingly overheard by anyone. Sharon arrived at the house shortly after seven, with another half hour or so of daylight remaining in the warm summer afternoon.

As they shared a glass of wine, she asked about the Whisenhunt appeal – she knew, as did everyone else at the Court, that it was under consideration, and she also knew how much time Jack was spending on the case. They briefly discussed some of the legal issues involved, and Jack informed her of various positions each respective party was taking. They continued their conversation while Jack began preparing dinner.

He made Caesar salads as the first course, followed by grilled veal chops with garlic potatoes and fresh green beans. The main course was accompanied by a bottle of Petit Syrah that Jack had picked up earlier at a local wine shop. As always, the dinner was excellent and Sharon took several opportunities to express her satisfaction and appreciation.

She could tell during dinner that Jack was becoming less talkative, and he began to stare off in other directions for periods of time. Something was on his mind, and she had known him long enough to know that he would require some prodding to get it out in the open. That was one of the other small things about him that irked her a bit, but she was growing accustomed to it.

"All right," she finally spoke up, "something is going on in that head of yours."

"What do you mean?" he said, turning his attention from the stairs back to her.

"You've started to quiet down again. I mean, you've hardly said a word over the last fifteen minutes and that usually means you have something bothering you."

"I'm fine," he lied.

"You aren't getting off that easy and you know it," she replied. "You should know by now that you can say anything to me, or at least I would hope you do." She was demanding his attention now.

"It's not that easy, Sharon." Jack was getting nervous again, wanting to avoid the rejection that would surely come.

"Nothing important to us ever is," she said, "but keeping it in isn't going to solve anything, so come on, out with it."

Jack leaned back in his chair and raised his arms overhead, stretching for a moment. He was clearly trying to find the right way to begin the conversation. He put both elbows on the table and clasped his hands together, "Do you find me attractive?" he asked.

Sharon let out a slight giggle, "Why would you ask such a question?"

"See," Jack replied, beginning to stand from the table. "If you're going to laugh, then…"

"Sit down, Jack," she cut in, trying to straighten her face. "I'm not laughing at you, I just can't believe you would ask me such a question. Of course I find you attractive – I wouldn't be here if I didn't."

"It's just that I've begun to wonder what exactly it is that you want out of this relationship," he said.

"I'm enjoying every minute of it. Well – except for a short while down at the beach." She tried to lighten the moment for a bit. "What do you think I want?"

"I don't know, that's why I'm asking."

"Well, what do you want, Jack?"

"I thought it was rude to answer a question with a question," he replied, trying to put on a grin.

"Fair enough then, I suppose I haven't actually sat down and thought about it. I love the time I spend with you. You've made me happy again and I guess I've been so preoccupied being content that I haven't really evaluated it any further. It seems you have though, so what is it you are asking me?"

No regrets. Never. Live every moment. "I've fallen for you, Sharon. Not just a little, but totally, and it's only fair to me and to you that you know it. I want you – that's all." The burden was lifting.

Sharon knew he cared for her, but he had never expressed it so honestly and deeply. She appreciated how hard it was for him to say what he had, and she knew that, deep down, she felt the same. "I love you, too, Jack."

Though he hadn't actually told her he loved her, which he badly wanted to, Jack couldn't believe his ears when she spoke. "You do?" he said, with a hint of doubt in his voice.

"Of course I do. Why would you think otherwise?" she asked.

"I don't know. I guess part of me wonders if I might be more of a father figure, a best friend type." He paused for a moment, looking her in the eyes, "I don't know."

It was all very clear to her now. She knew what had been troubling him over dinner, and he likely had been contemplating it for quite some time. If she was right about it, and she was certain that she was, trying to make him talk about the inevitable would be torturous for him. She had thought on a number of occasions how this would occur, but now she was going to wing it. "Do you have any more of that merlot?" she asked.

"I thought we were having a discussion."

"Please indulge me, Jack – the merlot?"

Jack went into the kitchen and returned with the merlot, pouring both of them a glass. When he finished, Sharon took him by the hand and began walking to the back porch. She led him on a walk around the pond that occupied the back of the property.

"May I ask what we're doing?" Jack said.

"Enjoying this beautiful night." Sharon looked him in the face as she said it, then turned her attention back to the wooded area that was his back yard, resuming her silence.

They circled the pond twice, walking slowly. When they had finished their drinks, Sharon led the way back to the house. As they entered, Jack headed for the kitchen. "What are you doing?" she asked.

"I was going to clean the dishes," he replied.

She couldn't suppress the giggle, "It figures you would pick now to do it."

"What's that supposed to mean?" Jack shot back.

"Nothing," she said, as she walked over and took his hand. "Come here."

Holding his hand, Sharon walked him into the master bedroom. She shut the door behind them and turned the lights down.

For the first time in more than fifteen years, Jack Garrett made love to a beautiful woman.

The following morning, Jack awoke a new man. Sharon was already up and making breakfast, draped in one of his long dress shirts – a most welcome sight to start a new day. They spent the rest of Saturday lounging around the house and doing some yard work. Saturday night would be spent in the same way as the prior evening, without as much talk.

TWENTY-SEVEN

The chief justice received a copy of the proposed opinion from Justice Callahan in the Whisenhunt appeal two weeks after his life had changed. Beth had, expectedly, come to the conclusion that Insure Pro had engaged in a scheme to deny valid claims and attempted to cover up the true nature of their expert. Furthermore, the pathetic arguments advanced by the company at trial had no merit, and the jury's verdict was proper and an adequate amount to accomplish the goal of punishing the company for its actions.

Jack studied the opinion carefully, reading every sentence as though he were proofreading his own work. He called Sharon in and asked her to review the case law cited by Justice Callahan; he wanted to make sure there was nothing missed or misquoted. Sharon completed her review within the day and notified him that, according to her, the reasoning was solid. Jack notified Beth Callahan personally that he was adopting the opinion as written. Now it was up to the remaining seven justices to determine the official result.

By late Thursday afternoon, the Court had come to its conclusion as to the appeal in Whisenhunt v. Insure Pro – by a vote of nine to zero, the verdict was affirmed – Stephen Whisenhunt was now officially entitled to almost eight and a half million dollars from his insurance company, unless the U.S. Supreme Court got involved.

* * *

Buck Padgett received a faxed copy of the opinion from the Supreme Court early Friday morning and immediately called Steve to give him the good news.

"Is it really over, or can they appeal again?" Steve asked.

"I don't think they will try to, but I haven't spoken with them yet," Buck answered, "and I certainly don't think the U.S. Supreme Court would hear the case if they did appeal. As soon as I talk with Mr. Vance I'll give you a call."

"Thank you so much for everything you've done, Buck."

"Congratulations, Steve."

* * *

Les Vance received his copy the same morning. He fully expected that his client would lose the appeal, but he was surprised to learn it was a unanimous decision. He had previously spoken with the powers that be at Insure Pro, and they, too, had come to the determination that further appeals would prove useless, regardless of the Court's decision.

Les was counsel of record in more than seven hundred pending cases against Insure Pro arising out of the Hurricane Peter fiasco – more than enough work to keep him busy for a long time, but his client was now in the sights of hundreds of lawyers who were doing everything in their power to track down the remaining fifteen hundred property owners who hadn't filed suit yet.

TWENTY-EIGHT

ONE YEAR LATER

Taylor Franklin had been out on bond when he got the news about the Alabama Supreme Court's opinion in the Whisenhunt case. The irony of the unanimous decision actually brought a strained smile to his face – his career and life were put on the line for nothing. He knew he had only himself to blame for what had transpired, and he fully accepted the responsibility.

With the help of Bill Hawkins, Taylor negotiated a plea deal with the U.S. Attorney. In exchange for his plea of guilty on the conspiracy charge and his agreement to testify against Daniel Spearman, he would be sentenced to five years in federal prison. The best estimate was that, with good behavior, he would be back at home within one to two years. Other than the time he would spend traveling to Georgia for Dan, he would spend the next year and a half at an Air Force base in San Antonio, at a minimum security prison. Taylor's punishment was far too severe, at least in his opinion. But when Dallas newspapers reported the story, Taylor Franklin was yet another example of white collar criminals getting the better end of the criminal justice system.

When he was released, Dee picked him up.

She never left him.

* * *

ONE YEAR LATER:

Dan Spearman was charged and tried for the murder of Cara Patterson in Georgia. Thanks to good old-fashioned police work by a couple of detectives in the Marietta Police Department, along with some help from the Georgia Bureau of Investigation, they were able to piece together enough evidence tying Ron Sullivan to Cara.

Kip testified about the requests Ron made to find her, and the timeframes matched the time of death. Taylor proved to be the nail in his coffin when he testified that Dan had confessed to the killing. Sitting on the stand and pointing at Dan as he told of the confession was the only satisfying moment for Taylor since the company lost the Whisenhunt trial. Dan Spearman was found guilty after thirty minutes of deliberation, and was later sentenced to seventy-five years in state prison.

Prosecutors in Alabama wanted him tried for the murder of Robert Powell. Bob's cremation presented the biggest problem, because, without an autopsy to determine the true cause of death, they were left with only the testimony of Taylor Franklin, a convicted felon who received a light sentence in exchange for his testimony. Once the Georgia jury convicted Dan of Ms. Patterson's murder, the case in Alabama was formally closed.

Dan Spearman died in the custody of the Georgia Department of Corrections four years later from injuries he suffered in a stabbing in the prison yard.

* * *

The Hurricane Peter Litigation Review Committee was called to formulate a plan to deal with the outstanding cases – and to try to bring closure to the mess that Taylor Franklin created in south Alabama.

The numbers were staggering. To date thirteen cases had gone to trial, resulting in a total of almost eighty million dollars in verdicts. A total of fifteen hundred lawsuits were pending in south Alabama and elsewhere. Even with some smaller verdicts, the exposure would reach at least three to four billion, just from the litigation. The average cost to rebuild each of the claims that were denied in the zone was four hundred thousand dollars. With a total of twenty-seven hundred denied claims, Insure Pro would have paid just over one billion dollars by now, and would have been done with it – if it were not for Taylor. Although roughly one thousand claimants had not filed suit, they couldn't expect them all to remain quiet. More would surely be filed, especially when the statute of limitations began to approach.

Leo Kirschberg turned the meeting over to Insure Pro's newly appointed Vice President and General Counsel, Luther Abercrombie.

Leo initially approached Les Vance for the position, but Les had strong ties to Alabama, and Melanie was firmly against uprooting the family and moving to Texas. Les suggested that Luther would be a perfect fit for the company, and Leo allowed Les to broach the subject with him. Luther's initial reaction was not to consider it, but after talking with his wife and taking into account the benefits, it became more attractive. Luther enjoyed litigation, but he was even better at management and policy making; and in recent years the stress of trying cases had begun to wear on his health. With his wife's blessing, he accepted the position and moved to Dallas in the midst of the Peter litigation crisis.

"The simple fact," Luther began, "is that we cannot afford to wait out the results of such a huge number of cases. Combine that with the knowledge that almost a thousand additional claimants are out there, many of which we can only assume will eventually file suit, and the unlimited exposure we face in this situation is unacceptable."

The other members of the committee were taking notes of everything Luther said. He continued, "I have come to the conclusion that a plan should be implemented that would address all outstanding cases, as well as the claims that haven't been filed. To that end, I have spoken with Sam Kingston about heading a task force designed to bring everyone to the table and put this matter to bed. After substantial begging on my part, Sam has agreed to help."

Samuel Kingston retired as an associate justice from the Illinois Supreme Court, having served twenty-four years on the state's highest court. During his tenure he was a well respected jurist, and particularly well known for his ability to bring about compromise on divisive issues. Luther had worked on a substantial number of cases in Illinois, Indiana and Ohio over the years, and had developed fairly close ties with a number of the lawyers and judges up north. When Sam retired from the bench, he took a position as "of counsel" with a large defense firm in Chicago in their mediation section. It so happened that Gibson Vance had asked his firm to assist them on a number of cases over the last several years.

At sixty-four, Sam was verging on full retirement. He still enjoyed his work, especially now that he was only conducting mediations, but he was closing in on the time when he would pass the torch and spend more time with his four grandchildren.

Luther had not misled the committee regarding having begged Sam to help mediate the Peter crisis. Sam recognized that, with a substantial number of lawyers in the fray, along with the outstanding claimants, finding common ground would prove difficult. The hardest part would be the few attorneys who had only one case or so in their office – knowing that one trial could result in millions of dollars in fees; it wouldn't be easy to persuade that group to accept a smaller figure. The power players, like Buck Padgett, were easier – the large volume of cases they were handling made a package deal quite appealing, and their clients still received enough money to rebuild.

Luther finally managed to convince Sam to head up the team, reminding him that Insure Pro's position was caused by the criminal activity of former employees, not a company-wide mentality.

Luther detailed the plan that he and Sam had put together for the committee, before turning to Leo, "Do we need to present this before the Board?"

"In light of the figures, I believe that they should be advised and given the opportunity to respond," Leo said.

Two weeks later Leo, Luther and Sam appeared before Insure Pro's Board of Governors and presented their plan to resolve the Hurricane Peter claims, making sure the Board fully understood the series of events that had placed the company in such peril. Following two days of discussion and debate, heated at times, the Board voted to approve the proposed action.

* * *

It would take almost a year before everything had been substantially finalized with the Peter settlements. There were a handful of claims that were still outstanding, all of which remained pending because, despite making every conceivable effort, the company had been unable to locate the policyholder.

Buck Padgett made out like a bandit. By the time the settlement program was in full swing, Buck represented nine hundred claimants. Each client received the full amount of coverage under his policy, plus an additional one hundred thousand dollars. Through negotiations, Sam and Buck finally reached an agreement that the trial lawyer would receive a lump-sum fee of fifty million, plus reimbursement of expenses incurred, for his services on all cases.

There were slightly more than six hundred other pending cases, each of which was settled with the policyholder receiving the full amount of coverage. Attorney's fees ranged from ten thousand to as much as eight hundred thousand dollars, depending on the number of cases each attorney had.

The other approximate one thousand claimants were contacted and sent a letter stating that additional review of their claims had been conducted, and that, upon further consideration, their claims were now approved. They would receive the full amount of coverage, plus interest from the date of loss. There were those who balked at the delay, some of whom requested additional money for having had to wait so long – they were handled by Luther and Sam, and the final estimate was that an additional five million was spent appeasing them.

At the Board's request, the final numbers were prepared and presented by Luther and Sam to the Board.

Taylor Franklin had denied the claims of twenty-six hundred homeowners in south Baldwin County. Had Insure Pro simply paid those claims outright, the total cost would have been one billion, forty million dollars, give or take. A review of all monies paid out in settlement to claimants, plus claimants' attorney fees, Insure Pro's attorney fees and expenses, and the generous payment to Sam Kingston, revealed that the company spent a total of one billion, seven hundred fifty million dollars.

They then presented the exposure estimates – had the litigation continued on a case-by-case basis – the lowest expected loss on all cases was calculated to be more than three billion dollars. In little more than a year on the job, Luther Abercrombie had saved his new employer more than a billion dollars. The Board voted unanimously to double his annual salary the following year.

Gibson Vance continued to receive the lion's share of Insure Pro's litigation in the southeast, with Les Vance as lead counsel in the majority of cases.

TWENTY-NINE

TWO YEARS LATER

Jack announced one year before the election that he would not be seeking a third term on the Court. He wanted to give potential candidates plenty of time to raise the money, and courage that would be required to be competitive – as well as get the lobbyists, whose calls came with substantial more frequency as elections approached, off his back. He had accomplished a great deal during his tenure, having brought the Court back from an extreme swing to the right to a moderate position. Justice in Alabama was more predictable for all parties, as a result of his influence. When the following year's elections were over, Republicans lost one seat – the Democrats now held a five-to-four majority, but Jack hoped that the spirit of compromise that he enjoyed in his later years on the Court would continue.

* * *

The Grand Opening, which was actually celebrated two months after the official opening, of Garrett & Waters, P.C., was a small affair. There were only a handful of attorneys who practiced law in Orange Beach, but from what they could tell, each and every one of them stopped by at some point during the day. They served coffee and juice with doughnuts in the morning, and appetizers with soft drinks were laid out in the afternoon. At four p.m., they provided some cocktails for those who showed up after work.

James Willingham made the drive down from Bay Minette, just to wish them both luck in the new practice. Even Ray Carlisle made the three hour drive from Montgomery, with the understanding that Jack would treat him to dinner after the ceremony.

Jack and Sharon used the party as an opportunity to meet the town's practitioners, some local judges and law enforcement and a few citizens, as well as for some low-cost advertisement. But more than anything, they enjoyed the moment. Though the dream was relatively new to them both, it had come true.

They had both talked about taking on a third partner. Despite Jack's insistence that Walter Broussard would love it at the beach, Walt said that Louisiana was home and he couldn't imagine leaving it. He appreciated the offer, but he loved his life in Kaplan.

Garrett & Waters operated as a general practice, handling a variety of legal matters – mainly for folks in south Baldwin County, but occasionally traveling to other south Alabama cities and towns. There had not been any more Eunice Johnsons, at least not yet – but that was fine, they made plenty to live and love on.

One year to the day after the opening of Garrett & Waters, Jack and Sharon were married on the beach, directly across from their paradise.

Walt Broussard was the best man.

FROM THE AUTHOR

I hope you have enjoyed reading The Cost of Justice. This is a piece of fiction. With the exception of some towns, cities and some other locations, everything in this book was a creation of my imagination. None of the characters, companies or events actually existed or occurred to my knowledge. Any similarities to actual people, or events, is unintentional on my part. I have taken some liberties with elements and appellate procedures in this book. My apologies to Judges Woodall and Vowell.

With that said, the underlying theme of this book, the corrupting influence of money in judicial elections in Alabama is far from being fictional. Numerous calls have been made to change the system into one of appointment based positions with qualifications being paramount. To date, these reforms have been opposed by whichever party is in control of the court at any given time. It is my hope that this will one day change. The Court loses its credibility with the public when Judges are forced to run campaigns on party lines, promising certain results if elected. It makes a mockery of what is expected to be an impartial branch of government.

As of the printing of this book, the latest race for the only Supreme Court position that was up for election in Alabama has not been decided. Between the two candidates, it was estimated that more than $5 Million, yes Million, was spent on the race. It was the most expensive judicial race in the United States. Outside agencies, political action committees and organizations claiming to be independent, contributed attack ads on both candidates. This election was so distasteful that the president of the Alabama State Bar has asked the Attorney General's office to investigate whether outside agencies violated state law in supporting certain candidates by issuing derogative ads about a candidate's opponent, and in stating that Alabama Bar Association had "graded" or "evaluated" either candidate, which it had not done.

It doesn't stop there. It was recently reported that, "in another indication of concern over the integrity of judicial campaigns, the United States Supreme Court has granted review in the case of Caperton v. Massey. In that case, a Justice on the Supreme

Court of Appeals of West Virginia refused to recuse himself from the Appeal of a $50 Million jury verdict, even though the CEO of the lead defendant spent approximately $3 Million supporting the Justice as a candidate, which amounted to over sixty percent of the total amount spent by the campaign. After winning the election, the Justice cast the deciding vote in a 3-2 decision overturning the verdict. The case will consider where the line is drawn to prevent a judge from hearing cases involving parties who made substantial campaign contributions." You can search the case style "Caperton v. Massey" to follow this very important decision.

No one wins when judges are selected in this manner...no one. The public loses its faith in the judiciary and, to an extent, the judiciary loses its credibility with the lawyers and public whom they serve. It is my hope that this divisive practice will soon come to an end. But for now, it is only a hope.

Mike Gedgoudas

ORDER EXTRA COPIES

THE COST OF JUSTICE

A Legal Thriller

▪▪

Name: _____

Address:_____

_____

_____

Email: _____

\# of copies at $15.95 each: _____

plus $3.00 mailing and handling: _____

Florida residents add: $1.12 state tax: _____

TOTAL: _____

EXCEPTION: If ordering four or more books,
Total S & H: = $10.00

Please send check for correct amount to:
Fireside Publications
13539 SE 87th Circle
Summerfield, Florida 34491

Or use Paypal to email address: **belois@comcast.net**

Please use this order blank or a facsimile.

OTHER AVAILABLE BOOKS FROM FIRESIDE PUBLICATION

AN AGENT SPEAKS by Joan West: $9.98
A Primer for unpublished Authors

ENGELHARDT by Gisela Engelhardt: $9.98
From ideal childhood to horror in Hitler's
Germany to America and life in the New
World.

BLESSED: MY Battle with Brain Disease
By Mary J. Stevens: $9.98
From life in a Convent to reintegration with
society as a wife and mother, all the while
seeking a diagnosis for her brain disease and
learning to live with it.

BEYOND FOREVER: Past Life Experiences
By Taylor Shaye $11.95
Shari searches through time for her soul mate.
TITLE_____ _____

TITLE_____ _____

TITLE_____ _____

Include # of copies& price of each book. Add $3.00 S & H
Per book. Florida residents, add 7% per book for state tax.
EXCEPTION: If ordering 5 to 10 books to same address, Total
S & H = $10.00.

TOTAL DUE: _____
Please mail check for correct amount to:
     Fireside Publications
     13539 SE 87th Circle
     Summerfield, Florida 34491